I0025265

The "desegregation" of English schools

MANCHESTER
1824

Manchester University Press

The "desegregation" of English schools

Bussing, race and urban space, 1960s–80s

Olivier Esteves

Manchester University Press

Copyright © Olivier Esteves 2018

The right of Olivier Esteves to be identified as the author of this work has been
asserted by him in accordance with the Copyright, Designs and Patents Act 1988.

Published by Manchester University Press
Altrincham Street, Manchester M1 7JA, UK
www.manchesteruniversitypress.co.uk

British Library Cataloguing-in-Publication Data is available

ISBN 978 1 5261 2485 2 hardback
ISBN 978 1 5261 4801 8 paperback

First published by Manchester University Press in hardback 2018

This edition published 2020

The publisher has no responsibility for the persistence or accuracy of URLs for any external or
third-party internet websites referred to in this book, and does not guarantee that any content
on such websites is, or will remain, accurate or appropriate.

Typeset by
Toppan Best-set Premedia Limited

We barely have time to react in this world, let alone rehearse.
(Ani Di Franco, "Letter to a John", *Out of Range* album, 1994)

In history there are no control groups. There is no one to tell us what might have been.
(Cormac McCarthy, *All the Pretty Horses*, 1992)

You can come up with statistics to prove anything, Kent. Forty percent of all people know that.
(Homer Simpson, in *Homer the Vigilante*, 1994)

As a kid I just thought that was it; racism as a concept never occurred to me, I never put two and two together. I just got on with it.
(Mel Jung, interview (Southall), 25 February 2016)

Pakis are just the same as people.
(White eight-year-old pupil from a Bradford suburban school where bussing operated, 1977)

Contents

Figures

Tables

Acknowledgements

In a five- or six-year project which seems to have taken for ever to materialise, it is inevitable that there should be names I am forgetting. To these unidentified helpers I am indebted too, and by them I hope forgiven. I also want to warmly thank modern technology for having made the digital camera possible; without that tool carrying out this research might well have proved impossible, especially for someone like me who lives and teaches in France, although a few miles away from Lille's Eurostar station.

The first people to be thanked in the Southall area are Balraj Purewal and Viney Jung, both of whom have given me ample logistical help, from contacts to curries. Without Balraj and his family in particular, this research would probably have been a no-hoper. I want to thank archivists Jonathan Oates and Piotr Stolarski, as well as Ranjit Dheer, Shakila Maan from Southall Black Sisters, Suresh Grover, Swarn Singh Kang, Tim Ottevanger, Ravi Jain and the people at Sri Guru Singh Sabha Gurdwara on Park Avenue (Southall). Also very helpful – and impressively knowledgeable – was Sarah Garrod from the George Padmore Institute in Finsbury Park (London), not to mention the many people who were instrumental in making what I hope to have been a success out of my urban odyssey through post-industrial England. In Manchester, I will never forget the keen and fruitful help provided by the Ahmed Iqbal Ullah Research Centre, particularly Ruth Tait. Still in Manchester, Barbara Lebrun, Jonathan Hensher, Joseph McGonagle and Rajinder Dudrah welcomed me warmly in their university, so I could travel comfortably to Huddersfield and Blackburn. In the former, Paul Thomas, Paul Ward and Joe Hopkinson were terrific hosts; in the latter, archivist Mary Painter and her staff were very helpful. In Bradford, I would like to thank Noorzaman and Jani Rashid, photographer Tim Smith, journalist Jim Greenhalf, sociologist Ludi Simpsons, entrepreneur Zulfi Hussain and all the staff at West Yorkshire archives and Bradford city archives, with whom I maintained regular contact asking for clarifications, documents, further details etc. In Leeds, my friend James House, a great historian and human being, also provided valuable help, especially when debating publishing issues. In Halifax documents mentioned by Tahira Iqbal really got the ball rolling in what otherwise looked like very unpromising terrain. In the West Midlands, apart from archivists at the Wolfson Centre in Birmingham, I would like to thank Shirin Hirsch (Wolverhampton), Billy Dosangh, Julia Foster and archival staff from Sandwell, Walsall and Wolverhampton.

Quite a few colleagues, mostly in France, Britain and the USA, have discussed some of the issues, have made appreciated suggestions, have proofread parts of the manuscript or have simply spurred me on with their encouraging talk and reading tips: Paul Silverstein, Matt Delmont, Brett Bebber, Darrell Newton, Timothy Peace, Romain Garbaye, Sally Tomlinson, Andrew Thompson, Raphael Eppreh-Butet, Audrey Célestine, Christophe Bertossi, Christian Ydesen, Julien Talpin, Sébastien Lefait, Sylvain Feucherolles and Florent Berthaut, with the latter two bringing their computer skills into the process. As the writing phase was approaching I got two new heads at my home university: my former department head, Delphine, my current department head, Christine, and my research team heads, Jean-Gabriel and Etienne, who in their respective ways have been true delights to work with and under. I also want to thank the secretarial staff in my Roubaix department, for their no nonsense, as well as unrelentingly humane, approaches to issues: Chrystèle, the Ferreira sisters, Sabrina, Sophie, Cora, Séverine and Bénédicte. Trouble-shooting Younes, Soëzic and Djazia at CERAPS have also been truly helpful and are simply great people to work with.

I am very glad to thank the many people who agreed to be interviewed about their experience and memories of being bussed; in their recollections, I often sensed how imperious my task was: to piece together and write a cohesive historical narrative which to a large extent had never really been put together before, at least not in such a purportedly exhaustive, detailed way.

Also decisive in their help have been all the staff at Manchester University Press I've been dealing with throughout my project. I have also had the chance to share elements of my project in academic or non-academic conferences in Chicago, Denver, Cleveland, London, Edinburgh, Nottingham, Ormskirk, Birmingham, Manchester, Leeds, Bradford, Huddersfield, Brussels, Amsterdam, Lille and Paris. I'm very thankful to all those who made these talks happen, from Kevin Myers to Elizabeth Buettner, from Andrea Stanton to Carol Helstosky. Importantly, the anonymous reviewers of my manuscript deserve a busload of gratitude: they spurred me on whilst pinpointing very obvious shortcomings which I hope to have revised satisfactorily.

Lastly, I want to warmly thank my family, my mum and dad who will never read this because it's in English but who have never given in to some of the political temptations at the root of dispersal, temptations which are so much stronger in France 2018 than in England 1963. And, to state the oh-so-very obvious, to Claire, Lucille and Ninon, the last to have leapt into this world and in many ways the loudest.

Abbreviations

BNP	British National Party
CIAC	Commonwealth Immigrants Advisory Council
CRC	Community Relations Committee
CRE	Commission for Racial Equality
DES	Department of Education and Science
ESL	English as a Second Language
ESN	Educationally Sub-Normal
ILEA	Inner London Education Authority
IWA	Indian Workers Association
LEA	Local Education Authority
NF	National Front
NUT	National Union of Teachers
RRB	Race Relations Board
URB	Uganda Resettlement Board
SEA	Smethwick English Association
SRA	Southall Residents Association
SYM	Southall Youth Movement
TGWU	Transport and General Workers Union

Introduction

On 25 May 1963, readers of *The Middlesex County Times (Southall Edition)* were taken aback by grisly news: the local Scout movement had recently lost as many as thirteen boys, all leaders of troops whose parents had fled to further suburban towns. W.J. Hubbard, the District Scout commissioner, acknowledged that "this was understandable", because "they feared that their children's education would be held back". The explanation given was quite straightforward: "We are losing many Scouters who have been living in that part of the town occupied by our Indian friends".

Since then, the demographic and ethnic development of places like Southall has sometimes been dubbed "White Flight". Although the phrase is convenient to counterbalance the deep-seated suspicion of pathological self-segregation[1] among ethnic minorities (Muslims especially), I believe it to be misleading for three reasons. First, the white versus non-white binary explicit in it fails to make sense of those who were by far the largest immigrant group post-1945, the Irish, whose influx into Britain was about seven hundred thousand during the postwar decades of prosperity,[2] a figure which dwarfs all West Indian and Indian subcontinent arrivals. Second, "White Flight" invites disingenuous parallels between England and the United States where it has rightly been called "the largest exodus in American history";[3] though "White Flight" has been an important mutation in English urban dynamics, its extent simply pales into insignificance when compared with its American (non-)equivalent. Third, it is also misleading as it implies that the move to suburbia is motivated only by race, whereas in actual fact a vast array of reasons have lured middle-class families away from the inner-ring areas of English cities.[4] For instance, some of this "White Flight" in areas at the heart of this book – Ealing in West London being one – was linked with the introducing of new schooling policies: after the conversion or closure of many grammar schools after 1965, more and more middle-class (white) families left London to move out to Slough, Maidenhead, Buckinghamshire, that is areas outside London which proved slower in implementing the move to comprehensive schooling. The parents of the above Scouts may have been repulsed by the prospect of what they saw as bad schooling in Southall, just as much as they may have been attracted by promises of good grammar schools a few miles to the north or west. That these were almost wholly white unlike Southall schools is only one element in a complex combination of causes.

It was the white movement to suburbia and its connection to ethnic minority clustering in areas like Southall and the inner cities of Bradford, Birmingham, Blackburn, West Bromwich and so on which were at the root of bussing, the subject of this book. Bussing itself was a form of social engineering initiated in a dozen Local Education Authorities, whereby immigrant children from primary school age upwards were (forcefully) dispersed to predominantly white suburban schools. The aim was twofold. First, and originally, to placate white fears of an immigrant demographic takeover in areas such as Southall where the number of Asians had dramatically soared in a few years. Second – dispersal's official *raison d'être* – to make sure that those mostly non-Anglophone Asians "integrated", that is, that they efficiently addressed their English-language 'handicap' and internalised the British/English way of life at a time when, a few decades before devolution, almost everyone south of the border saw these two terms as synonyms.

With some exceptions, bussing proved a failure. One reason was that dispersed, marooned and unwelcome Asian youths faced racist bullying in schools from two to seven miles away from their neighbourhoods, even ten miles in some cases in the borough of Ealing.[5] As a postcolonial aftertaste, it also confirmed to many Asians that somehow they were lesser breeds without the law, since bussing white children to the multiracial inner cities was never an option. This is what Riaz Ahmed, a Bradfordian bussed for a few years in the late 1960s, bitterly recalls:

> It was a failure primarily because it was a one-way traffic, not a two-way traffic, I remember it was a couple of lads like me going to white schools, there were ten or twelve of us, and I remember we got bullied, it was terrible, and these are your formative years, you see, very important for your mental development ... There should be bussing, but it has to be a two-way traffic, otherwise it will fail.[6]

The US analogy

Riaz Ahmed's point finds illuminating echoes across the Atlantic. In localities where bussing[7] was a one-way traffic, some African-Americans who were bussed to white suburban schools inveighed against the gross inequalities whereby in order to get a decent education, they had to be transferred to faraway schools and hurled into an often toxic school environment where they were the butt of racism. In Norfolk (Virginia), one Clarence Garrett inquired: "Why are new schools always built in white sections in the city and Negro students bused?" Garrett's classmate Dwight Davis opined, "I feel that busing black students to a white community to attend school and not busing the white students to a black community is unjust".[8] There were analogous views aplenty in nearby North Carolina, but also in New York or Detroit.[9] This was the first problem with American bussing in the places where it was introduced.[10] In his book *Stayin' Alive: The 1970s and the Last Days of the Working Class*, Jefferson Cowie states that "on busing, policy makers continued to believe that moving people was a better and easier solution than moving money and resources".[11] Or, in the words of Genevieve Mitchell from the Black Women's Center in Cleveland (Ohio): "I have said time and again, 'bus the Money, honey!'".[12] With hindsight, these damning statements sound obliquely appropriate for England. In his report on "dispersal", professor of public policy Maurice Kogan found that the schools Southall Asians were bussed to were of much better quality than the Southall schools these youths had been bussed from. So much so that, as Kogan put it, "There was none of the receiving schools in which I would not gladly see my own children educated"[13] – an encomium he would not have extended to Southall schools, to state the obvious.

The US analogy is inevitable when discussing English bussing. This is despite the fact that bussing in England was about immigration, integration or assimilation and deficiency in English, whereas in the United States it was about desegregation and the righting of a historical wrong for African-Americans who, to state the obvious again, were not immigrants: they were a submerged community for whom the federal state, states, school districts and school boards had for generations painstakingly preserved "a system of compulsory ignorance".[14] Why this parallel is inevitable is because, for better and often for worse, "America" has provided for decades a convenient cognitive map to make sense of immigration and racial issues in Britain.

More importantly perhaps, the practice or the mere prospect of bussing in the United States filled countless headlines, and framed how the desegregation of schools, particularly in the northern states, was discussed: this was bound to have an international impact, not least in England, where "bussing" was introduced and debated. Across the Atlantic, bussing could make you (hope to) win elections or a Pulitzer Prize. Nixon, Ford and Reagan were three presidents who made negative statements about it to rally whites against what was often dubbed "forced busing". J. Anthony Lukas's book on bussing, *Common Ground: A Turbulent Decade in the Lives of Three American Families*,[15] won a Pulitzer prize, as well as Stanley Foreman's photo "The Soiling of Old Glory", displaying a white anti-bussing

Figure 1: Stanley Forman's Pulitzer Prize-winning photograph "The Soiling of Old Glory", Boston, 1976

activist using an American flag against a black man in Boston (1976, see Figure 1). Probably more than any other historical development, it was "bussing" which made "White Backlash" a mainstream phrase in public debate, a phrase feared by Johnson and then cunningly instrumentalised by Nixon. It was, for many Blacks, "a phony issue which obscured the causes of educational inequality, and that school buses had long been used to maintain segregated schools". According to historian Matt Delmont, "With 'busing', northerners found a palatable way to oppose desegregation without appealing to the explicitly racist sentiments they preferred to associate with southerners".[16] Delmont finds "busing" so potent a smokescreen that in *Why "Busing" Failed* he uses the word hundreds of times always with quotation marks. These I also use in the title of this book, as "desegregation" is appropriate for the United States but not for England. Yet this is how bussing came to be legitimated by public authorities, in a bipartisan effort to stave off the proliferation of "ghetto" schools. However muddled they were, parallels with the US situation along the British corridors of power will have to be returned to.

At a remove from the national furore around bussing in America, bussing in England was a very low-key practice, affecting some twelve thousand pupils in a dozen or so LEAs. Circular 7/65 issued by the Department of Education and Science only *recommended* the implementation of dispersal in areas which had more than 33 per cent of immigrant children. Without compulsion, the four LEAs with the largest number of immigrant children – the Inner London Education Authority, Birmingham, Brent and Haringey – refrained from introducing dispersal altogether. Consequently, whereas a number of monographs by scholars on American bussing do exist, this is the very first book about bussing in England, despite the substantial number of essays on race and schooling, above all in the field of sociology. Unsurprisingly then, I found when carrying out this research that librarians and archivists contacted across England in areas which operated bussing were often unaware of the existence of this policy in their own communities. And, just as unsurprisingly, the only two places where I did not have to describe what English bussing was were Ealing (Southall) and Bradford, the two areas where it was fairly widespread.

Going where the archival silence is

The paucity of sources on bussing in England is a daunting challenge for the social scientist. In the early stages of the archive-collecting process, it oddly felt like a better idea to write a novel rather than a historical monograph about it. Soon enough though, it appeared that this dearth of archival material proved germane, and was an open invitation to "read against the grain", or read against the grain when there is no grain.[17] Unquestionably, a 1960s consensus prevailed that some race-relations policies ought to be kept outside the public gaze, both not to elicit critiques from ethnic minorities and, for the indigenous majority, not to convey the feeling that ethnic minorities and immigrants were themselves being given preferential treatment simply because they were treated differently. To give one example: Birmingham practised a policy of housing dispersal from 1969 to 1975. One Housing Committee member of the Birmingham Corporation confided to researcher Hazel Flett that "it was a fairly quiet policy – deliberately ... The Corporation believed, along with so many agencies in race relations, in doing good by stealth."[18] An analogous approach prevailed in education, as is shown by David Kirp in *Doing Good by Doing Little: Race and Schooling in Britain*.[19]

In the years when bussing was introduced in Ealing, Bradford and West Bromwich, a real reluctance still existed as to the collecting of racial information and to the differential treatment of social groups on the basis of racial identity, and it is also how this stealthy approach must be understood. After all, by the late 1960s, it still seemed unnatural to introduce racial provisions in the British legal framework, which some still regarded as "the quintessence of colour-blindness"[20] despite the Race Relations Acts of 1965 and 1968. The general Welfare State philosophy was also underpinned by a broad universalism whereby social needs were to be addressed irrespective of group or individual characteristics,[21] despite the discriminatory bias within welfare provision and the fact that its achievements fell short of its universalist claims.[22]

Locally, such cautiousness was illustrated by the way authorities begrudged giving information on bussing to the race-relations busybodies interested in whether the system operated on the basis of immigrant children's deficiency in English, in which case bussing could hardly be called discriminatory according to the Race Relations Act (1968), or whether it rested on purely racial or colour criteria, which, on the contrary, could be declared illegal on the same grounds. Historian Brett Bebber, in what appears to be the only article published on English bussing for decades, states: "The [Ealing] Council was notoriously secretive about its educational decisions, even denying the local Community Relations Council basic information about education decision-making and funding".[23]Ealing's secretiveness was then also due to its awareness that bussing was on the fringe of legality, not solely to its determination not to spark controversy among whites as well as Asians. Much the same comment could have been made about other local authorities (such as Walsall), whose secrecy was challenged by the Race Relations Board in 1975–76.[24] Similarly, at national level, the DES never really carried out a national inquiry into the bussing system. Pamela Fox, a DES civil servant, candidly confessed in 1976 that "We have never made a survey to find out how many districts were dispersing or how many children were involved".[25]

The upshot of all this is clear. It is wellnigh impossible to tell with any degree of certainty how many LEAs dispersed, and when dispersal began and ended in LEAs which operated it. In Southall, bussing lasted from 1963 to 1981, in Bradford from 1964 to 1980. Beyond this it is all guess-work, since in LEAs where bussing was low-key local archives are very sparse and local newspapers quite often did not cover it. What's more, most studies of dispersal, which generally run to only a few pages, cagily baulk at venturing an exhaustive list of dispersing LEAs, often referring to the two notorious cases (Ealing, Bradford) next to convenient words or phrases like "including", "among others" or "to quote a few". An analysis of all the available sources looked into for this book suggests that, between 1964 and 1986, twelve LEAs opted for dispersal, mostly in order to "desegregate" some schools with a large intake of immigrant children (30 per cent quite often). These are, in alphabetical order: Blackburn, Bradford,

Bristol, Ealing (Southall), Halifax, Hounslow, Huddersfield, Leicester, Luton, Walsall, West Bromwich and Wolverhampton. There is uncertainty as to whether three other LEAs really operated dispersal: these are Croydon, Dewsbury and Smethwick. Dispersal took many different forms, especially in places like Bristol or Leicester, which are not, unlike Bradford and Ealing, at the heart of this study. It is also important to keep this in mind when reading the section below on terminology: a single word could easily cover different realities.

There is one last reason why there is such a paucity of sources on bussing or dispersal: the policy's introduction coincided with the move to comprehensive schools. It is understandable that for policy-makers interest in such a hoped-for wholesale reform trumped dispersal. A mere 569 schools out of a total of 26,000 accommodated more than one-third of immigrant children in 1971.[26] Small wonder then that, in educational archives from 1965–66, circular 10/65 which introduced comprehensive schooling largely overshadowed the soon infamous circular 7/65, whose paragraph eight promoted dispersal for immigrant children. To give one example among many: the Anthony Crosland personal papers held at the London School of Economics archives contain nothing at all about dispersal, despite the fact that Crosland was secretary of state for education and science from 1965 to 1967. On the other hand, there is a plethora of documents about comprehensive schools, which is understandable given the intended scope of the reform, and since Crosland privately confided that he was hell-bent on "the destruction of every fucking grammar school in the country".[27] Similarly, the Sir Edward Boyle papers held at the University of Leeds archives have precious little about bussing, despite the fact that he, as a secretary of state for education before Crosland, actually put dispersal on the political agenda in October 1963 following a visit to a Southall school.[28]

Positioning an academic project

This bussing project positions itself at the crossroads of various social sciences, whose disciplinary porosity and interconnectedness it serves to highlight: history, political science and sociology, borrowing methods and concepts from each of the three. Its object of study brings together the history of English public policies at micro- and macro-level, the history of education and immigration, the sociology of social movements and transdisciplinary urban studies as well as the history of postcolonial England. It focuses on the negotiation and devising of top-down policies as well as the variegated ways in which people navigate through these policies, and by "people" I mean parents and children themselves, variously as agents, actors or subjects, to borrow from Michel Rolph-Trouillot's useful triad.[29]

It is a contribution to the history of immigrant and ethnic minority experience in the field of education, a sub-discipline within the history of education for which, until recently, there was a "paucity of material" which has constituted, according to Kevin Myers, "a puzzling and rather disturbing silence".[30]This is largely owing to a methodological nationalism among historians for whom, for a long time, the "general idea of migration" was deemed "exceptional, unimportant or somehow problematic".[31]

Despite the above-mentioned paucity of archival material, this project relies heavily on primary sources and interviews, and hopefully weaves a narrative of ethnic minority and immigrant experience which tackles head-on the complexity, ambivalence and multi-faceted lived realities of Asians and (to a lesser extent) West Indians in the field of education. As will be shown, this very ambivalence reaches beyond the well-known binary of the (mostly Asian) immigrant keeping a low profile versus collective resistance against institutional racism. This archaeology of the black box of bussing also tries to reach beyond inside and outside visions of "shared identities", both at meso-level (LEAs had different stories to tell) and at micro-level, since it will be seen that many individuals reacted differently to the demands made by the dispersal policies. Kevin Myers invokes sociologist Bob Carter's phrase "experiential empiricism" as well as Bill Schwarz's insistence on the need for a "'detailed, situated and historical story' that helps to make clear how immigrants encountered and responded to the logics of racial thought".[32] It is one of the ambitions of this book to provide something resembling that.

The project finds its place in postcolonial and postwar history, and it is to be lamented that, as Jordanna Bailkin has argued, these two dimensions are too often perfunctorily juxtaposed without being brought together.[33] For one thing, the history of the British Welfare State was largely shaped by both postcolonial and postwar realities, and it is worth remembering that the concept of "parental choice", which was to be so crucial in how public actors engaged with "bussing", was reinforced *during* the war rather than after it, with the Education Act of 1944.

The national backcloth to the introduction of English bussing is also, or above all, a postcolonial one. This must be understood literally: the question of the education of immigrant children from the Indian subcontinent came *after* British colonial rule in India, and bore certain traces of past colonial domination. In the words of Geoffrey Bindman and Anthony Lester, "Post-war immigration from the new Commonwealth has transplanted to the old Mother Country prejudices and patterns of behaviour which could conveniently be ignored or righteously condemned so long as they flourished only within an Empire beyond our shores".[34] In top-down terms of public policy, the postcolonial dimension took the form of white bureaucratic decision-making with little or no consultation of Asians,[35] or through cultural and linguistic normative policies to implement assimilation. In bottom-up terms of Asian appreciation of English schooling and of educational policies, postcoloniality was evidenced by a tendency to keep a low profile often brought directly from former colonies. To explain why her parents never thought about challenging bussing and racism in schools, one interviewee for this book, Anjuna Kalsi, an Asian originating from Kenya, states that "in Africa there was very high respect for teachers in general. So you naturally reproduced that in England. More generally, you came from that place where you generally accepted authority."[36]

So, despite the pragmatic way in which "postcolonial" is apprehended in the following pages – itself a way of keeping at arm's lengths some cryptically theoretical debates about postcolonialism seldom rooted in experience – it is clear that the move from being parts of the empire to independence was no smooth path, both overseas and in the metropolis.[37] Beyond that, Anjuna Kalsi's statement, echoed by other interviewees, validates the way researchers in the field of "new imperial history" have striven to transcend "home" and "overseas" into "a single conceptual category and insisted upon moving beyond a restricted, national-bound approach to modern Western Europe".[38] Although these points will rarely be returned to, they provide a grid of intelligibility to make sense of the history of dispersal as it unfolded in England.

What's in a word?

Clarifications about the words "dispersal" and "bussing" are needed. First of all, the two terms are not strictly synonymous for, technically, "bussing" is only one form of "dispersal". In January 1964, West Bromwich introduced a measure of dispersal, "first for children walking to school and later by bus".[39] In 1967, Denis Howell, Labour MP for Small Heath and joint parliamentary under-secretary for education and science, was scathing about Birmingham's adamant refusal of dispersal and insisted that there were almost wholly white schools not far from the city's northern segregated ethnic enclaves (Handsworth, Soho, Rotton Row) as well as from its southern ones (Small Heath, Sparkbrook, Balsall Heath).[40] Consequently, in order to "desegregate" schools in these places, a form of dispersal without resorting to bussing was possible and desirable according to Denis Howell and Roy Hattersley, who was then Labour MP for Sparkbrook.

For all these nuances, dispersal and bussing were mostly understood as synonyms in the 1960s and 1970s. But their connotations were different. "Dispersal" is a fairly abstract concept mobilised by local and national bureaucracies who endorse or actively promote a policy of encouraged or forced assimilation. By using "dispersal", policy-makers could always convey a feeling of protectiveness towards South Asian pupils deficient in English and cultural integration. After all, wasn't the evacuation of British children from Blitz-torn London in the Second World War sometimes called "dispersal"?[41] Such terminological associations, however indirect, did play a part among political authorities who in the 1960s had all been through the traumatic experience of war.

On the contrary, "bussing" is a concrete term which was used by critics of dispersal at grassroots level, that is multicultural or anti-racist associations, Asian parents, community relation activists, politicians and so on. Bussing refers directly to the experience of being herded away from a neighbourhood school where one feels one naturally belongs, it is about a quantity of human bodies being shovelled into seemingly or actually unwelcoming places. Whilst many Asians either had fun with their peers on the buses or were simply dozing, many experienced daily racist bullying in predominantly white schools, and this is what "bussing" encapsulates. Likewise, "bussing" seethed with controversy, particularly when one thinks of the (white) American struggle against it. Although it took a radically different form in Southall or Bradford, "bussing" was likewise made, by those who fought against it and by some media, into a red-button concept, a sort of boo word.

These lexical nuances were not lost on public actors. In a 1975 interview for the London Broadcasting Company, Usha Prashar, then conciliator for the RRB, was asked by anchorman Tony Tucker: "Where are they being bussed to? It's an unfortunate expression that – bussed – I think because it conjures up so many other attitudes, but I mean where are they being taken?"[42] In the same way, faced with mounting criticism of bussing, Ealing Council issued a press release on 4 December 1974 which ran: "After careful review of these changed circumstances, the Council accepts that the best interests of all children in the borough would now be met by bringing dispersal – as we prefer to call it – to an end as soon as is practicable".[43] The local authorities in Bradford were likewise very averse to the use of "bussing"; "dispersal" was what they did.[44]

These hesitations around a word seem to betray a degree of self-consciousness among authorities and in academia, which is why other words, phrases and metaphors were used in order to debate the parameters of the recommendations made in circular 7/65. Thus, the circular itself mentioned "spreading the children" besides "dispersal", the National Union of Teachers (NUT) promoted "distribution schemes", Nicholas Hawkes in his *Immigrant Children in British Schools* referred to "spreading" and "purposeful distribution", [45] social anthropologist Sheila Patterson to a "benign quota" policy,[46] the Bow Group think-tank to "quota system".[47] Maurice Kogan talked repeatedly of "coaching",[48] *The Daily Mail* of "a rationing policy"[49] and, in 1965, a Birmingham consultative document entitled "A First Report on the Educational and Social Problems of the Coloured Immigrants" upheld dispersal by calling it "unscrambling the omelette".[50]

As opposed to these motley circumlocutions, Asians and whites who mobilised against dispersal in Bradford and Southall nearly always singled out one enemy which they generally called plain "bussing". This is important since in the 1970s immigrants and ethnic minorities tended to be objects rather than subjects of public discourse. Hence, the majority of words and concepts used in the debate on immigration and integration were often none of their choosing. Algerian sociologist Abdelmalek Sayad, in line with the concept of "symbolical violence" by Pierre Bourdieu (with whom Sayad worked), insists on how immigrants are frequently tricked into using the very concepts which in public debate are exploited in order to question their citizenship, deny their integration, suggest their backwardness and so forth. If anything then, the choice of "bussing" is a telling sign of lexical agency from among the Asian minority, whose keeping of a low profile has too often been exaggerated in classic historiography. It is a telling sign that the subaltern, indeed, *can* sometimes speak.[51]

One last comment on this lexical ambivalence, for the more practical purposes of this book. Both "bussing" and "dispersal" will be used, depending in most cases on whether the focus is more top-down or bottom-up.

No panacea

One of the ironies about dispersal in schools is that most of those who defended it tooth and nail, often by importing frightening Jim Crow metaphors about "segregation", were themselves never convinced that dispersal would prove an efficient remedy to the schooling separation of immigrant children. The truth is that they had no better local solution than bussing to come up with.

Two apparently "commonsense" solutions were recommended to stave off over-concentration of immigrant children in schools: one was to close the door on further immigration, the effect of which would be dramatic although not immediate, the other was to spread the immigrants themselves, that is to implement housing rather than schooling dispersal. Regarding the former solution, it is of course no coincidence that the Commonwealth Immigrants Act (1962) was implemented one and a half years before Edward Boyle's visit to Southall which was to inspire schooling dispersal.[52] The "beat-the-ban effect" in the eighteen months that preceded the enactment of the law has been well researched by historians;[53]

the mere threat that doors would soon be closed did cause a massive New Commonwealth rush to England, which had not been the case after the British Nationality Act (1948).[54] The demographic consequences in Southall, Bradford and all of the LEAs which were to introduce dispersal were immediate and profound. Just before and after the legislation was passed, the press in Southall and Bradford was full of wake-up calls to end immigration *now*, which evinced the frustration and powerlessness of local political authorities over policy choices which, by their nature, were national.

As for housing dispersal, its hoped-for efficacy rested on what psychology and sociology generally call the "contact hypothesis" or "bridging social capital", here summarised by a Birmingham Labour councillor: "If (coloured) people were dispersed they would go to different schools, use shops that Birmingham people used and go to the pubs".[55] This contact hypothesis was taken up again in the Cullingworth Report on housing (1969), and it was believed to lead naturally to an assimilation of immigrants. More concretely, housing dispersal was made possible by the fact that in the 1960s approximately one-third of the housing available was run by local authorities in the form of council housing.

The housing dispersal idea faced two stumbling blocks. One was the spatial concentration of specific immigrant groups next to large industrial employers: for instance, the many Pakistani immigrants employed in the gigantic textile mills of Bradford made up an army of labour that simply had to live in the vicinity, all the more so as almost none of them had cars and as many of them were on night-shift. The second stumbling block is as natural and is often disregarded by those, in the 1960s as today, who readily pathologise the tendency among minorities or immigrants to stick together: any human community is characterised by what sociologists call the "homophily principle", whereby individuals have a natural proclivity to "gravitate towards those that share a great deal in common".[56] This is all the more true for migrant groups established in a foreign land whose language they don't speak, where they may feel unwelcome, whose weather they regard as very inclement and so on.

To insist on housing dispersal is key in a book on schooling dispersal since, even in Ealing where bussing was to become a massive issue, most local press articles before and after Boyle's visit to Southall in October 1963 dealt not so much with schooling questions but rather with housing ones. The 1964 general elections locally were fought mostly on overcrowding, "Rachmanism",[57] quality-of-life issues and the ghettoisation of areas like Hambrough and Dormer Wells. Two and half months before Boyle's visit, a petition of some 140 local residents, from ten specific streets, urged the council to buy properties in the area "which were likely to be bought by coloured people". In mid-August 1963, two months before Boyle's visit, the General Purposes Committee of the Town Council was presented with a petition by 625 residents claiming that the town must use "compulsory purchase powers to buy up vacant houses", in order to prevent these houses from being bought by immigrants.[58] The general feeling bought into conspiracy theories of some "peaceful penetration" of Indians aided by the "folly" of "liberal do-gooders". In late August 1963, Ealing councillors were mobbed by some Southall petitioners. Irate residents from the Beaconsfield area cried out against councillors: "We want peace and quiet in our road – not Indians!"[59]

In general terms, the debate on and policy of housing dispersal reveals some compelling commonalities with bussing. Three of them can be looked into here. First, they are connected with liberal attempts at "integrating" immigrants by desegregating a dilapidated, overcrowded urban space which itself comes to embody the immigrant presence, although this inner-city dilapidation largely preceded it historically. Such a mental construction is facilitated by what Charles Wade Mills in *The Racial Contract* has called a racial "circular indictment": " 'You are what you are in part because you originate from a certain kind of space, and that space has those properties in part because it is inhabited by creatures like yourself' ".[60] This liberal, integrationist framework is not incompatible with illiberal, "White Backlash" mobilisations at grassroots level. In Birmingham for instance, it was the threat of a white council tenants' rent strike in Botany Walk (Ladywood) against the arrival of West Indians which eventually enacted the stealthy housing dispersal locally, whereby not more than one in six council flats or houses in a given area could be allocated to a Black tenant. Five out of six property cards for council housing bore a cryptic "N/C" (not coloured) inscription by the Housing Department. Another troubling concomitance was that these housing dispersal plans to integrate immigrants efficiently were devised locally only one week after the: so-called "Rivers of Blood" speech by Enoch Powell (20 April 1968).[61]

A second parallel between bussing and housing dispersal is that in the few cases where minorities were either consulted or active in the process, or when this rested on a voluntary basis discussed with the minorities themselves, then the policy was understandably much more likely to be accepted and successful. In this respect, the opacity of Birmingham's housing dispersal is to be contrasted with that in Nottingham, where, by the mid-1970s, a fair-housing officer, originally funded by the Gulbenkian Foundation, worked with ethnic minorities who placed confidence in the local dispersal scheme in housing estates.[62] An identical contrast could be drawn, in terms of schooling dispersal this time, between say Ealing and

Leicester, where local involvement by ethnic minorities in policy-making was substantial.

The last parallel to be made between housing and schooling dispersal is that, local disparities notwithstanding, both evidently failed to achieve their goals. In housing, one reason is that it was supported only half-heartedly. Even in Ealing, after Labour MP George Pargiter had suggested it in 1964, some retorted that housing dispersal was "quite alien to the British democratic set-up".[63] One Indian Workers Association representative also pointed out that "it is highly undemocratic and against the Commonwealth's spirit".[64] Susan J. Smith summarises the situation thus: "Despite a broad commitment to interventionism in most areas of government, legislators were reluctant to introduce special programmes for migrant minorities, especially in housing".[65] In a 1964 correspondence between the Southall General Purposes Committee and the Home Office, one reads that there was "no power to compel them [Commonwealth immigrants] to live and work in particular areas or to compel them not to settle in places where their compatriots were already living, and the Government would not think it right to seek such powers".[66]

There are two other powerful limits to housing dispersal. One is that the further one went into (white) suburbia the more council estates adopted strict suburban approaches to a form of self-conscious respectability which in effect was racially exclusive.[67] On top of this, immigrant and ethnic-minority groups either were unfamiliar with how council housing operated or they could not qualify (in Birmingham in the 1960s there was a five-year residence clause) or else they were simply not interested in council housing, like so many Asians who would rather buy more or less dilapidated property by borrowing from within their *biraderi* (extended family). Lastly and more importantly, the private market was (and is) totally uncontrolled, and the prejudices exposed by Elizabeth Burney's seminal analysis are more likely to be exacerbated there.

Who cares about bussing anyway?

Here I want to make two points. First that bussing as a historical object of study does matter. Second that it does matter a lot today.

At a talk given at Huddersfield University in 2016, one of the participants in the debate, historian Paul Ward, remarked that the disturbing thing about bussing was its apparent normality. This view is important: many thousands of pupils have indeed been bussed up and down the country, in urban and rural areas, in the 1960s just as today. In the United States too, white anti-bussing militants rallied around the "tradition" of "neighbourhood schools" but in fact their slogans were largely spurious, for by 1970 nearly half of all American public school students had to ride buses to school.[68]

On top of all this, there is a "racial" form of "normality" involved. A 1988 CRE report entitled *Learning in Terror* insists on how shockingly routine racial bullying, racist violence and name-calling were in British playgrounds. "British" is in order here rather than "English", for a study of the Scottish situation in the mid-1980s revealed that "Asian children face a daily barrage of abuse and physical attacks in Glasgow's multi-racial schools".[69] Therefore, some South Asian people from Tower Hamlets, Manchester or Sheffield who were never bussed could logically cry out that their own experience of being racially bullied was astonishingly identical to that of Southall, Bradford or Blackburn Asians who were bussed.

With all this background in mind, what is different – albeit seemingly "normal" – about bussing is that many thousands of Asian pupils were *forcefully* transported to faraway schools, especially in Ealing and Bradford, that their parents had little or no say in it, or did not know they could have a say, and that most of these children were of primary school age. In Ealing in particular, thousands were bussed from two to ten miles away from the age of four to the age of eleven. Bussing was an outright denial of "parental choice" as recognised by the Education Act of 1944 (section 76).[70] In a rare twist of historical irony, in order to become like others, in order to be integrated and learn some English, Asian pupils had to go through a long phase, in their crucially formative years, during which they were less equal than others, different, "the Pakis on the bus" as they were sometimes called.

That bussing does matter as a historical object also needs to be proved for demographic reasons. We already know that it was a minority practice targeting an ethnic minority deficient in English and "integration", and that the suggestion to disperse cut no ice with the four LEAs having the largest number of immigrants in the 1960s. However, regardless of whether bussing was introduced in LEAs with a large intake of immigrant children, the concept of dispersal was passionately debated in many places and this sheds light on issues of integration, assimilation, ghettoisation and desegregation which were to shape multicultural politics in the decades that followed. Whether militants, academics or politicians, many of those who were pivotal race-relations actors in the 1960s and 1970s had something to say about bussing and often said it loud. They included E.J.B. Rose and Nicholas Deakin; sociologist John Rex; Labour party figures Maurice Foley, Roy Hattersley and Denis Howell; race-relations expert Anthony Lester (the co-founder of the Runnymede Trust); Maurice Kogan and West Indian militants such as Bernard Coard and Jeff Crawford; but also conservative headmaster Ray Honeyford, who was to become an English national martyr in the eyes of the assimilationist right in the 1980s. Not to mention that it is also very likely that in his so-called "Rivers of Blood" speech, when saying that his constituents "found their wives unable to obtain hospital beds in childbirth, their children unable to obtain school places",[71] Enoch Powell himself was actually referring to Birmingham and some of the major West Midlands towns where pressure had been mounting for a few years to introduce dispersal. Lastly, it was often the experience of being bussed that sharpened the political consciousness of some of the Asian youths in Southall and Bradford. And it is no coincidence that much of the 1970s–80s Asian militancy, from the "Bradford Twelve" case to the Southall Youth Movement, actually originated from these two places.[72]

The policy of bussing in the 1960s and 1970s also illuminates some highly topical debates on class, ethnic and religious segregation in British schools. In Bradford, thirty years after the last nail had been hammered into dispersal's coffin, the city erupted into riots the like of which had not been seen since 1981 in London (Brixton). In the backwash of the 2001 disturbances, Muhamad Ajeeb, the former lord mayor of Bradford who had campaigned against bussing twenty-five years before, travelled to London and consulted with Lord Falconer, then minister of local government. He suggested that locally a 70 per cent limit to the number of Asians in schools should be set, and that a two-way-process type of bussing ought to be considered because, he claimed, "my argument has always been that we should make a mutual effort; if we want to understand each other, we should make those sacrifices, even if it's a very explosive issue. We should really think about the long-term consequences rather than the short-term benefits."[73]

The point developed here is congruent with Elizabeth Anderson's in *The Imperative of Integration*: "Students who attend more racially integrated schools lead more racially integrated lives after graduation: they have more racially diverse co-workers, neighbours, and friends than do students who attend less diverse schools".[74] Yet, against this belief in "integrationism",[75] Veit Bader states that "whether the effects of interaction are beneficial depends partly on the voluntariness of interaction and on contextual variables such as (the absence of) threats, (patterns of) discrimination, socio-economic inequalities and negative-sum games".[76] This issue will be further developed in the Conclusion, but among the "sacrifices" evoked by Ajeeb, there was the looming threat of "white-bashing" (or "gore-bashing") by Asian youths in schools where they now made up a huge majority, a kind of historical revenge for the Bradford bussing years of their parents' generation.

Muhamad Ajeeb was aware that he was probably fighting a losing battle: on the English education market, "parental choice" was by 2001 an unshakable guiding principle, and is now even more so as this book goes to press. In addition, the events of 9/11 and then 7/7 did generate a massive, knee-jerk type of Islamophobia. More importantly, which white middle-class parents from the outskirts of Bradford would want their children to be educated in ailing schools of run-down Manningham? In an English school system which has been more and more compartmentalised, on the basis of fierce competition reliant on league tables (introduced under John Major in 1993), and with even fiercer job competition in the offing, being sent to "ghetto schools" in Bradford or elsewhere would unleash a deterring storm of litigation.

Today, in the Holme Wood and Bierley estates around Bradford, a few double-decker buses drive daily to Tong High School. Most of those who ride these buses are Asian students who do not live in the vicinity of these predominantly white housing estates. On the face of it, the situation is evocative of 1960s–70s quotidian scenes, but in the present case those who take the bus do it on a *voluntary* basis, which changes just about everything. What this (and, to be sure, analogous situations around the country) highlights is that the provision of unequal education facilities will inevitably keep the bus going for many years, except that carbon emission now brings a further element of complexity to the debate.

In June 2016, the chairman of the Sutton Trust charity, philanthropist Sir Peter Lampl, suggested that children in run-down areas be bussed out to "good" schools in an effort to improve their education.[77] He was only echoing calls by some London headteachers who had promoted bussing since 2012 in order to challenge a social segregation which is blighting education.[78] Sometimes, it is also claimed that dispersal could prove a useful tool to address linguistic deficiency in areas like London, where unprecedented immigration since 2004 has made the British capital a veritable Tower of Babel. In an essay on "White Backlash" perceptions in Youngstown (Ohio) and Barking and Dagenham (East London), Justin Gest reproduces a very long letter sent to David Cameron by an angry white constituent, Nancy Pemberton. In the course of this four-page document, one reads: "In a class of 24 you have maybe one or two English children these days; how terrible is that. 67 languages spoken at our local primary school! One language should be spoken – English – this is still, just about, England."[79] Whether or not this constitutes one unpalatable side of super-diversity, this testimony provides an amplified echo of comparable issues raised in Southall in the early 1960s, as we will shortly see.

Bussing has seemed like a solution to be contemplated not only to curb social inequalities or address linguistic deficiencies among immigrants but also to tackle self-ghettoised communities living parallel lives, generally meaning "Muslims". Trevor Phillips, whose 2005 "sleepwalking to segregation" speech at Manchester (rightly) came under fire from some sociologists,[80] suggested on Channel Four in April 2016 that in schools with more than 50 per cent of Muslims there ought to be bussing in order to bring about an enforced mixing.[81] Needless to say, in the wake of the disastrous 2014 Trojan Horse affair, when the regulator OFSTED claimed to have found evidence of Islamist infiltration of some twenty-one schools in Birmingham, such recommendations had an air of muscular common sense about them, despite the disturbing complexity of the issues involved. It is fairly obvious that neither Lampl nor the former head of the CRE appears to be cognisant of the shady side of bussing's history in England. This book, then, is also for them.

Notes

1 Shamim Miah, *Muslims, Schooling and the Question of Self-segregation*, London: Palgrave Macmillan, 2015.

2 Enda Delaney, *The Irish in Post-war Britain*, Oxford: Oxford University Press, 2007, p. 4.

3 Ronald Formisano, *Boston against Busing: Race, Class and Ethnicity in the 1960s and 1970s*, Chapel Hill: University of North Carolina Press, 1991, p. 11.

4 See Ludi Simpson and Nissa Finney, *Sleepwalking to Segregation: Challenging Myths about Race and Migration*, Bristol: Policy Press, 2009, pp. 128–9.

5 See *Middlesex County Times (Southall Edition)*, 30.7.1971.

6 Olivier Esteves, *De l'invisibilité à l'islamophobie : les musulmans britanniques (1945–2010)*, Paris: Presses de Sciences-Po, 2011, p. 83.

7 In the United States, 'bussing' is spelt with one 's', in Britain with two.

8 Matthew F. Delmont, *Why Busing Failed: Race, Media and the National Resistance to School Desegregation*, Oakland: University of California Press, 2016, p. 177.

9 For a thorough list of American cities and towns which had one-way bussing, see *ibid.*, pp. 90–1.

10 Despite the national furore around it, bussing affected only between 2 and 5 per cent of American schoolgoers in the 1970s (see *ibid.*, p. 5, p. 214).

11 Jefferson Cowie, *Stayin' Alive: The 1970s and the Last Days of the Working Class*, New York: The New Press, 2010, p. 245.

12 United States Committee on the Judiciary, *Effectiveness of Mandatory Busing in Cleveland*, London: Forgotten Books, 2015, p. 65.

13 Maurice Kogan, *Dispersal in the Ealing Local Education Authority Schools' System*, Report to Race Relations Board, 1976, p. 14.

14 Meyer Weinberg, *A Chance to Learn: The History of Race and Education in the United States*, Cambridge: Cambridge University Press, 1977, p. 11.

15 J. Anthony Lukas, *Common Ground: A Turbulent Decade in the Lives of Three American Families*, New York: Vintage Books, 1985.

16 See Delmont, *Why Busing Failed*, p. 171, p. 3.

17 On the appropriateness of this metaphor, see Ann Laura Stoler, *Along the Archival Grain: Epistemic Anxieties and Colonial Common Sense*, Princeton: Princeton University Press, 2009.

18 Hazel Flett, "The Politics of Dispersal in Birmingham", Working Papers on Ethnic Relations, no. 14, Birmingham, 1981, p. 14.

19 David Kirp, *Doing Good by Doing Little, Race and Schooling in Britain*, Berkeley and London: University of California Press, 1979.

20 This is a phrase by E.J.B. Rose *et al.*, quoted in Erik Bleich, *Race Politics in Britain and France: Ideas and Policy-making since the 1960s*, Cambridge: Cambridge University Press, 2003, p. 42.

21 On this point and its connection with the specific treatment of ethnic minorities, see Catherine Jones, *Immigration and Social Policy in Britain*, London: Tavistock, 1977, p. 39.

22 Jordanna Bailkin, *The Afterlife of Empire*, Oakland: University of California Press, 2012, p. 4.

23 Brett Bebber, "'We Were Just Unwanted', Bussing, Migrant Dispersal and South Asians in London", *Journal of Social History*, vol. 48 (3), 2015, p. 657.

24 On the Walsall/RRB controversy, see *Birmingham Post*, 1 December 1976.

25 See Lewis Killian, "School Bussing in Britain, Policies and Perceptions", *Harvard Educational Review*, vol. 49 (2), 1979, p. 196.

26 National Archives (Kew), CK2/515, Race Relations Board *vs* Blackburn education authority (1972–1974), RRB general committee report, 2.5.1972.

27 Susan Crosland, *Tony Crosland*, London: Jonathan Cape, 1982, p. 148.

28 *West Middlesex Gazette*, 19.10.1963.

29 Michel Rolph-Trouillot, *Silencing the Past: Power and the Production of History*, Boston: Beacon Press, 1995, pp. 23–4.

30 Kevin Myers, "Immigrants and Ethnic Minorities in the History of Education", *Paedagogica Historica*, vol. 45 (2009), p. 801.

31 *Ibid.*, p. 815.

32 Kevin Myers, *Struggles for a Past: Irish and Afro-Caribbean Histories in England, 1951–2000*, Manchester: Manchester University Press, 2015, p. 2.

33 Bailkin, *The Afterlife of Empire*, pp. 2–3.

34 Geoffrey Bindman and Anthony Lester, *Race and Law*, Harmondsworth: Penguin, 1972, p. 13.

35 On this point, and the contrast with the United States, see Kirp, *Doing Good by Doing Little*, p. 26.

36 Interview (Southall), 19.10.2016. A place-name is given in parentheses for those interviews which were not telephone or Skype interviews. References are given at the first occurrence of interview excerpts.

37 Elizabeth Buettner, *Europe After Empire: Decolonization, Society and Culture*, Cambridge: Cambridge University Press, 2016, pp. 4–5.

38 *Ibid.*, p. 7.

39 *Birmingham Post*, undated newspaper cuttings, Birmingham City Library / Wolfson Centre, Indian Workers Association archives.

40 *Birmingham Post*, 23.1.1967.

41 See Carlton Jackson, *Who Will Take Our Children? The British Evacuation Programme of World War II*, Jefferson, N: McFarland Publishing, 2008, pp. 18, 149, 179.

42 "Immigrant School Children", LBC, Radio scripts, Report RRB no. 429, Ahmed Iqbal Ullah race relations centre, Manchester Public Library.

43 Kogan, *Dispersal in the Ealing Local Education Authority*, appendix IV (unpaged).

44 See Brenda Mary Thomson, *Asian-named Minority Groups in the British Schools System: A Study of the education of children of immigrants of Indian, Pakistani or Bangladeshi origins from the Indian subcontinent or East Africa in the city of Bradford*, PhD dissertation, University of Bradford, 1991, p. 206.

45 Nicholas Hawkes, *Immigrant Children in British Schools*, London: Pall Mall Press, 1966, pp. 28–9.

46 Sheila Patterson, *Immigration and Race Relations in Britain 1960–1967*, Oxford: Oxford University Press, 1969, p. 256.

47 Christopher Brocklebank-Fowler, Christopher Bland and Tim Farmer, *Commonwealth Immigration*, London: The Bow Group, 1965, pp. 16–21.

48 *Ibid.*, p. 7, p. 17, p. 22, p. 24.

49 *Daily Mail*, 16.6.1965.

50 On this last phrase, see Ian Grosvenor, *Assimilating Identities: Racism and Educational Policy in post 1945 Britain*, London: Lawrence & Wishart, 1997, p. 118.

51 The reference here is to Gayatri Chakravorty Spivak's "Can the Subaltern Speak?", a foundational document of postcolonial studies, in Cary Nelson and Lawrence Grossberg (eds), *Marxism and the Interpretation of Culture*, Urbana and Chicago: University of Illinois Press, 1987, pp. 271–315.

52 The law came into effect on 1 July 1962, and Boyle's visit to Southall was 15 October 1963.

53 For instance, Randall Hansen, *Citizenship and Immigration in Post-War Britain, The Institutional Origins of a Multicultural Nation*, Oxford: Oxford University Press, 2000, pp. 118–19.

54 The record 136,000 New Commonwealth rush to Britain in 1961 needs to be seen in proportion to the net population of England and Wales, 46,104,548 according to the census of the same year.

55 Flett, "The Politics of Dispersal", p. 7.

56 Michael Merry, *Equality, Citizenship and Segregation: A Defence of Separation*, New York: Palgrave Macmillan, 2013, p. 11.

57 After Peter Rachman (1919–62), a notorious Notting Hill slumlord. "Rachmanism" came to signify overpopulation in slums, terrible hygiene conditions, rent racketeering of immigrant and white working-class tenants, etc.

58 For both petitions, see *West Middlesex Gazette*, 17.8.1963.

59 *West Middlesex Gazette*, 24.9.1963.

60 Charles Wade Mills, *The Racial Contract*, Ithaca and London: Cornell University Press, 1997, pp. 41–2.

61 On all these points, see Flett, "The Politics of Dispersal", pp. 10–13.

62 See the Race Relations Board's newsletter *Equals*, 3, August–September 1975, pp. 4–5.

63 *Middlesex County Times (Southall Edition)*, 18.1.1964.

64 *Middlesex County Times (Southall Edition)*, 15.2.1964.

65 Susan J. Smith, *The Politics of "Race" and Residence*, Cambridge: Polity Press, 1989, p. 125.

66 Ealing archives, Southall borough minutes, Meeting of the General Purposes committee, 12.3.1964, p. 642.

67 See Elizabeth Burney, *Housing on Trial: A Study of Immigrants and Local Government*, Oxford: Oxford University Press, 1967, p. 76.

68 Thomas J. Sugrue, *Sweet Land of Liberty: The Forgotten Struggle for Civil Rights in the North*, New York: Random House, 2010, p. 483.

69 Commission for Racial Equality, *Learning in Terror: A Survey of Racial Harassment in Schools and Colleges in England, Scotland and Wales*, London, 1988, p. 9.

70 This says: "So far as is compatible with the provision of efficient instruction and training and the avoidance of unreasonable public expenditure, pupils are to be educated in accordance with the wishes of their parents".

71 The full script of the speech is available at: www.telegraph.co.uk/comment/3643823/Enoch-Powells-Rivers-of-Blood-speech.html (accessed 20.12.2017).

72 See Anandi Ramamurthy, *Black Star: Britain's Asian Youth Movements*, London: Pluto Press, 2013. The Bradford Twelve case was a high-profile case in the history of the anti-racist movement. The Bradford Twelve were members or supporters of the United Black Youth League who had marched in July 1981 through Manningham (Bradford) to defend themselves against the National Front. Having prepared petrol bombs which they had stocked in nearby buildings, they were put on trial on conspiracy charges. They were finally acquitted, having repeatedly used the slogan 'self-defence is no offence'.

73 Interview, 20.10.2015.

74 Merry, *Equality, Citizenship and Segregation*, p. 32.

75 *Ibid.*, pp. 6–7.

76 *Ibid.*, p. 32.

77 Sally Tomlinson, *A Sociology of Special and Inclusive Education: Exploring the Manufacture of Inability*, London: Routledge, 2017, p. 145.

78 *Evening Standard*, 1.10.2012.

79 Justin Gest, *The New Minority: White Working-class Politics in an Era of Immigration and Inequality*, Oxford: Oxford University Press, 2016, p. 61.

80 See for instance, Simpson and Finney, *Sleepwalking to Segregation?*, pp. 94–5.

81 Channel Four, "What British Muslims Really Think" (Trevor Phillips), 20.4.2016.

1

"To allay people's fears on numbers":[1] the introduction of dispersal in Southall

The national picture

Bussing's introduction followed the vote of the Commonwealth Immigrants Act (1962), which aimed to close the door on further immigration from the New Commonwealth by issuing work vouchers to specific countries and commensurate with specific skills. Therefore, the 1963 visit to a Southall primary school by education secretary Edward Boyle, which is at the heart of this chapter, took place in a context when immigration and the pressing need for "integration" had become a red-hot topic in parliamentary debates as well as in the mainstream media. Restriction was the order of the day, and the 1962 legislation was only the logical outcome, precipitated by the racial outbreaks of violence at Notting Hill and Nottingham (1958), of years of immigration control programmes debated at Parliament and Whitehall. As Abigail Beach and Richard Weight put it, the law "was the culmination of the politics of citizenship and nationhood operative in Britain since at least 1945 and by which some Britons were perceived to be more British than others".[2] Rather than constituting an actual disruption, the urban disturbances of Notting Hill and to a lesser extent Nottingham in 1958 were needed catalysts to introduce legal distinctions which would dent the very concept of British citizenship. This was itself a postcolonial manifestation of a national identity resting on race and on a race-based "Anglosphere", which was "distributed across the metropole, Canada, Australia, New Zealand, East Africa, Central Africa, and most problematically of all, South Africa".[3] West Indians as well as Asians, those likely to be bussed, were outside this race-based national identity, regardless of their passports or Commonwealth affiliations. Later legislation on citizenship and immigration would only serve to emphasise this (in 1962 of course, then 1971, and 1981).

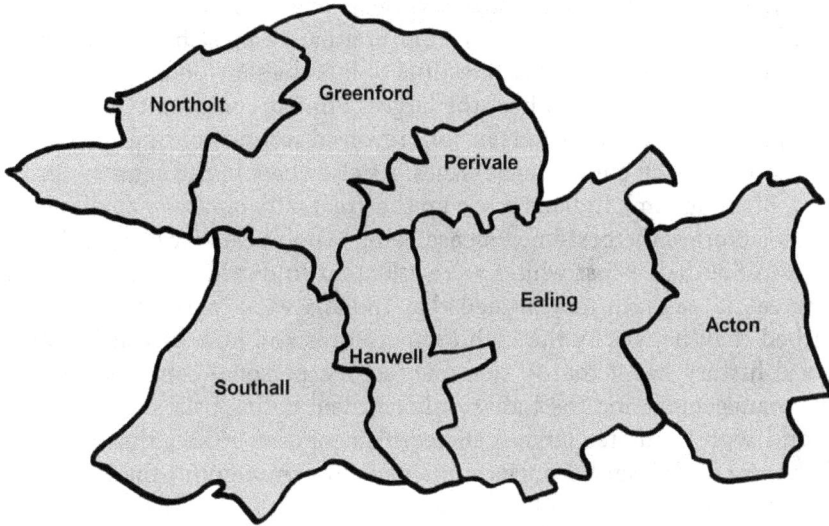

Figure 2: The borough of Ealing after the 1965 reforms

The local picture

Southall, until it was incorporated into Ealing in April 1965 (see Figure 2), was a middle-sized western borough of London. Geographically, its strategic position on the Uxbridge Road (London to Oxford) and on the main railway line to Reading had attracted many light-engineering companies and various manufacturing plants, not to mention Heathrow airport's huge business magnet to the south-west, past the borough of Hounslow.

For all these assets, the borough's population had been on the decline since about 1945, from 55,896 (1951 census) to 52,983 (1961 census). In 1951, only 300 (0.6%) of the whole were born in Commonwealth countries, colonies and protectorates. One decade later, the figure had risen to 2540 (nearly 4.8%), with 2259 from India, Pakistan and the West Indies. In the years that followed 1961, Southall's overall population increased slightly again, but this was due to the migrant influx. The Town Clerk's department, basing its estimate on health, sanitary and education figures, reckoned that the number of "coloured immigrants" had nearly trebled from 1961 to 1964, from about 2500 to about 6500, with a great majority of Punjabi Indians from the districts of Jalandhar and Hoshiarpur to the east of Amritsar, and some four hundred West Indians as well as four hundred Pakistanis.[4] From 1960 to 1964, the number of immigrant children locally soared from 1% to 15% of the whole, being established at 1130 by January 1964 (with one hundred West Indians, and the rest Indians).[5] Taken together, these figures – added to the local concentration of South Asians in a limited number of streets *within* Southall – must be kept in mind when considering the backlash leading to bussing's introduction. In just a few years, Southall would host the largest Punjabi community in Britain.

Most immigration-related tensions revolved around housing and education, not so much employment issues. As elsewhere in the country (Bradford, Birmingham), Indians made up the great bulk of labour employed in some factories, the best-known case being Woolf's Rubber plant in Hayes next to Southall. Most whites were reluctant to do these jobs post-1945, whereas it was routinely argued that Indians were "naturally" less disturbed than natives by the high temperatures and humidity at Woolf's.[6] Local history has it that in this one factory, personal contacts between the management and the Indian subcontinent dating back to the Second World War[7] facilitated large-scale recruitment after 1955, a time when, in fact, most Middlesex boroughs contained more immigrants than Southall.

In political terms, Southall was a rather safe Labour seat, until and even after its incorporation into Ealing. George Pargiter was the local MP from 1950 until his retirement in 1966, at which time Sydney Bidwell succeeded him as Ealing Southall MP until 1992. Despite this long hold on power, Labour often walked a political tightrope, having to sound tough on migrant overcrowding and other race-related issues to their core white working-class electorate whilst needing to placate Indian interests, locally embodied by an Indian Workers Association whose influence on elections was to become pivotal like nowhere else in the country. In the 1960s, the Tories trailed behind political actors who played the race card more uninhibitedly than they did, whether the British National Party itself[8] or the Southall Residents Association (which never actually ran for elections). Given this polarised situation, it is no coincidence that MP George Pargiter, partly to appease the Indian electorate, was one of the most vocal opponents of the Commonwealth Immigrants Bill (1961), which many immigrants denounced as an outright colour bar, whereas Barbara Maddin, the local Conservative leader in Southall, was counted among its most outspoken advocates. Nevertheless, the very same Pargiter, at an SRA meeting held on 10 January 1964, recognised that it was only natural, among British natives, to "be entitled to look after our own people" and that "there cannot be this free-for-all any longer".[9] This electoral Janus-like attitude testifies to what Justin Gest calls "the twin pulls of populism and pluralism"[10] characterising Labour in many multi-ethnic areas.

Eighteen months later, the Conservative minority in Southall moved an amendment stipulating that, to get public housing, immigrants would have to have been residents for fifteen years. Margaret Maddin and her colleagues knew full well this was a cheap political trick, the number of migrants on the housing list being less than negligible.[11] By contrast, this move was also a way to expose Labour as totally "out-of-touch" with the grassroots situation. To conclude on the 1960s local political context, it is no exaggeration to suggest that, with the Birmingham conurbation (notably including Smethwick and Wolverhampton), Southall was the most polarised English area in matters of race and migration.

"Farewell to Bingo" and the new White Man's Burden

In his essay on Boston bussing, historian Ronald Formisano argues that white working-class and middle-class rage against what Alabama segregationist George Wallace called "the senseless, asinine busing of schoolchildren to achieve racial balance"[12] has to be apprehended as one key struggle within a large spectrum of local crusades. Formisano talks of bussing as part of "a continuation of wars waged in recent years against the depredations of highway construction, urban renewal, and airport expansion promoted by civil engineers, bureaucrats and, above all, outsiders".[13] Indeed, if bussing itself is tightly bound up with race, most of these other issues are not, or perhaps might be, but indirectly so.

Much the same could be argued about Southall's political and social scene in the early 1960s, a decade which has been rightly designated "the Golden Age of Residents' Associations".[14] Some of these associations mushroomed into existence in nearby Greenford, Hounslow, and further afield in Hornsey, Brixton, Heston, High Wycombe, Pinner, Wembley, North Gifford.[15] In all these places, thousands of (mostly) white tax-payers endeavoured to push quality-of-life issues into the local authorities' agendas, and often issued serious warnings about uncontrolled immigration. The year 1960 was when some noise-abatement societies formed in Ealing, and local MP George Pargiter was pressured to take action against unnecessary noise (sports car roars, ice-cream sales chimes, radios blaring). Other residents' associations were formed to address vandalism (in Hanwell, Southall), yet others campaigned to slow down traffic (in Ravenor Park). There were proposals in favour of anti-spitting by-laws pushed forward by some residents' associations,[16] which evidences very prosaically the culture clash between Asians and white natives. By and large, local mobilisations challenged certain aspects of what was seen as "permissive society", also some negative side-effects of consumer and technology-driven society, as well as deficient public services and, of course, developments directly linked with the new demographic dynamics brought about by New Commonwealth immigration. Quite often immigration-related, these "perceived outrages", to quote Bill Schwarz's hugely important analysis of British White Backlash, were "proximate and sensuous: they [could] be smelt, heard, seen". They would serve to devise "a peculiarly homely racism" for which "the neighbourhood worked as principal axis",[17] and which, in a few years, would raise Enoch Powell into a national icon for many.

As far as the ailing state of public services is concerned, the London Transport network was regularly upbraided by Southallians wondering whether it was "quicker to walk",[18] whilst the 1962 reduction in the number of part-time teachers in the borough as a whole made some tax-payers fear that the County Education Committee had deliberately decided to lower the standards of education, especially in the Southall area.[19] Those part-time teachers would really help the pupils with serious difficulties, taking them apart from the rest of the class in very small groups. This would be less and less possible in the near future.

The introduction of comprehensive schooling, that is the Labour-promoted abandonment of the three-tier system that had been cautiously preserved by the Education Act (1944), was associated by the most con-servatively minded with the era's permissive society.[20] Despite dogged Conservative opposition locally, the Labour-controlled new borough of Ealing (somewhat artificially bringing together the former Middlesex bor-oughs of Acton, Ealing and Southall) aimed at being "one of the leading education authorities in the London area"[21] in the field of comprehensive schooling. If "dispersal" was soon to be associated with "integration", "comprehensives" were coterminous with "modernity".

Southall's demographic and ethnic development meant that some local institutions passed to Indian hands, unleashing a chorus of "there goes the neighbourhood!" among middle-aged or elderly whites who had been born and reared in the area. Quite tellingly, local ethnographic fieldwork con-ducted by Nicholas Deakin in the early 1960s concluded that among those who felt very strongly about immigration (i.e. those who mentioned immi-gration as a key issue without being prompted to discuss the issue at all) were long-established Southallians, "and the longer they had lived there the more often they tended to mention immigration", claimed Deakin.[22] A few years later, the nationally held Community Attitudes Survey (1969) showed that "there is a tendency for a greater proportion of electors of a lower socio-economic status to have lived in the 'home' area for over 20 years".[23] Hence, those Southallians who could summon up recollections of their quaint western nook of London were more likely to be more vulner-able categories of society, who could not or would not move out.

In her essay *India Abroad: Diasporic Cultures of Postwar America and England*, anthropologist Sandhya Shukla indirectly challenges the memo-ries of quaintness shared by elderly folks in the 1960s. Indeed, Southall had already been a bleak, heavily industrialised London suburb for a few generations, a change in some way embodied by the spelling "Southall" instead of the hitherto used "Southolt". Shukla's views chimed with George Orwell's, for he too would have dismissed such pre-urban nostalgia: as a teacher in 1932–33 in nearby Hayes, the author of *Nineteen Eighty-Four* grew to hate that area of Middlesex, which he camouflaged lightly as West Bletchley in *Coming Up for Air* and as Southbridge in *A Clergyman's Daughter*. In the former, published in 1939, his main character George Bowling sees much of Ealing as an epitome of suburban dreariness, with its "miles and miles of ugly houses, with people living dull, decent lives inside them".[24] But however dreary, the high street of Southall was filled, in Orwell's time, with British-owned shops, and this is primarily what was looked back upon with melancholy a few decades later.

One generation after Orwell's death in 1950, most urban developments locally were apprehended through the lens of Punjabi immigration. The year 1965, which saw the ministerial sanction of dispersal of immigrant children, was also the year when the Dominion Social Centre and adjacent cinema on the main street (called "The Green") was sold to Indians.[25] This farewell to Bingo was a mere three years after the Working Men's Club premises on Featherstone Road had been transformed into the Indian Workers Association's headquarter. There was suspicion of foul play when some indignant Southallians demanded to know "where the money comes from".[26]

Admittedly, some grievances were not race-related, but they seldom failed to be exacerbated by some local immigration specificities. For instance, and to quote from above examples, some lamenting the poor state of London transport could point to the "shocking" fact that young dispersed Asians were bussed freely to schools, whilst others who bemoaned the decreasing number of part-time teachers could draw contrasts with the recruitment of teachers for non-Anglophones, whose number steadily increased throughout the 1960s. Although not related to race, both situations encouraged "White Backlash" contrasts between so-called "natives" and Asians, all the more so as, in general terms, areas where immigrants clustered were often areas characterised not only by a real labour shortage but also by deficiencies in housing and in the main public services.[27]

Perusal of Ealing newspaper archives from the period provides constant evidence of Dominic Sandbrook's claim that, during the decade, while a "small group of affluent, self-confident young people ... welcomed change, millions of others clung firmly to what they knew and loved".[28] Among those millions were a few thousand in Southall who would not or could not afford to leave the area. They were those who must have felt a pang of estrangement when listening to Prime Minister Harold Macmillan's well-known postwar injunction to feel happy: "Indeed let us be frank about it – most of our people have never had it so good" (Bedford speech, 1957). The growing number of Asians and what was perceived as their outlandish ways, on top of the "permissive society" and other unwelcome developments, were experienced as a theft of enjoyment by them, who felt they deserved yet did not have a place among Macmillan's "most of our people". The "permissive society" and "theft of enjoyment" were not unrelated to postcoloniality and race: the former was easily connected with lily-white hippies but also with the seemingly strange manners of Asians and disorderly manners of West Indians. As Bill Schwarz puts it, "The racial encodings of order, as whiteness, and disorder, as blackness, were endlessly repeated".[29] To Bill Schwarz, there was a great deal of colonial nostalgia in such an order/disorder dialectic: in the present case, to ruefully witness the way Southall evolved in the 1960s was, whether consciously or not, to hark back to times when non-whites knew their geographical as well as metaphorical place, when things were in their right and hierarchically based racial order. As for "theft of enjoyment", it confirmed the sense of Southall (and England) as being a neighbourhood (or nation) under siege, where the white majority was prevented from reaping the fruits of liberal society, where "pursuit of happiness" should be untrammelled. And we also know after Žižek that enjoyment is often raised into a condition for the Nation itself to exist.[30]

Many white Southallians were unsure whether they should embrace wholeheartedly the tenets of the postwar consumer boom, and yet there was one thing they were sure about: they were annoyed that the immigrant presence itself was putting the history clock back. There was a bitter irony in this perception: some Southallians would have loved to make their neighbourhood what it was like a few decades back (before the Asian 'invasion') whilst they blamed these for putting the clock back. In a 1965 letter of complaint to Edward Boyle (still education secretary), a woman living in Slough referred to the immigrant presence as a major threat to "our own people, whose standards have been put back ten years over this immigration".[31] Albert Cooney, SRA's leader, went further when claiming that "Southall has gone back fifty years in five".[32] Typically, it was that type of argument, with exactly the same words ("standards", "being put back"), which was used to describe Asian over-concentration in a few schools and to legitimate bussing.

Southall's rapidly changing face altered some whites' local sense of pride, especially on days when they were supposed to enjoy some free time. Like Bradford for Pakistanis in the north, Southall did attract, at the weekend, large crowds of Asians coming to visit friends or relatives and marvelling at the endless displays of exotic foodstuffs in ethnic shops. These two powerful Asian magnets made some whites feel as if their area was colonised by foreigners from outside Southall or Bradford coming to visit the foreigners who had already too massively clustered in the area. This confirmed that the two places had already become, in the eyes of some, wholly Asian areas, as is shown in Figure 3. Elderly natives were particularly sensitive to this, for many of the shops they had patronised had disappeared and a lot of their friends had passed away or gone to live elsewhere, as is exemplified by this testimony of a social worker from the area: "There is the feeling of being alone and that Southall has become untidy, over-crowded, shops are run by foreigners, main roads are congested by traffic … To sum up in one lady's words, 'Southall has become the Mecca of the Asians'."[33]

The national reputations of places like Southall or Bradford elicited a sense of local shame among whites who bitterly resented the Asian presence. In an article called "Southall, the Town of Shame?", one I.A. Darling bitterly confided: "When I meet people and they ask me where I live, I am ashamed of living in Southall".[34] It is clear from this that theft of enjoyment could easily translate into theft of local pride, and a feeling that being a Southallian meant having stepped down a few rungs on the social ladder, which weakened their own sense of social positionality (the feeling of being beneath some but above others).

The Southall Residents Association and the crystallisation of local resistance

In many debates on integration and race-relations issues in the 1960s (as well as today),[35] the key to manage to press certain arguments is not so much *what* you say, rather *where* you actually live to say what you say. This is because ordinary voters have a keen sense that those they elected to the Commons often do not live in the areas they represent, a fact made possible by quite unrestrictive British election laws in this respect. On top of this, many local public figures concerned with race-relations questions, such as the (white) executive members of Community Relations Councils, often live in houses comfortably away from the multi-ethnic and decaying inner cities whose "racial harmony" they are meant to promote.[36]

In June 1969, a BBC *Panorama* debate between Mark Bonham-Carter (chairman of the Race Relations Board) and Enoch Powell led one Wolverhampton housewife in the audience to argue that immigrants do not want

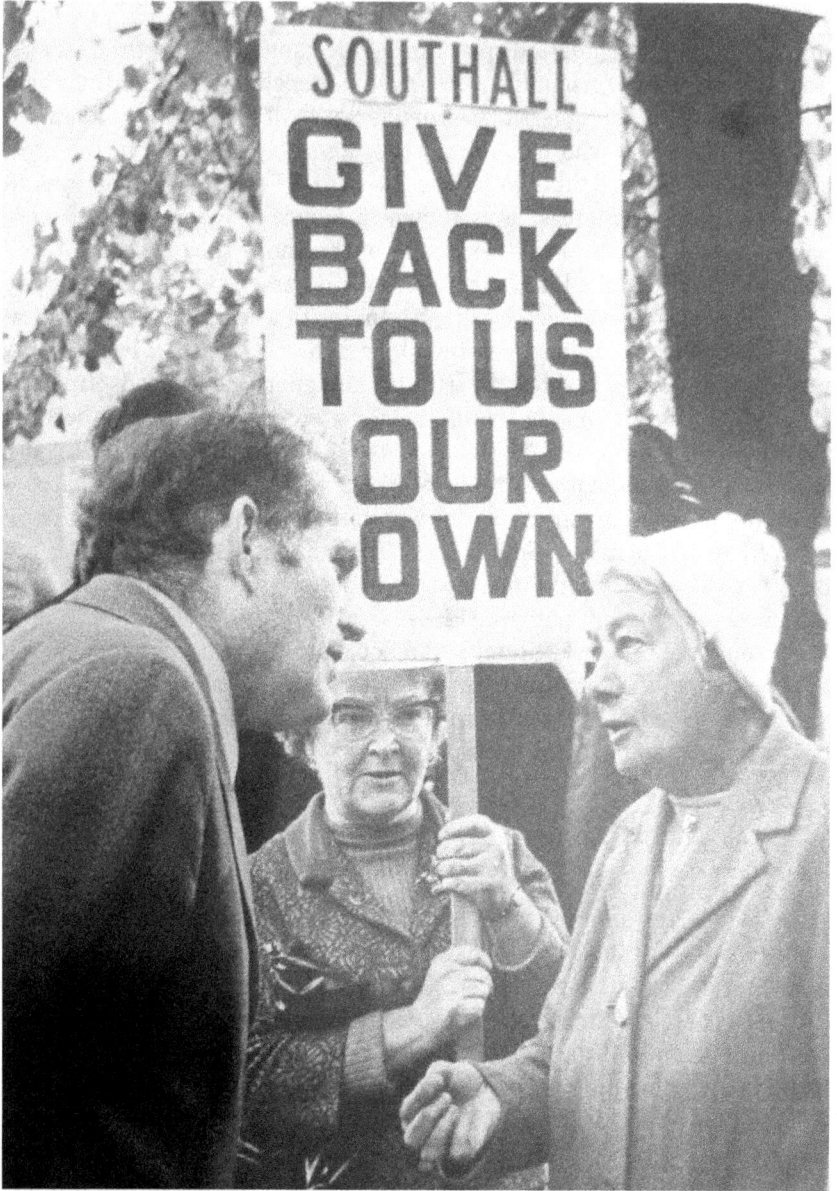

Figure 3: Labour MP Sydney Bidwell debating with two Southall women in 1975

to integrate and that the local population simply have to put up with them, before striking a more personal note:

> My son is one of three white children in a class of 37 pupils. The rest, of course, are immigrants. His education, apparently, is of no consequence to you but to me, it is of vast importance. I do not blame the immigrant people for this shocking state of affairs, but I do lay the blame fairly where it belongs, with the Labour government for allowing the masses in, and I also blame people who theorise, without any real knowledge of the facts.[37]

All of this was sweet music to Powell's ears, a man who lived in very fashionable South Eaton Place (London) and yet repeatedly claimed to "live within the proverbial stone's throw of a street which 'went black'",[38] whereas to Mark Bonham-Carter, Prime Minister Herbert Asquith's grandson, the residential reminder must have been terribly annoying.

Such claims to legitimacy based on territoriality are key to understand Southall's urban dynamics. In 1961, at a time when the debate on the Commonwealth Immigrants Bill was gathering momentum in the Commons, one Labour Party Southall councillor, T.J. Steele, warned of the possibility of race riots if more Indians continued to live in "colonies", and if these made "no efforts to integrate with local residents".[39] A "popular councillor" according to Paul Foot,[40] Steele lived in the Hambrough ward of Southall. He received a hefty rebuttal from some of his colleagues. One of these, MP George Pargiter, blamed Councillor Steele's "unsocial approach" but his words carried little weight: when Pargiter decided to leave Dolphin Square in fancy Pimlico, it was not to go and live in Southall but rather to move to select Caterham in Surrey.[41]

It is this focus on territoriality as a form of political legitimacy to express "commonsense" viewpoints about immigration which led to the creation of the Southall Residents Association (SRA). In September 1963, the residents of Palgrave Avenue saw a house for sale sold by a young couple. A grassroots mobilisation immediately crystallised against the selling of the house to coloured people, with the formation of a Palgrave Avenue Residents Association which was to become, the very next month, the Southall Residents Association. At its helm was originally a prominent Conservative, Mrs Penn. Thanks to a petition signed by nearly all Palgrave Avenue residents, the Labour-controlled authority was pressured into buying the house. The council placed a compulsory purchase order on the house and had one of its medical officers move into it.[42]

Very early on, Mrs Penn was sidestepped for she favoured conciliation with the Indians, and aimed to liaise with the IWA to promote quality-of-life issues for both natives and Asians. Albert Cooney, a vehicle builder who had been living in Southall for thirty years, became the muscular chairman of the SRA. His approach was more of the vigilante, self-defence type facing the Asian "silent invasion".[43] When hearing about "threats" to natives, Cooney cried: "If ever such a threat is taken up, we shall not hesitate to take the law into our own hands. We shall not stand aside."[44] Cooney was close to the BNP, whose 1963 local election candidates in Southall he was central in nominating. One of these candidates was John Bean, who had solid far-right credentials and liked to call himself a "British Goebbels".[45]

In February 1964 four out of the twelve members of the SRA's committee resigned, including its founding member Mrs Penn. A further two resigned in the next few months, one because he left the area, the other to become a local election BNP candidate.[46] The association became ever more focused on the "Asian peril" locally, so much so that, in early 1966, it was dismissed by Ealing Labour MP Sydney Bidwell as having fallen into the hands by "some crude racialists".[47] Understandably, the IWA in its turn chose to take a more radical stance in local politics, in order to take on the hard-liners of the SRA. And, in 1963, the Southall International Friendship Council was created in order to counter the SRA's hateful discourse; naturally, it attracted left-leaning members sympathetic to the Indian presence.[48]

The SRA's political itinerary in the mid-1960s invites us to take the multi-issue concerns discussed earlier in this chapter with a pinch of salt. Indeed, in order to counter any accusation of racism, R. James, one of the SRA's board members, gave the list of all the issues it was actively involved in, including "housing, rates, trees in the streets, health, traffic problems, litter, parking nuisances, and crime". Committees were set up to deal with "traffic, air pollution and transport".[49] The truth, however, was more monothematic: race and immigration were the SRA's veritable *raison d'être*, and key non-racial issues (housing, health, litter, crime) were always looked at through a racial lens. In the SRA's rhetoric, the multi-issue focus was a smokescreen to deracialise race.

With hindsight, two central points are worth making about the SRA. First, its focus on locality and the grassroots (as opposed to unwelcome outsiders, whether bureaucrats or Asians) should not blind us to the fact that only Southallians who agreed with its immigration agenda were accepted as members. Probably because of the disappointment at Mrs Penn's volte-face, to be a *resident* was not enough to be made member.[50] The second point is that, besides being residents with a specific type of politics, members of the SRA proved to be residents with influence. It is remarkable that, after only a few weeks' existence, the association should have been instrumental in sending a delegation to the Department of Education and Science, and then in having Sir Edward Boyle, the education secretary, visit Southall to discuss Asian over-concentration in schools on the ground.

When Boyle comes to town

Sir Edward Boyle was the one pivotal actor in the introduction of bussing. A moderate Conservative, Boyle had decided to resign as a junior minister in the Eden Cabinet because he disagreed with the British handling of the Suez affair and, more to the point, he was one of the 25 Conservative MPs to abstain on the vote of the Race Relations Bill in 1968.[51] He spoke out against Enoch Powell repeatedly. Boyle was also MP for multi-ethnic Handsworth (Birmingham) from 1950 until his retirement in 1970. With first-hand knowledge of race-relations issues and new Commonwealth immigration, Boyle remained actively engaged in debates on integration and education. For instance, he accepted to become the chairman of the conciliation committee of the RRB in Yorkshire and the North-East in September 1970, a gesture which was saluted by Mark Bonham-Carter.[52]

Boyle had excellent credentials in the eyes of most moderates in Ealing, whether white or Asian, Labour or Conservative. A decade or so after the introduction of bussing, by the time it had spawned a great deal of opposition and had become "a racist policy though it started from the best of intentions", Labour MP Sydney Bidwell made it clear that Boyle, one of its founders, "could not by any stretch of the imagination be called a 'racist'" since "he was an outstanding opponent of racism whether it showed in the Midlands or anywhere else".[53] Piera Khabra and other leaders of the IWA would certainly have agreed with this.[54] But Boyle's appreciation of the education and integration issues raised in Southall (or in his constituency of Handsworth) was also typical of the period and framed in vigorously assimilationist terms. Furthermore, as historian Brett Bebber points outs, "Boyle, just like many American segregationists, cast the influx of South-Asian and Afro-Caribbean children as a problem, a drain on educational resources. Implicitly, 'immigrant' children proved unequal, saddled with less natural educational acumen, and a challenge to 'native' homogeneity."[55]

In *Immigration and Race Relations in Britain 1960–1967*, Sheila Patterson makes the point that the education of immigrant children was a non-issue for years.[56] In Southall, it started to crystallise only in 1962–63. The local press and council minutes from 1960 to 1962 and even 1963 have very few references to education as such,[57] much of the debate being centred on housing, overcrowding, multiple occupation, hygiene, overcharging by (Asian) landlords and so on. Indeed, there is anecdotal evidence aplenty to support the view that, before 1963, the presence of Asian

immigrant children in Southall schools, even Beaconsfield and Featherstone schools which were to be at the heart of bussing's introduction, was
indeed a strain but that it was not enough to translate into organised
resistance by white native parents. For instance, one Ealing journalist
visited Featherstone County Secondary School, exactly one year before
Boyle's visit to Southall. Expecting a "Little Rock Atmosphere",[58] the journalist interviewed headmaster G. Down and came to the realisation that
a great deal of racial harmony prevailed, the only very isolated incidents
being caused by parents who themselves were known racists.[59] Similarly,
in November 1961, at a time when one out of three pupils at Beaconsfield
Road Junior School was already Indian, headmistress E.A. Webster admitted that "the situation came to a point where special provision had to be
made so that the rest of the school could function normally" and felt
"encouraged for virtually no serious complaint [had] been received from
parents".[60] Arguably, the interests of the schools administrations locally
were not to paint too dark a picture, if only to cultivate peaceful race relations and contain the acceleration of "White Flight" to suburbia. Yet, it is
clear that until 1963 harmony and benevolence prevailed.

That year was when a tipping point was reached, when the situation
started to become untenable in the eyes of a growing number of white
parents, whose sense of frustration and fear about the future (of their
children) was actively whetted by the SRA. On 5 July 1963, a general
meeting was organised with the local education officers and the parents
of Beaconsfield Road schools. A deputation was set up to contact the Minister and asked to be received, in order to be "treated as a special area",
with extra teachers and extra resources. At this early stage, and against
the suggestion that Asians should be forcefully segregated, education
officer Mrs Jones warned that "we could not try to deal with the question
in the same manner in which the colour problem was being dealt with in
South Africa and America".[61] Then, on 1 August 1963, Sir Edward Boyle
received in his DES office a Southall deputation of five people including
the local education officer and E.A. Webster, headmistress of Beaconsfield
Road Junior School.

Two points may be made about this meeting. First, the possibility of an
Indian-only school was seen as a problem in itself but almost only from
the standpoint of white parents who were afraid about the lowering of
schooling standards. Second, the prospect of dispersal or bussing does not
seem to have been envisaged at this stage. To allay the fears of autochthonous parents, references were made to the hiring of extra teachers, to the
creation of reception classes for non-English-speaking immigrant children, and more generally to the "problem of parents wishing to transfer
their children to schools outside their appropriate catchment areas".[62]

Other meetings, held at Southall, shed further light on white parents' motives for wishing to get transfers to other catchment areas. It was during one of these, on 8 September, that an educational sub-committee meeting with parents came up for the very first time with the suggestion of dispersal or bussing, in rather unclear terms. Provided they got the ministerial go-ahead, "immigrant children might be diverted from Beaconsfield Road Primary School to other schools in the borough".[63] But the idea of dispersal of immigrant children really crystallised at a later meeting held on 7 October, one month later, to prepare for the ministerial visit scheduled the following week. At that Ealing meeting, "consternation was expressed at the high proportion of immigrant children": 58 per cent immigrant children in both departments of Beaconsfield School. This school would "inevitably become a 'coloured' school within two years unless very drastic steps [were] taken". To reduce this proportion "would entail transporting some of the immigrant children to other schools in the borough",[64] and contacts with another Southall school (Lady Margaret's) were already being made with a view to alleviating Beaconsfield. At the same time, a proactive policy needed to be introduced to make sure the white schoolchildren already there would remain. One of the ways to try to do this was by recommending that no new immigrant children be accepted at Beaconsfield in the year 1964–65.[65]

It was during the meeting at Edward Boyle's London office on 1 August 1963 that the idea of a ministerial visit to Southall was confirmed, on 15 October of the same year. Back then, that kind of event was a rarity, and Labour MP George Pargiter was key in bringing it about. Southall Grammar School was chosen for what was described repeatedly as a "private talk" between the minister himself, some local representatives and the concerned parents from Beaconsfield school, in particular. Letters of invitation were sent to all parents, a crowd of some eight hundred people was expected, but only four hundred indicated their intention to attend.[66] The IWA got to meet Boyle at 7.30 in the school's staff room before parents followed suit at eight o'clock. Although both had claims which were little different in nature, since the IWA at that time was broadly assimilationist, the separation confirmed that parents to be listened to were primarily white indigenous ones, who needed to be cajoled into remaining in multiracial Southall.

Another important point was the insistence on a *private* meeting with Boyle, which was caused by mounting racial tensions locally. During the ministerial visit, a police van was outside the grammar school and a bunch of BNP hardliners were chanting slogans like "Keep Britain White!", "Britain to the British!". Inside the building, some parents insisted on the need for a separate provision of educational facilities for natives and for immigrant children.[67] The SRA stalwarts, like Cooney, favoured segregation in schools.[68] Faced with this segregationist suggestion which was anathema to him, Boyle promoted a one-third scenario: once a school had reached what the minister called "the educational danger-point",[69] dispersal to other schools should be initiated.

According to many people present, the meeting itself went quite well. Boyle, in his speech to the Commons six weeks later, admitted that "in a political life of about thirteen years in this House, it was one of the best public meetings that I have attended".[70] Both the local councillors present and the members of the IWA were satisfied with the dispersal proposal. This should come as no surprise since in those years the IWA was focused, in the words of anthropologist Brian Keith Axel, on cementing "a regime of national normativity and mimicry"[71] among Asians, that is on making them "more British than the locals".[72] Piera Khabra, for one, stated that "it was a very successful meeting. We stressed the necessity of spreading our children out to all schools, and Sir Edward seemed to agree with us. I think he satisfied everyone."[73] This included other ethnic-minority public actors, for instance the British-Caribbean Association, whose secretary Felicity Bolton wrote to Boyle: "I am certain I am writing on behalf of our entire membership in thanking you for the stand you took with regard to the school situation in Southall. It is immensely encouraging to all of us who are trying to find ways to overcome racial prejudice to have a lead on this issue from the minister of education in Her Majesty's Government."[74] That point is important to make since a few years later, when it became evident that bussing was a failure, the IWA as well as others would backtrack and rally against it.

Boyle's move was even regarded as quite progressive, at a remove from the "Jim Crow" (i.e. segregationist) solutions pushed forward by some backlash conservatives and the angriest parents. In this whole debate, before, during and after the introduction of bussing, the United States was conjured as a potent racial foil. There were routinely ill-thought parallels between "England" and "America" (sometimes even to Apartheid South Africa), and Boyle made clear in his 27 November 1963 speech in the Commons that, the very week when President Kennedy had been assassinated, he entertained the hope that "the House [would] never be attracted by the spuriously respectable doctrine which has gone by the name of 'separate but equal'".[75] Boyle thought that inaction in this field would be unthinkable and almost criminal, and that action was very urgent. As he put it, "*laissez-faire* acceptance of what one might call *de facto* segregation"[76] simply was not an option. He then told his colleagues in solemn tones: "I must regretfully tell the House that one school, Beaconsfield Road

School, must be regarded now as irretrievably an immigrant school. The important thing to do is to prevent this happening elsewhere."[77]

The apparent progressiveness of dispersal as suggested by Boyle in 1963 may be gauged by the backlash of parents in favour of segregation or of repatriation who, a few years after its introduction, laid a bitter emphasis on how grossly inappropriate dispersal was proving as a method for solving racial issues in Southall. Boyle's personal correspondence has some anecdotal evidence of that. In one letter dated 9 March 1965, a Mrs R. Easter, now living in Slough, was scathing against the now former minister:

> Much of the blame for the explosive situation ... which lies across our path like a stick of dynamite must be laid at your door Sir Edward, for your approach and answer to the parents of Southall worried over the effects immigration was having on their own children's education, shocked and horrified everyone living in areas where immigrants had been allowed to congregate with no previous arrangements made beforehand to absorb them.[78]

To which Boyle curtly retorted: "I spoke to a crowded meeting of 5–600 people on what I fully recognised was a difficult and sensitive subject. I had an absolutely quiet hearing, followed by about ¾ of an hour of serious and thoughtful questioning."[79] Another letter exploited the "exile-at-home" motif so central to White Backlash talk and also, just as typically, invoked memories of the World Wars. This man, promoting segregation instead of dispersal, wondered "what right has Sir Edward Boyle to determine that these conditions must be accepted by the Native, to the extent that they are turned out from their Homes, education of their children neglected. We did not fight in two wars for this end product."[80] Maurice Foley and Harold Wilson likewise received letters in exactly the same vein, once the Labour administration pursued the policy of dispersal after 1965. Some SRA members complained about the immigrant menace to "decent living people", who had no other choice but "to move away, thus becoming refugees in their own country".[81] Such dynamics produced an urban and educational vicious circle: the more these (white) "decent living people" moved from Southall, the larger the proportion of Asians was, and the greater pressure for schooling dispersal was, in order to forestall the emergence of urban "ghettos".

The introduction of dispersal in Southall

Plans to set up dispersal were laid out immediately after Boyle's visit. The major concern, as a first step, was to sharply decrease the proportion of immigrant children in Beaconsfield schools (Junior Mixed and Infants) and to increase this proportion in Southall schools that had virtually no Asians. Table 1 highlights the local contrasts, and shows that not all Southall schools had a large intake of Asians. In fact, only Tudor Road Infants School, Featherstone Boys School and the Beaconsfield Road schools were above the official 33 per cent threshold suggested by Boyle. For instance, St Anselm's Catholic School had only six Asians for a total roll of 465 in the year 1965. There is a geographical irony in the fact that, in the years to come, thousands of Asians would be herded miles away from Southall whilst St Anselm's, being a denominational school, would obdurately remain white-only.

The table also indicates that Lady Margaret's Junior Mixed and Infants schools, as well as Dormers Wells (Junior Mixed) had a proportion of immigrant children equal to or lower than 10 per cent, which is why the Southall education authorities prioritised these schools when transferring children from Beaconsfield. Note that these figures are for 1965, a time when bussing had already started, albeit timidly, in Southall.

One month after Boyle's visit, an explanatory meeting was held at St Margaret's Primary School. Councillor P.G. Southey, chairman of the Divisional Education Executive, announced the introduction of an eighteen-pupil reception class in a school with an official maximum quota of four hundred pupils, a quarter of which was not filled. Nevertheless, six months later, the very same P.G. Southey expressed his satisfaction about the provision of a double classroom hut (for Asian reception classes) in the same school.[82] If the school building was not occupied to full capacity (three-quarters), why then build these huts? There as elsewhere Asian pupils with special needs implying special classes were not only "the kids on the bus", they were also "the kids in the huts", which underscored their radical Otherness in the eyes of native pupils in Ealing.

At the Lady Margaret's Primary School meeting, Southey faced an angry audience of three hundred parents who were afraid that the intake of some Asians into their children's school might "hold them back" and jeopardise their health at a time when fear of tuberculosis was rampant. With a total school roll of 316 in 1963, nearly all parents had gathered to hear the local authorities painstakingly promote the integration of Asians. The vehemence of the parents' reaction can be gauged by the fact that only a *reception class* was being planned, that is Asians, whatever their number, would remain in the same non-white (and hutted) class to learn English. This segregation for integration notwithstanding, many parents were afraid that Lady Margaret's might "degenerate" into another Beaconsfield. One father, to loud applause, told Southey: "You have assumed you will get our goodwill in promoting this class. But I do not want my children edu-cated with Indians", whilst another one wanted to know whom

Table 1 Distribution of immigrant children in Southall schools (early 1965)

School	Total roll	Indians and Pakistanis	Other immigrants	Total immigrants as a percentage of total roll
Beaconsfield Road (JM)	261	135	19	59
Beaconsfield Road (I)	175	93	9	58
Clifton Road (JM)	177	19	6	14
Clifton Road (I)	189	20	12	17
Dormers Wells (JM)	245	23	1	10
Dormers Wells (I)	231	28	5	14
Featherstone Road (JM)	321	32	8	12
Featherstone Road (I)	254	20	29	19
George Tomlinson (I&J)	330	49	4	16
Lady Margaret (JM)	356	4	4	2
Lady Margaret (I)	345	30	4	10
North Road	469	52	32	18
Saint Anselm's	465	6	7	3
Tudor Road (JM)	388	101	11	28
Tudor Road (I)	242	67	17	35
Dormers Wells Boys	521	97	9	20
Dormers Wells Girls	518	67	16	16
Featherstone Boys	576	189	8	34
Western Road Girls	402	85	8	23
Southall Grammar	768	7	NIL	0.9

JM: Junior Mixed; I: Infants.
Source: Southall LEA; Christopher Brocklebank-Fowler, Christopher Bland and Tim Farmer, *Commonwealth Immigration*, London: The Bow Group, 1965.

"segregation would harm". Southey appealed to their sense of humanity and charity, reminding them that "everyone here is supposed to be a Christian. Christ was a Jew, he was coloured you know", but this only unleashed a chorus of guffaws. Also with a view to placate the parents, the school's headmistress, Mrs Vann, admitted that she could cope "quite comfortably with a third of my school composed of immigrants".[83] Most of the crowd facing her could not cope with what to them was the ugly prospect of 6 or 7 per cent of Asians in a separate class within the school, or just outside the school's main building.

From this point until the publication, on 14 June 1965, of circular 7/65 which made dispersal official ministerial policy, a few other reception classes were opened in Southall or Ealing schools that Asian children were bussed to. The major one was in Northolt, which also caused some resentment among native parents, who felt resentful that their old and "already decrepit" school should have been selected as a site of social engineering.[84] There as elsewhere, though, major renovation works were done which started to improve everybody's lot, regardless of age, sex and race. For example, the bussing of Asians implied a need for larger spaces for the midday meal, since because of distances none of these children could go back home before returning to school early in the afternoon.[85]

It was probably serendipitous timing that the incorporation of Southall into the newly created borough of Ealing in April 1965 facilitated a process of dispersal validated by ministerial circular 7/65 only two months later. Councillor P.G. Southey welcomed the merger of Acton, Ealing and Southall into the new Ealing and stated that contacts had already been made with schools in Greenford, Northolt and Ealing to speed up dispersal.[86] No mention was ever made of the need to send children to schools that were as close as possible, to avoid undue strains for these children. On the contrary, in February 1964, the Southall borough contacted its Ealing counterpart and said it was "anxious that the large number of immigrant children resident in Southall should be spread in schools as widely as possible, so as to limit the numbers in the individual schools".[87] What was key therefore was to assuage white parents' fears by placing as few Asians as possible in individual schools, rather than make sure that "dispersal" could be achieved by as little "bussing" as possible. Often not informed about where their children went to school, Asian parents would probably not make themselves heard, unlike the angry crowd at Lady Margaret's primary school.

In practical terms, to alleviate already congested reception classes in the Southall area, others simply had to be introduced elsewhere. In July 1965, two reception classes were created: one in Downe Manor (Gifford), the other one in Northolt Primary School. In September of the same year, three others were announced: one in Brentside Secondary Boys School (Hanwell), Islip Manor Junior School (Northolt) and Barantyne Junior (Northolt).[88] Then in January 1966, three additional reception classes were agreed upon, to be opened immediately at Islip Manor (Brentside) and Acton Wells Primary School. All of these depended on the bussing of Asian children.

By 1964–65, in other words before circular 7/65, bussing was already a well-oiled system in Southall (and in Bradford), in spite of the practical difficulties that frequently arose. What comes to mind in the reading of the local press and archives is that, in order to become like others, that is speak English and interiorise the British/English "way of life", Asians had to be treated differently "for some time", it was hoped: they had to be transported by bus from more or less faraway homes and often had to be schooled in poor-quality hutted accommodation, thereby limiting contact with the natives. Once they had acquired enough English, in a process lasting from six months to eighteen, these Asians would get into mainstream classes, but most of them would continue to be bussed nonetheless, to maintain the artificial ratio.

What is also clear is the sheer horror that "segregation" elicited among policy-makers and the media. The natural ethnic clustering of Asians in Southall was, to the Boyles, Southeys etc. tantamount to Jim Crow Mississippi or South-African Apartheid. The imperative of "integration" understood as "assimilation" blinded the Establishment to distinctions which are self-evident a half-century later: Asians chose to come together and therefore were schooled together, they were not trapped or forced into segregated schooling as they would have been in the south-side of Chicago or in Birmingham (Alabama). Nevertheless, on both sides of the Atlantic, ethnic-minority parents were made into passive recipients of policies that affected their children directly. In England, Asian parents were not consulted about bussing and their main representatives (the IWA) initially backed dispersal schemes, only to backtrack a few years later; in the United States, Blacks struggled actively to become pivotal actors within education administrations which had always blissfully ignored them, in order to introduce a real form of desegregation with or without "busing".[89]

But the wrong-headed parallels between Southall's demographic dynamics and segregation in Dixieland may also be explained differently. England's local and national authorities could always take pride in actively thwarting any segregated scenario and wrap their policies with humanistic, integrationist soundbites. This was more palatable than having to express consent with Southall whites, some of whom cringed at the idea of having a dozen Asians in their children's schools, even if they were placed in "hutted accommodation". Instead of publicly endorsing "White

Backlash" mobilisations, these public actors would rather trumpet their integrationist concerns and humanitarian paternalism for the sake of Asians themselves, since, in their eyes, this had always been the British/ English way of doing things. In the words of Sir Archer Hoare, chairman of the Middlesex County Council committee, "A separate racial community in our midst would be contrary to the British way of life".[90] An Asian "ghetto" in the heart of England would be all the more repugnant to a certain view of Britishness as other forms of integration were at work in the early and mid-1960s, whether through comprehensive schooling (social class integration) or co-educational schooling (gender integration).

In an effort to gauge how exceptional the borough of Ealing's situation was, the divisional education officer sent letters to some of his colleagues across the country, in Cardiff, Liverpool, Birmingham, Bristol, Glasgow and Smethwick. What emerges from the responses received is that Birmingham and Smethwick did indeed share some of the issue Ealing was facing, albeit not on the same scale. This led Ealing to conclude that the problem at Beaconsfield Road was "not being met to the same degree anywhere else in the country and no solution to the dilemma has been suggested".[91] Simultaneously, the Bow Group, a moderately conservative think-tank, gathered statistics on the percentage of immigrant children (European and non-European) in all schools, which are reproduced in Table 2.

Table 2 Immigrant children (European and non-European) in schools (%): the LEAs' response (early 1965)

Hornsey (borough of Haringey, North London)	28.0
Southall	18.4
Smethwick	11.2
Greater London	9.3
Birmingham	7.8
Nottingham	5.9
West Bromwich	4.5
Bradford	3.6
Heston and Isleworth (Middlesex, including Hounslow)	2.9
Leeds	2.6
Walsall	2.0
Dewsbury	2.0
Oldham	0.9
Manchester	0.04

Source: Southall LEA; Christopher Brocklebank-Fowler, Christopher Bland and Tim Farmer, *Commonwealth Immigration*, London: The Bow Group, 1965.

The information in Table 2 is probably incomplete and relies on the goodwill of LEAs which chose to send responses to the Bow Group for its research. Notice, for instance, the absence of Wolverhampton, Liverpool or Slough. Whilst Southall is second and comes after Hornsey in North London, it must be emphasised that in Southall the immigrant group was much less diverse and less Anglophone than in North London.

Overall, such realisations are important for they underline what seemed like the unique situation in Southall, and how dispersal or bussing came about as a partly improvised solution to what was perceived as an unprecedented emergency situation. Although a decade later it came to be vilified as a racist policy with various detrimental consequences, dispersal was originally a measure of practical politics, however half-baked, discriminatory, tinged with hypocrisy and untenable in the long term. This is also how comparisons with the above towns should be read.

Notes

1 This title is a phrase from an oft-quoted Margaret Thatcher interview for Granada TV, 27.1.1978. She borrows from some of Powell's favourite themes and vocabulary.
2 Abigail Beach and Richard Weight, *The Right to Belong, Citizenship and National Identity in Britain, 1930–1960*, London: I.B. Tauris, 1998, p. 239.
3 Buettner, *Europe After Empire*, p. 49.
4 For all these figures, see Nicholas Deakin (ed.), *Colour and the British Electorate, Six Case Studies*, London: Pall Mall Press, 1965, pp. 32–3. It is worth mentioning that, unlike in other London boroughs, West Indians made up a minority among New Commonwealth migrants in Southall.
5 *Ibid.*, p. 34.
6 Ralph Fevre, *Cheap Labour and Racial Discrimination*, Aldershot: Gower Publishing, 1984, pp. 110–11.
7 Jonathan Oates, *History and Guide: Southall and Hanwell*, Gloucester: Tempus, 2003, pp. 112–13.
8 In the 1963 local elections for instance, the BNP came second in two Southall wards, Dormers Well and Hambrough, a fact which is very striking for a London borough in the 1960s.
9 Deakin (ed.), *Colour and the British Electorate*, p. 49.
10 Gest, *The New Minority*, p. 54.
11 See Patterson, *Immigration and Race Relations*, pp. 228–9.
12 Dan T. Carter, *The Politics of Rage: George Wallace, the Origins of the New Conservatism, and the Transformation of American Politics*, New York: Simon & Schuster, 1995, p. 447.
13 Formisano, *Boston Against Busing*, p. 3.
14 Piotr Stolarski, *Ealing in the 1960s*, Gloucester: Tignarius, 2013, p. 191.

15 Paul Foot, *Immigration and Race in British Politics*, Harmondsworth: Penguin, 1965, pp. 216–17.
16 Patterson, *Immigration and Race Relations*, p. 229.
17 Bill Schwarz, *Memories of Empire: The White Man's World*, Oxford: Oxford University Press, 2011, p. 37, p. 47 respectively.
18 See for instance *West Middlesex Gazette*, 17.12.1965.
19 *West Middlesex Gazette*, 14.4.1962.
20 This is true although a substantial number of Conservatives had little time for the eleven-plus tests and realised it was very much this education issue which precipitated their electoral defeat in the 1964 general elections.
21 *Middlesex County Times (Southall Edition)*, 8.1.1965.
22 The ethnographic work was on a sample of 200 voters locally. See Deakin (ed.), *Colour and the British Electorate*, pp. 48–9.
23 Michael Hill and Ruth Issacharoff, *Community Action and Race Relations: A Study of Community Relations Committees in Britain*, Oxford: Oxford University Press, 1971, p. 66.
24 *The Complete Novels of George Orwell*, London: Penguin Classics, 2000, p. 602
25 *Middlesex County Times (Southall Edition)*, 24.12.1965.
26 *Middlesex County Times (Southall Edition)*, 31.12.1965.
27 Patterson, *Immigration and Race Relations*, p. 253.
28 Dominic Sandbrook, *White Heat: A History of Britain in the Swinging Sixties*, London: Little Brown, 2006, p. 798.
29 See Schwarz, *Memories of Empire*, p. 11.
30 Slavoj Žižek, *Tarrying with the Negative: Kant, Hegel, and the Critique of Ideology*, Durham, NC: Duke University Press, 1993, pp. 201–2.
31 University of Leeds archives, Boyle papers, race relations files, MS 660/28009.
32 *West Middlesex Gazette*, 28.3.1964.
33 Ealing archives, Nigel Spearing papers, 1972 memorandum written by Amarjit Khera for Ealing CRC.
34 *Middlesex County Times (Southall Edition)*, 5.11.1965.
35 See comments by Justin Gest in his fieldwork on Barking and Dagenham in *The New Minority*, p. 124, p. 199.
36 That fact is evident from the fieldwork in eight distinct English areas in Hill and Ishacharoff, *Community Action and Race Relation*, p. 108.
37 Manchester Central Library, Muhamad Iqbal Ullah Research Centre, Race Relations Board archives, *Race Relations Board* newsletter, no. 4, June 1969.
38 *Daily Telegraph*, 7.2.1967.
39 *Middlesex County Times (Southall Edition)*, 25.11.1961.
40 Foot, *Immigration and Race in British Politics*, p. 164.
41 See the comments made by one Isabel Mason (Park Avenue, Southall) in *Middlesex County Times (Southall Edition)*, 1.6.1963.
42 Foot, *Immigration and Race in British Politics*, pp. 210–11.
43 *Middlesex County Times (Southall Edition)*, 17.8.1963.
44 Foot, *Immigration and Race in British Politics*, p. 212.
45 *Ibid.*, pp. 207–8.

46 Deakin, *Colour and the British Electorate*, p. 36.

47 Patterson, *Immigration and Race Relations*, p. 229.

48 Hill and Issacharoff, *Community Action and Race Relations*, p. 222.

49 *Middlesex County Times (Southall Edition)*, 19.11.1965.

50 See the insightful comments made by one A.E. Cracknell in *Middlesex County Times (Southall Edition)*, 18.1.1964.

51 Sir Edward Boyle, *The Politics of Education, Edward Boyle and Anthony Crosland in Conversation with Maurice Kogan*, Harmondsworth: Penguin Books, 1971, pp. 54–5.

52 Muhamad Iqbal Ullah Research Centre (Manchester), Commission for Racial Equality archives, *Race Relations, quarterly bulletin of the Race Relations Board*, Winter 1970–71.

53 Sydney Bidwell, *Red, White and Black: Race Relations in Britain*, London: Gordon & Cremonesi, 1976, p. 19.

54 See *Middlesex County Times (Southall Edition)*, 19.10.1963.

55 Bebber, "'We Were Just Unwanted'", p. 641.

56 See Patterson, *Immigration and Race Relations*, p. 253.

57 See, for instance, Ealing archives, Southall Council minutes, 1963, pp. 240–5.

58 This is a reference to the infamous 1957 episode when nine college students had to be escorted by the National Guard to enter their school in Little Rock (Arkansans). On the influence of this event in the race-relations debate in Britain, see Kennetta Hammond Perry, "'Little Rock' in Britain: Jim Crow's Transatlantic Topographies", *Journal of British Studies*, Vol. 51 (1), 2012, pp. 155–77.

59 *Middlesex County Times (Southall Edition)*, 27.10.1962.

60 *Middlesex County Times (Southall Edition)*, 11.11.1961.

61 *Middlesex County Times (Southall Edition)*, 6.7.1963.

62 *Middlesex County Times (Southall Edition)*, 3.8.1963.

63 *Middlesex County Times (Southall Edition)*, 3.8.1963.

64 Middlesex County Council, Education committee, Ealing archives, Report of sub-committee meeting with parents (7.10.1963), pp. 6–7.

65 This is what the borough did, with the proviso that children of five, who were reaching school age in 1964–65, should be accepted. See Ealing archives, Middlesex County Council, Education committee, Report of sub-committee (6.7.1964).

66 *Middlesex County Times (Southall Edition)*, 12.10.1963.

67 See Bebber, "'We Were Just Unwanted'", p. 640.

68 *Middlesex County Times (Southall Edition)*, 22.2.1964.

69 *Middlesex County Times (Southall Edition)*, 19.10.1963.

70 Hansard, *House of Commons Debates*, 27.11.1963, vol. 685, p. 441.

71 Brian Axel Keith, *The Nation's Tortured Body, Violence, Representation and the Formation of a "Sikh" Diaspora*, Durham, NC: Duke University Press, 2001, p. 178.

72 John DeWitt, *Indian Workers Associations in Britain*, Oxford: Oxford University Press, 1969, p. 1.

73 *Middlesex County Times (Southall Edition)*, 19.10.1963.

74 Leeds University Special Collections, Edward Boyle Papers, MS 660/27991.

75 Hansard, *House of Commons Debates*, 27.11.1963, vol. 685, pp. 440–1.

76 *Ibid.*, p. 439.

77 *Ibid.*, p. 441.

78 Leeds University Special Collections, Edward Boyle Papers, MS 660/28009.

79 Leeds University Special Collections, Edward Boyle Papers, MS 660/28009.

80 Leeds University Special Collections, Edward Boyle Papers, MS 660/28096. The letter is by one F. Billson (Hatch End, Middlesex), and is dated 22.4.1968, at a time when Boyle was refusing to vote against the Race Relations Bill that Enoch Powell had just vituperated against in his "Rivers of Blood" speech.

81 Quoted in Bebber, "'We Were Just Unwanted'", pp. 643–4.

82 *West Middlesex Gazette*, 11.4.1964.

83 For these quotes, see *West Middlesex Gazette*, 16.11.1963.

84 *West Middlesex Gazette*, 23.7.1965, 30.7.1965.

85 *West Middlesex Gazette*, 26.2.1965.

86 *West Middlesex Gazette*, 26.3.1965.

87 Borough of Ealing, Education Committee minutes (1964), p. 120. Other archives of the same period qualify this by stating that schools near Southall ought to be prioritised, which is why, at this very early stage, schools in further-away Acton were not seriously envisaged (see Ealing archives, Report of the divisional education officer, 7.12.1964, p. 3).

88 *West Middlesex Gazette*, 10.9.1965.

89 Delmont, *Why Busing Failed*, pp. 168–9.

90 *West Middlesex Gazette*, 2.11.1963.

91 Middlesex County Council, Education Committee, Ealing archives, report of the divisional education officer, 12.5.1964, p. 3.

2

Improvisation in high places? Setting the national framework for bussing

The aim in this chapter is to make sense of how, among national policy-makers, dispersal came to be regarded as a "necessary evil".[1] One school organiser summed up the dilemma many LEAs faced by describing it as "ethically wrong but educationally essential".[2] With this background in mind, what need to be analysed are the forms of legitimisation of bussing, as well as the ways the stumbling blocks around dispersal were under-stood. The key ones are: What exactly lay behind the cryptic "about one-third" of immigrant children? Was the phrase "immigrant children" defined and if so how and by whom? Should statistics be collected on this? Should dispersal be based on linguistic deficiency and/or on racial or ethnic difference? Lastly, why should "immigrant children" be the only ones to be bussed out? On this and a few other questions, many public and education actors had a say and said it loud: ministers, teachers, schools inspectors, academics, the press, MPs, local councillors and DES civil servants as well as think-tanks like the Fabian Society or the Bow Group.

Bussing is one of those issues that testify to how, historically, questions pertaining to immigration and integration have often been objects of consensus among the two main political parties in Britain once they are in power. Introduced in 1963 by Edward Boyle, a moderate conservative, dispersal was officially sanctioned and administered in 1964–65 by Harold Wilson's moderate Labour government. The key players in this political continuum were Edward Boyle (1923–81) of course, then Denis Howell (1923–98), joint parliamentary under-secretary for education and science under Harold Wilson. Also, though to a lesser extent, Anthony Crosland (1918–77), secretary of state for education and science from 1965 to 1967, and Maurice Foley (1925–2002), junior minister at the Home Office from 1966 to 1967, with special responsibility for immigration. Foley and Howell were MPs in constituencies, respectively West Bromwich and Small Heath (Birmingham), which vehemently debated dispersal, to the point that the former actually embraced the so-called "purposeful distribution of immi-grant children", quite controversially as it turned out.

The 1964 general elections gave Labour a paper-thin majority at Parliament (four seats only) and were very hotly contested, with race-relations issues being top of the agenda in some constituencies accommodating large New Commonwealth communities, such as the Birmingham conurbation and Southall. Undoubtedly, the most notorious campaign locally was in the industrial town of Smethwick (West Midlands), where Tory candidate Peter Griffiths defeated the shadow foreign secretary Patrick Gordon Walker, notably by using, in some leaflets, the slogan "If you want a nigger for a neighbour, vote Labour".[3] All this is quite well-known.[4] The Labour administration's embracing of dispersal must be considered with this general background in mind: the election was held on 15 October 1964, and circular 7/65 was published eight months later (on 14 June 1965).

"Seeing like a state": the political framework of dispersal

Whitehall established the political framework of dispersal between 1963 and 1965. The necessity for devising efficient tools and policies to teach English to immigrant children was framed by the broader objective to both limit (coloured) immigration into Britain and to assimilate those already in the country.

Four documents deserve a mention: *English for Immigrants*, a Ministry of Education pamphlet published on 29 November 1963 (six weeks after Boyle's visit to Southall); the Second Report of the Commonwealth Immigrants Advisory Council (published 6 February 1964); the Department of Education and Science Circular 7/65 entitled *The Education of Immigrants* (14 June 1964), and the White Paper *Immigration from the Commonwealth*, published on 2 August 1965. The exchanging of draft versions in Whitehall and the closeness of the publication dates make it almost possible to see these four as a single document outlining a cohesive whole.

Regarding *English for Immigrants*, suffice it to say that it contained suggestions on how to improve the teaching of English as a second language, based on on-the-ground observations made by HM inspectors. Tellingly, the document betrayed the absence of a really national perspective on a crucial question, as well as the absence of any thorough, nationwide research into the specific needs and the best methods to promote English for immigrants. The Slough-based National Foundation for Educational Research bemoaned the lack of funding available to carry out such research. If it had about £10,000 to £12,000 a year for three years, it claimed it could comprehensively investigate the national situation rather than just tinker at the edges of a daunting task.[5]

Parallel to this, there was in the early 1960s a worrying dearth of properly trained staff to teach such pupils, with only the University of Leeds giving training to would-be teachers of non-Anglophone students. On top of this, the educational apparatus already proved very strained: the annual report of the Department of Education and Science for 1964 revealed that 26 per cent of all classes in state schools had more than the recommended number of pupils.[6] That type of strain was much more likely to be felt in the already crowded districts that acted as magnets for immigrant settlement, such as Southall, a fact which was emphasised in a 1965 Fabian Society pamphlet critical of dispersal,[7] but which went unreported in the four documents presented here. There is also evidence of vast local discrepancies in the amount of public money spent on education.[8]

The second document was the Second Report of the Commonwealth Immigrants Advisory Council (CIAC), which dealt with education issues. The CIAC had been created by R.A. Butler under the pressure of Labour after the vote of the Commonwealth Immigrants Act (1962). This was the first government attempt at dealing directly with issues created by the presence of immigrants, and probably a half-hearted attempt, for the CIAC staff was part-time and unpaid. Nevertheless, its second report was not just shrugged off by education authorities, for its unflinchingly assimilationist common sense set the tone for circular 7/65 and much of the early years of dispersal.

An oft-quoted part of the report reads that "a national system of education must aim at producing citizens who can take their place in society properly equipped to exercise rights and perform duties the same as those of other citizens … A national system cannot be expected to perpetuate the values of immigrant groups."[9] Elsewhere in the report, it is stated that "if their parents were brought up in another culture and another tradition, children should be encouraged to respect it, but a national system cannot be expected to perpetuate the different values of immigrant groups".[10] Both the Schools Council and the NUT were critical of this apparent confusion between "cultures" and "values", and of the assumption that immigrants' values were necessarily distinct from those of indigenous whites.

Some parts of the report are more evident harbingers of dispersal. Paragraphs 25 and 26 underline the "contact hypothesis" which is seen as a *sine qua non* for integration: by being in touch with Anglophone (white) natives, immigrant children would get to learn the language and interiorise the British/English way of life more easily, to the ultimate benefit of everybody. But on the contrary, "the presence of a high proportion of immigrant children in one class slows down the general routine of working and hampers the progress of the whole class, especially where the immigrants do not speak or write English fluently". As a consequence, "we were concerned by the evidence we received that there were schools in certain parts of the country containing an extremely high proportion of immigrant children". [11] The spectre of ghetto schools having nothing to do with the English/British way of doing things was raised a little further on, hence the suggestion that there ought to be "arrangements to send children to some alternative school in order to preserve a reasonable balance". The Council regarded this "as a last resort but … preferable to *de facto* segregation, which is something to be avoided at all costs". [12]

What often comes through is a sense of one-sided, reified national identity that immigrant children are called upon to interiorise, especially in such phrases as "introduction to life in Britain", "introduction to British life". The mores, behavioural norms and cultural references are those of some (white) middle-class Briton who typifies life in the country as a whole. Of course, teachers were expected to act as the principal vectors of this acculturation: "The teachers see their role as putting over a certain set of values (Christian), a code of behaviour (middle-class), and a set of academic and job aspirations in which white collar jobs have higher prestige than manual, clean jobs than dirty". [13] This is but a telling grassroots illustration of the Marxian notion that at all times the ruling classes enjoy the ruling ideas and "the means of mental production", a concept which Antonio Gramsci would develop with his "hegemony". [14] In the present case, exhorted to don the mantle of reified Britishness, immigrant children whose parents were often small peasants or working class were also pressured to internalise the ways of the middle classes in what, ideally, was an obliteration of *both* their geographical and their social class backgrounds.

Enter circular 7/65. Among its eighteen paragraphs, three are directly about dispersal, in what is actually the largest part of the document. The introduction makes the claim that in no way are immigrant children to be treated as second-class citizens, and that they too, under the 1944 Education Act, "should enjoy all the opportunities enjoyed by other children and that they should be given a knowledge and understanding of our way of life which will enable them to regard themselves, and to be regarded, as full members of the community to which they each make their own contribution". The method (dispersal) devised by the DES to make the second part of the sentence possible (being regarded as "full members of the community") necessarily meant reneging on the claim made in the first part of the sentence, enjoying "all the opportunities enjoyed by other children", generally known as "parental choice". [15]

The circular resulted from a cursory analysis of the situation in Southall and in the West Midlands, with a focus on Asians rather than West Indians. [16] Also crucial was Bradford, which like Southall had introduced dispersal before the circular, and whose approach to immigrant children Denis Howell eulogised. Upon the understanding of these situations, "experience suggests" that, "apart from unusual difficulties (such as a high proportion of non-English speakers), up to a fifth of immigrant children in any group fit in with reasonable ease, but that if the proportion goes over one third either in the school as a whole or in any one class, serious strains arise". All efforts must therefore be geared towards the redrawing of catchment areas when this proves possible, that is when a district is not already inhabited by a very large number of immigrants. In any other case, "every effort should be made to disperse the immigrant children round a greater number of schools and to meet such problems of transport as may arise". To ensure the success of this policy its "reasons should be carefully explained beforehand to the parents of both the immigrant and the other children, and the cooperation obtained". Then, in what is the only part of the circular fully in italics, one reads: *"It will be helpful if the parents of non-immigrant children can see that practical measures have been taken to deal with the problems in the schools, and that the progress of their own children is not being restricted by the undue preoccupation of the teaching staff with the linguistic and other difficulties of immigrant children"*.[17]

Why the italics? There is no doubt that the circular's main concern was to assuage those whites in Southall, West Bromwich and Bradford who were fearful that their sons and daughters might be "held back" by Asians. The education of immigrants was almost solely apprehended through the lens of its alleged effects on white indigenous children. This is also how the official focus on linguistic deficiency among immigrant children may be construed. Surely, linguistic needs are not the be-all and end-all of the educational integration of immigrant students, since, as John Power put it, "an immigrant child, even of younger secondary age, is still a child with the ordinary emotional and psychological needs of children".[18] But this linguistic deficiency was the one problem probably most likely to constitute a strain on other, i.e. native, children. Hence the need to disperse the non-Anglophones to reassure white parents that their children would get the sustained attention of teachers.

Two other major issues arise from the reading of circular 7/65, which a few contemporaries were quick to expose. For one thing, no definition of "immigrant children" was provided, and it was left to the LEAs to devise their own definition, a perilous task eight months after the general election. Then, just as worryingly, the one-third quota was given regardless of the obvious fact that until then the DES had not collected statistics on immigrant children. It was only from 1 January 1966 that such statistics started to be gathered, and even then with some real difficulty, some LEAs clearly baulking at the task.

To be sure, reading this document with all this information in mind suggests that this was improvisation in high places. Some lost no time in pinpointing the circular's patent shortcomings. The Brent Friendship Council, which liaised with immigrants in a borough accommodating a very large multi-ethnic population, sent the DES the following questionnaire:

1/ How many schools in the country have more than the recommended number of immigrant children?
2/ How many non-English speaking children are in the schools?
3/ How many children, classified as immigrant, are there in the total school population?
4/ How many children, classified as immigrant, have been born in this country or born overseas?
5/ What is the age distribution of immigrant children at school?
6/ What objective studies have been made of the 'serious strains' referred to in paragraph 8 of the circular?
7/ What demographic evidence is there concerning the concentration of immigrants in certain neighbourhoods?

The ministry honestly answered the Brent association "that there were no statistics of this kind".[19] And as we know Brent was never to introduce dispersal.

In the wake of the circular's publication, both the moderately conservative Bow Group and the Fabian Society made some scathing comments, particularly on the way circular 6/75 oversimplified a vast array of causes into a single-issue initiative, that of "spreading the children". Although it stressed how important the degree of proficiency in English was, never did 6/75 take into account such variables as: the age of arrival in a school, whether children had or had not attended school before, the pre-existing conditions in the schools prior to the immigrant influx, whether these children were literate in another language or another alphabet, lastly, whether they were born in Britain or overseas.

The two think-tanks' comments are worth quoting at length. The Bow Group's conclusion was that:

The disadvantages of the quota system are such as to make it almost impossible to operate fairly. We feel that it can only be justified as a short term measure in exceptional cases, where educational difficulties would arise in a given school if more children with language difficulties arrived. Only on a basis of language ability should quotas be applied, any other criterion is almost certainly contrary to the provisions of the 1944 Act. The temptation to impose quotas as a result of parental pressure based on colour prejudice must be resisted, even where this leads to demands for transfers.[20]

The Bow Group would have agreed with the Fabian Society's conclusion, part of which is reproduced below:

> Problems that arise in schools in immigrant areas are going to be solved by education not logistics. Many schools and local authorities are getting on quite happily with percentages of immigrant children far in excess of that recommended by the Circular. Redistribution in itself is not a solution. The arrangements made within each school after the bus draws up at the door, wherever the bus comes from, are the vital point.[21]

The fourth document to be discussed was the White Paper on *Immigration from the Commonwealth* (1965), which aimed at curtailing the number of vouchers to reduce the flow of skilled workers, however badly needed these might be. *The Guardian* called it "the indefensible White Paper":[22] within the suggestion made of 8,500 vouchers a year, Maltese immigrants were reserved one thousand, which was grossly disproportionate. Then, Irish immigrants were not included in this limitation, as this would have probably created some bad blood between North and South and caused issues on the Irish border. These provisions are important because they run parallel with some debates on whom to include as "immigrant children" in the dispersal policy. Also, they were sorry signals to New Commonwealth immigrants already in Britain that the White Paper, a political aftermath of Smethwick, could hardly have been any whiter indeed. If some Labour MPs such as George Pargiter (Ealing) or Roy Hattersley agreed with its restrictionist approach, the document did cause much of a stir with some other figures. Some Labour councillors and CRC officers resigned in protest against what they saw as the "infamous" White Paper. MPs David Weitzman (Hackney North) and Norman Atkinson (Tottenham) said the document rested on "muddled thinking" on race and immigration.[23]

Part 3 of the White Paper was called "Integration" and promised some government grants for Community Relations Councils, or liaison officers, if local authorities were committed to help by providing office accommodation and secretarial staff. One paragraph ("Conditions of Success") lays great stress on the need to arrive at decisions through mutual consent between "host" and immigrant communities: a liaison committee should be a joint project "in which immigrant and host community are both fully involved".[24] Some contemporaries, such as Dipak Nandy, were quick to expose the myth of mutual decision-making; at best there was native paternalism, or agreements struck with non-representative, self-appointed immigrants, "Uncle Tom" Asians or West Indians. Dipak Nandy also believed that much of the vocabulary mobilised to promote racial harmony was spurious, such as "liaison" (as in Voluntary Liaison Committees), which "suggests a symmetrical, two-way relationship that does not obtain in real life".[25] Such critiques struck a particular chord when thinking of the way dispersal was introduced, despite the fact that the IWA (Southall) agreed with it.

What's in a figure?

The concept of "quota" when applied to minority groups is itself fraught with ambiguity. "Quotas" are broadly seen by public opinions (in Britain, in America notably) as protective of subordinate groups whilst they also, in some cases, apply to supposedly undesirable groups whose presence is resented and should be curtailed, such as quotas on the number of Jews at Harvard prior to the Second World War.[26] Regarding dispersal, quotas were apprehended as "protective" (to allow immigrant children to integrate by being bussed) as well as "stigmatising" (surely, more than 30 per cent or so was unpalatable to the native whites).

From the outset, the one-third quota was envisaged as flexible. It simply had to be for, astonishingly, the DES chose as a model for its circular a rather atypical outer London district, Southall, with a single, non-English-speaking population whose number had skyrocketed in only three years.[27] Not all LEAs faced the same situations, although, among the variables and parameters compounding or easing difficulties on the ground, the DES was only able to identify the most obvious one: the extent of deficiency in English. Sometimes the one-third quota referred to specific classes within schools, sometimes to a school population as a whole. H.E.R. Townsend, in a late 1960s study conducted for the National Foundation for Educational Research, discovered that, among the LEAs which had taken up dispersal, the quota varied from 10 per cent in one case to 40 per cent in another.[28] Another reason was simply that LEAs enjoyed broad leeway: just as they were merely advised to introduce dispersal, they could interpret the "about one third" suggestion as they saw fit. In this respect, the DES's general attitude was best summarised by one of its spokespersons interviewed in 1963: "We're leaving it to the local authorities, who have different and esoteric problems".[29]

Depending on local circumstances, the one-third quota was slightly altered either (originally) out of choice or (soon enough) out of necessity. Bradford deliberately opted for a 25 per cent quota even before the circular was issued, whereas Ealing, faced with the soaring number of Asian children in the mid-1960s, felt by July 1966 that its sole option was to change 33 per cent to 40 per cent.[30] Another upshot was that, whilst there remained some vacant places in Southall schools, some Asians were dispersed by bus to try to maintain the desired quota artificially.[31] In a comprehensive

1968 study of dispersal locally, the Ealing International Friendship Council stated: "It is clear that the quota system is already breaking down, and if the ratio of immigrants to host the community in Southall continues to rise, even the dispersal system as operated at present cannot prevent almost all-immigrant schools".[32] At the same time, had dispersal not been implemented, some schools would already have become 100 per cent Asian by 1968.[33]

There is evidence aplenty that even the 40 per cent ratio was untenable. In 1972, Ealing councillor Michael Elliott avowed that "we have tried to adhere to that figure, but one or two schools have always exceeded it".[34] The best example was Beaconsfield Road School, which the Ealing borough dismissed as "hopeless" only one month after circular 7/65 was issued.[35] There is a baffling irony in the fact that the one school which was at the origin of dispersal's introduction proved unable, from the very start, to stick to the ministerial "about one third". Unsurprisingly, in the late 1960s Bradford was also faced with a dispersal system bursting at the seams. Although the 25 per cent ratio was adhered to, in some schools 33 per cent was the norm, and even this was difficult to preserve. The only viable option was either to disperse whites in order to let more Asians in or to spend more money on welcoming extra Asians. Or else to "abandon dispersal to allow the vacant places in the central area schools to be filled by immigrants which would in due course mean the creation of virtually immigrant schools". This prospect was deemed "most undesirable".[36]

Another bone of contention was the apparently unscientific character of the one-third proportion. As was exposed by the Brent Friendship Council, doubts could be raised as to the grounds on which this ratio rested. As for the DES, it was at pains to prove otherwise, despite the fact that, in archives, some HM inspectors had already suggested, by May 1963, that one-third was an acceptable boundary.[37] An editorial from *Education*, published three days before the circular, stated that the document had drawn extensively from "the collective experience" of LEAs covering "about 30 towns", which went unnamed.[38] Denis Howell himself, who masterminded the circular, was pressured in the Commons to give details on how this complex issue had been investigated, if at all. Reginald Freeson, Labour MP for Willesden East (Brent), asked to be further informed. The exchange between the two Labour figures fittingly encapsulates the suspiciousness of the opponents of dispersal as well as the defensive position of those who advocated it:

Mr Reginald Freeson: asked the Secretary of State for Education and Science upon what statistical or other evidence based on social and educational studies he concludes that there is a need for organised dispersal of immigrant children by local education authorities, as would be required by the implementation of his Circular 7/65.

Mr Denis Howell: The Secretary of State [Anthony Crosland] is in constant touch with the local education authorities who are carrying the main responsibility for the education of immigrant children. Detailed information and advice about the educational and social considerations which apply is also available to him from H.M. Inspectorate of schools. He has concluded from a close study of this information, and on the professional advice of those most closely associated with this problem, that the difficulties in both schools and classes are manageable where the number of immigrants is generally not in excess of 30 per cent of the total number of children. Practical experience in the schools shows that when this figure is exceeded the proportion of immigrant children tends to increase rapidly and such a situation militates against a policy of integration which is the main aim of the Government.

Mr Reginald Freeson: Is my hon. Friend aware that in fact this is not the general experience in all areas – and I choose my words carefully – where there are immigrants settling in this country, while it may be true in certain specified areas. Are we to take it from my hon. Friend's reply that there have been no properly designed social surveys and studies made as a basis for this circular?

Mr Denis Howell: My hon. Friend is quite wrong to say that. There is the overwhelming evidence of the professional people involved – and I know this from my own practical experience of sending my own children to such a school. These problems are manageable up to a certain percentage, after which a considerable difficulty arises.[39]

Howell's autobiographical quip was a rhetorical device to silence those among his colleagues who lived in leafy suburbia or sent their children to private or denominational schools. Clearly, his point was to show that, unlike the elite of the so-called "race relations industry" routinely vilified by the radical right, his own social and urban environment was the very same as that of those white families who had campaigned against the "invasion" of Asian children in "their" schools.

Reading Howell's autobiography published twenty-five years after this debate invites us to take his House of Commons claim with a hefty pinch of salt. He was a key national figure in the administration of sport, and his book has only a few pages on education issues. But these make for compelling reading. First, debates on dispersal and on the necessary ratio to initiate dispersal were not merely abstract musings for him. Indeed, Howell speaks about how his own children's schooling, which spanned eleven years from 1964 to 1975, reflected the swift increase of immigrant children in the inner rings of Birmingham. Andrew, Michael, Kate, David and his four children experienced dramatically contrasted situations. Andrew, the eldest, went to Park Hill school at a time when 10 per cent of the children schooled there were immigrants, whereas David, ten years later, told his father upon coming back from school: "this has been a great day, another white boy has joined our class, there are now two of us". Howell also elaborated on the scale of 'White Flight' in these Birmingham areas.[40]

But more to the point is that, prior to the elaboration of the circular, Howell dithered a great deal over the actual percentage of immigrant children to be agreed upon before dispersal was recommended. Then Howell talked to Mr Labon, the headteacher of Park Hill School where he sent all his children, and Mr Labon, in whose experience Howell trusted, suggested that 30 per cent was a maximum, taking into consideration all sorts of linguistic, cultural, sociological, class elements: "he [Mr Labon] thought he could maintain standards at that level but he would be very concerned if it went much higher". Then Howell acknowledged: "My officials appeared incredulous when I explained all this to them but they could not produce any challenge on professional grounds so that was that".[41] Needless to conclude that Reginald Freeson and the Brent Friendship Council were completely right to expose the unpreparedness and lack of exhaustive research at the DES.

Defining and quantifying "immigrant children"

The absence of definition of "immigrant children" further complicated the issue, as well as the absence of statistics on their actual number. These two facts confirm the general feeling of unpreparedness which permeates this chapter.

Deprived of any specific guidance by the DES on how to interpret "immigrant children", LEAs were given broad – and dangerous – leeway to define the phrase as they saw fit. This is shown by an embarrassment about referring to race as such,[42] that is by using the term "colour(ed)", but the way the circular was construed certainly does confirm the impression of a colour bar. This racial slant was nurtured by the perception that white immigrant children were not meant to be a problem. As had been the case already with the White Paper *Immigration from the Commonwealth*, Irish immigrants were specifically excluded from the category. Except for specific places on the British mainland where religious sectarianism was still rife (Glasgow and Strathclyde, to a lesser extent Liverpool), only on very rare occasions were the Irish seen by the administration as actual *immigrants* in the way West Indians or Pakistanis were. Shared war memories and the perception of a shared popular culture undergirded this belief.

As "internal others",[43] the Irish therefore were not seen as enough of a problem to be included as *immigrants*. Much the same could be argued for Italians. Indeed, Bedford, with its substantial Italian population geographically concentrated in a very specific area, also had a large population of non-Anglophone immigrants. But these being white and of "European stock", the question of whether Bedford should or should not introduce dispersal never seems to have been a matter of debate. To Sheila Patterson, these Italian children were "presenting just as great social and educational difficulties [as in Southall], though they lacked publicity value".[44] No surprise, then, that in 1968 the Ealing International Friendship Council should have deplored that "it does not seem to have been thought out clearly at any stage whether the justification for the quota system and dispersal lies in language, culture or colour differences".

Two years earlier, the DES had finally managed to give a definition for "immigrant children", which ran thus:

1/ Children born outside the British Isles who have come to this country with, or to join, parents or guardians whose countries of origin were abroad;

2/ Children born in the United Kingdom to parents whose countries or origin were abroad and who came to the United Kingdom within the last ten years.

But despite such (belated) guidance, some LEAs still chose to apply their own (more restrictive) definition. Such was the case for Birmingham. In a 1970 letter to Enoch Powell, who was demanding statistical information about immigrant children, education officer Mr Stickland provided the following details regarding the way Birmingham education authorities were asking their schools to evaluate their number:

Whether or not to classify a child as an "immigrant" for the purpose of this inquiry must be in some measure a matter for the Head's own judgement, but you are asked to use the following as a guide:

(a) : all pupils of non-European stock (one or both parents) should be regarded as "immigrants" even if they were born here.

(b) : European children – and this applies especially to Irish children– should be regarded as "immigrants" (wherever born) if their background leads to any substantial difficulties or problems, educational or social.

If however, they are well enough assimilated to fit in to the school without special help or consideration, educational or social, they should not be regarded as "immigrants" for the purpose of this inquiry.[45]

Part (b) in the Birmingham reinterpretation of part 2 from the ministerial definition is nothing but a more radical form of racialisation of "immigrant children". In both, children born in the UK are still, under certain circumstances, considered as immigrants, owing to the widespread belief in the mid-1960s that New Commonwealth people were cultural Others lacking in integration, either being culturally deprived (the estranged West Indians who did not really know who they were) or having too much culture (Indians and Pakistanis). That mindset made it possible to regard (British) children of immigrants as immigrant children, raised by parents who had not assimilated. More broadly, it was an affirmation of *jus sanguini* congruent with the evolution of British legislation in this respect, say, from the British Nationality Act of 1948 to that of 1981. This is what is meant by "racialisation", the ascription of race identities to particular groups as though they were fixed and immutable. This was at play in political debate, in legislation designed to control immigration, but also in the field of education policy and practice, in health care and in policing, as applied to groups defined primarily in terms of their colour or (allegedly) immutable culture. That view of racialisation chimes with the specific definitions of "ontology" as given by Ann Laura Stoler and Ian Hacking, the former seeing it as "that which is about the *ascribed* being or essence of things, the categories of things that are thought to exist or can exist in any specific domain, and the specific attributes assigned to them", the latter highlighting for his part "what comes into existence with the historical dynamics of naming".[46] Such powerful mental processes largely shaped bureaucratic practices at the root of dispersal.

A great many public actors dealing with education issues were unhappy with this racialising approach, and that included Southall and Hanwell MP Sydney Bidwell, who criticised this definition in no uncertain terms, since it gave grist to the anti-Asian mill locally. The Brent Community Relations Council dismissed it as "inaccurate and arbitrary", and stated that statistics should be first and foremost collected to make sense of the provision of education and of the general outlook of the student population.[47]

The Birmingham city approach could hardly have been more different. Indeed, part (b) in the Birmingham definition amounted to a conceptual straitjacket: to be counted as an immigrant, you had to constitute a living problem, whether educational, social, behavioural, an urgent problem but one which could be mended only at great cost by taxpayers etc. Birmingham's appraisal, therefore, was a public institutionalisation of prejudice in the second city of England. Although it never introduced dispersal, that type of definition meshed quite well with certain critiques of dispersal, such as this one by multicultural educationalist David Milner, from a book that was vastly influential in academia:[48] "Policies like dispersal institutionalise the recognition of the disparity between the races. They allow that white people's wish to remove immigrants from their neighbourhood schools is a permissible sentiment; by actually implementing this desire they confirm the immigrants' second-class status and officially endorse the prejudice."[49] Such definitions as Birmingham's definition of immigrant children nurtured a performative stereotyping of "race", rooting even more deeply certain widely held beliefs in what is a socially constructed vicious circle redolent of the classic W.I. Thomas theorem: "If men define situations as real, they are real in their consequences".

It is precisely the looming threat of an analogical racial vicious circle which accounts for the local reluctance to collect statistics on immigrant children, that is, once the definition had been provided by the DES. In January 1966, about six months after the circular, new forms called "7i schools forms" were sent to the 146 LEAs as supplements to the customary annual returns of all pupils.[50] It was only the Southall crisis which had precipitated this willingness to statistically evaluate the demographics of race and education in England, as Denis Howell was to admit in 1967: "the Department were without definite evidence of the number and distribution of immigrant children, and a delicate political decision was needed before a statistical count could be undertaken".[51] Without Southall then, the DES would not have felt compelled to reach this extremity.

Here, the pros and cons run parallel to the broader debate about the collecting of ethnic (and religious) statistics. Those in favour argued that the collection of such statistics would help educational efficiency and facilitate the distribution of local and ministerial funds, which was a matter of justice for the children involved. Those against feared that the public revelation of substantial proportions of immigrant children would act as a deterrent to white parents, accelerate "White Flight" and confirm the belief that some Southall, Bradford and West Bromwich neighbourhoods were blighted, problem areas with an ailing population in need of special assistance. In the early 1970s, the Brent Community Relations Council and the Brent Teachers Association expressed their concern in no ambiguous terms: "However well-intentioned the motives of those who support the collection of such information may be, the *effect* is to highlight and stress the 'problems' of one section of the school population and divert attention from the real needs of all teachers and children". The Ealing Community Relations Council loudly agreed with this statement. The Brent and Ealing bodies therefore pressured the NUT to instruct its members to "refuse to provide information about their pupils which can be used against the children".[52]

Tellingly, this opposition reflected the broader, age-old dilemma about the actual finality of statistics. These are alternatively understood as a control tool used by the establishment, a device in the hands of scientific or pseudo-scientific governmentality to naturalise the cultural and the social, or as a "weapon of the weak" mobilised by progressive militants wishing to emancipate subaltern groups. Classic works by Alain Desrosières and Tod Porter lay great emphasis on this historical duality,[53] which has a specific relevance for Britain, a country whose history is tightly linked with the emergence and evolution of public statistics,[54] and whose modern Welfare State would witness the proliferation of statistics and experts auditing the efficiency of welfare provision in many domains.[55]

Another moot point is that, in the 1960s, the British legislative framework was still envisaged as the "quintessence of colour-blindness".[56] When sociologist Ruth Glass argued in 1960–61 that ethnic statistics should be mobilised to gauge as accurately as possible the extent of discrimination in England, she was painfully aware of how marginal her voice was.[57] Also, the use of "race" raised a concern about sounding "racist" or "racialist"; therefore circumlocutions were prioritised over explicitly racial terminology, one of the best-known being "New Commonwealth" to refer to black and brown immigrants who came from India, Pakistan, Jamaica, and not from the white "Old Commonwealth" of British stock. In the field of education, the DES preferred "non-English speaking", "culturally deprived", "educationally disadvantaged" rather than explicitly racial phrases. Furthermore, the use of racial references also clashed with the move towards comprehensive education: its very inclusiveness, trumpeted by the Wilson government, tended naturally to favour a colour-blind approach to the education of non-whites.[58]

Despite this real ministerial concern with racial references, circular 7/65 failed to *clearly* objectify the problem as one of linguistic, rather than racial-cum-cultural, deficiency. In paragraph eight of the circular, descriptions of non-Anglophone children are to be found at the beginning ("the number of immigrant children who are proficient in English") and at the very end ("the linguistic and other difficulties of immigrant children") but nowhere is it said in so many words that, for instance, immigrant children (whether defined or undefined) are to take a test of English proficiency and that, should a large enough proportion of these fail the test, then dispersal becomes a recommended option. Hence the accusation that the circular was discriminatory in nature, thrown by the Fabian Society (7/65 "fully deserves being branded as discriminatory")[59] as well as the Bow Group ("it is obvious that the quota can all too easily be based on a colour bar").[60] The 1965, 1968 and 1976 Race Relations Act would provide the opponents of dispersal with a legal framework to combat it in court. But finding individuals to sue would prove another story, as will be explored shortly.

Why not the white children?

Only on very rare occasions were white students bussed out in England. And when they were, it was solely in the few town centres, such as Bristol, where overcrowding had led to the moving of non-immigrant *as well as* of immigrant pupils.[61] But whites were never dispersed in an attempt to achieve something approaching what Americans debating the desegregation of schools in the northern states would call "racial balance". Therefore, dispersal was criticised from its very early stages as unfair because it was a one-way process, and from its very inception advocates of dispersal did their utmost to legitimate what was indeed a major flaw which, ten years later, Asians would mobilise against. In his House of Commons speech on Beaconsfield School (Southall), Edward Boyle acknowledged that "it is both politically and legally more or less impossible to compel native parents to send their children to a school in an immigrant area", before adding that "one must recognise the perfectly legitimate anxiety of many of the parents".[62] Despite that, archives show that the NUT did discuss, in 1965, the feasibility of "distribution schemes" including the dispersal of whites, but this was swiftly nipped in the bud. To John England, Birmingham headmaster and expert in education, the suggestion created a furore which acted as a powerful deterrent: "It was heartily damned, it met with such violent emotional opposition that we did not feel it prudent to put the proposition forward".[63]

Though imaginable in theory, bussing white children to forestall "ghetto schools" would stumble against (white) parental choice as upheld in the 1944 Education Act, a principle which was already inscribed in the Foster Act of 1870. Furthermore, the triumph of consumer society in the 1960s started to entrench in white middle-class families the view of an "education market" which the Thatcher years would later crystallise for good. In this market, white upper- and middle-class families who had "never had it so good" were top of the pile whereas immigrant families in need of assimilation were placed at the very bottom. Interestingly, at a time of assimilationist consensus, the view that white students themselves, if placed in racially mixed schools, might actually fare better academically and as citizens in a multi-ethnic society was almost never voiced.

Contemporary legitimisations of dispersal as one-way traffic often rested on a belief in the deficient citizenship of immigrants. These were primarily immigrants *before* they were citizens, despite the fact, almost never mentioned in public debate, that they were all under the British Nationality Act (1948) "citizens of the United Kingdom and Colonies". Actually, that (white) consensus in Britain clashed with the self-definition of a substantial number of "immigrants" from the West Indies, for whom there is vast anecdotal evidence that they felt British before anything else.[64] This was to the point that some baulked at regarding themselves as "immigrants" at all: one West Indian interviewed by Nicholas Deakin held the view that "we are not immigrants in the true technical sense:

after all, we are members of the Realm, we are British".[65] Nevertheless, the unclear wording of circular 7/65 meant that in certain areas (West Bromwich being the best example) English-speaking immigrants with a strongly interiorised sense of British citizenship such as West Indians were bussed out alongside non-Anglophone Asians.[66] According to educationalist Nicholas Hawkes, nothing better than the West Bromwich case "could illustrate ... the confusion between colour and real educational issues which bedevils the whole question of immigrant children in schools".[67]

West Indian self-identification as British was at loggerheads with the native white justifications of one-way dispersal. Anteriority of presence (being "natives" instead of "newcomers"), being tax-payers, being citizens worried that newcomers ought not to take advantage of native hospitality were all recurrent themes vindicating double standards in their eyes, as is shown in these statements by three Ealing borough councillors made at different times:

> Dispersal in Ealing was a policy adopted by whites, and for whites. The white children were here first.[68]

> There is a difference on this point between England and the United States. You've got there black children and white, but they're all American citizens. Here they have come from overseas ... They're guests, and it's a little unreasonable to impose a very great disadvantage on the English community.

> They're here because of a constitution laid down in Victoria's time saying that they were Commonwealth citizens; now they've taken advantage of it.[69]

Although not explicitly evidenced just above (but implicit enough in the use of "guests"), the tax-paying argument was a potent one since it helped to deracialise the debate at a time when referring explicitly to "race" still went against the British grain and to confirm the deficient citizenship of New Commonwealth immigrants. Whites were not dispersed for the very reason that they were fully fledged citizens who paid taxes and rates. It was a way to suggest that Asians did not, or not nearly enough, a fact that was publicised in the notorious cases of income-tax evasion among Asians, which in turn facilitated the massive sending of remittances back home to Pakistan and India.[70] Traditionally brandished as an argument by political minorities (from suffragettes in the 1910s to Asian immigrants in the 1980s) in order to get political justice and equality and to assert their full belonging to the nation,[71] the tax-paying argument was also employed by the white-dominated establishment, but this time in order to deny immigrants full citizenship and to claim that, in effect, double standards for whites and immigrants were only a matter of plain common sense and justice. That kind of rationale has already been analysed in US debates on bussing and the desegregation of education, here by historian Camille Walsh in a statement which has a potent resonance for England:

> The use of taxation and "taxpayers' rights" as a principle to uphold segrega-tion was implicitly premised on the idea that African Americans must proportionally pay less in taxes, and therefore were not entitled to the same benefits as whites. A sense of paternalism toward African Americans was often connected to the belief among whites that the public tax funds really belonged to whites to distribute. Whites repeatedly asserted that they paid "more" taxes than blacks and therefore had the right to be heard by courts and legislatures. This sense of "buying" services from the government through tax payments was connected to an idea that African Americans were "lesser" taxpayers and therefore "lesser" citizens.[72]

One last point may be made, about dispersal as an acculturation strategy to assimilate immigrant children. Since, as has been said before, the accul-turation model was a vaguely reified, middle-class British-cum-English identity, it could conceivably be claimed that, deprived of middle-class cultural references and of the canons of respectability that are prerequi-sites for upward mobility, working-class or poor whites ought to be dis-persed to middle-class areas to receive their schooling, to be rightfully acculturated to a national (and social class) norm. Odd though it may seem, it was probably that point which was touched upon by Maurice Kogan, who was commissioned by the RRB in 1975 to write a report on the discriminatory nature of dispersal. The professor of public policy studies at Brunel University stated that, unlike an English language test, a test in "English lore and culture" was hardly imaginable, that it would not be as efficient as a test in English and that nobody seriously thought about putting white children to this type of test. He went on to add that "there are probably indigenous white people in Southall who are not dis-persed although their enjoyment of English lore and culture might be minimal".[73] It is impossible to tell whether in Kogan's eyes this cultural deficiency was owing to the immediate ethnic environment of these white children in Southall or because of social class criteria and imagined norms of respectability. But be that as it may, the exhortation to interiorise British culture, norms and landmarks must sound odd with hindsight.

A hard sell

The fact that Birmingham and above all London (Inner London Education Authority) rejected dispersal from the outset will be analysed separately in Chapter 4, for these two LEAs were by far those accommodating the largest number of immigrants' children (about seventy thousand in 1965, as opposed to the twelve thousand dispersed nationally) and, as such, wielded decisive influence on debates nationwide. From the very publication of circular 7/65, it appeared that those who were most adamant about the necessity for dispersal had actually started to introduce it even *before* the circular was out: these are, as we know, Ealing and Bradford. A great many other LEAs with a large immigrant population were lukewarm at best.

For instance, Charles Smyth, chief education officer for Eton and Slough, argued against bussing, for parents were very reluctant to send their children far away from their homes and "anyway we haven't got the transport". In Bedford, Eric Walker, the town's education officer, stated that "head teachers here are not in favour of dispersal".[74] Brent, despite an immigrant children population of 25.1 per cent in 1968, was absolutely opposed to any concept of dispersal. The Brent CRC went so far as to ask the question: "Why shouldn't schools in predominantly immigrant areas be predominantly immigrant?"[75] Mostly, the Outer London borough was keenly aware of the ailing state of education in inner-city areas, notably when stating: "we feel that dispersal will not help the situation which will only change when deprived areas are replanned and rebuilt".[76]

In Manchester too, disapproval was massive. Edwin Wetton, headmaster in a Moss Side school with more than 50 per cent immigrants, argued: "I disapprove of their dispersal in several schools as suggested by the Ministry". As for J.K. Elliott, chief education officer in the city, he implicitly disavowed dispersal by stating that "Manchester's policy for immigrant children has been to attach them to normal classes and to allow them to work with their classes as far as possible".[77] A similar approach prevailed in Nottingham and in Leeds, with the latter enjoying the added advantage of hosting a very active department in its university which, under the aegis of educationalist June Derrick, devised innovative methods and tools for the teaching of English as a second language.[78] In Leicester, education officer Elfed Thomas believed that the overriding priority was to generate confidence and mutual trust between the schools, the local authorities and the parents of immigrant children, a need which was all the more crucial as the apparently permissive atmosphere of English schools appeared very unsettling to many parents. "Every effort should be made to encourage contact" between parents and schools, he argued, before adding that "at best, a policy of dispersal particularly as applied to pupils of primary school age, would seem to us likely to create as many problems as it seeks to solve and should only be embarked upon, therefore, after the most careful and cautious appraisal of all the relevant factors".[79] Having said that, Leicester would reconsider its education policy towards immigrant children when faced, a few years later, with the influx of Ugandan Asians, although most of these were Anglophones. As for Reading, its chief education officer W.L. Thomas acknowledged the town's comparative geographical good fortune by not having neighbourhoods where non-Anglophone immigrants were overly concentrated, before adding: "I would in any case uphold the principle of non-dispersal since I am convinced that eventual acceptance of and tolerance towards a different racial group in the community depends very much on people living in their localities".[80]

What this last point highlights is that the decisions made locally depended on two parameters: first, the broad local philosophy in defining the education of immigrant children, education in general and citizenship, which owed a lot to which specific individuals held power at which given time; second, the local geographical distribution of immigrant children in specific wards and specific schools. Reading the latter, Table 3 sheds light on how different localities in the country fared in terms of distribution of immigrant children. Again, these figures are somewhat difficult to compare and interpret since the cases of Bradford and Ealing tell us how much a micro-approach is needed (which specific schools in which wards are affected) to make sense of the local vehemence for calls for dispersal. More tellingly, the figures in Table 3 provide a stark contrast with some inner London boroughs such as Hackney, Haringey or Islington, where the statistics for immigrant children ranged from about 20 per cent to nearly 30 per cent. None of these introduced dispersal.

Faced with the at best reluctant approach to dispersal in many LEAs, Denis Howell, the parliamentary under-secretary for education and science and a staunch advocate of dispersal, announced in the House of Commons on 19 January 1967 that he was about to try anew to convince Birmingham in particular, but also London, Leeds and Nottingham.[81] This involved a tour of some industrial towns of England which had substantial immigrant children populations, including a congratulatory visit to Bradford. Howell was also personally chafed that his home city of Birmingham

Table 3 Percentage of immigrant children in schools of other English boroughs (%) (January 1968) (localities in bold types introduced dispersal)

Birmingham	9.0	**Bradford**	8.2
Derby	10.0	**Huddersfield**	9.8
Leicester	9.9	Manchester	4.7
Nottingham	7.4	Warley*	9.6
West Bromwich	5.3	**Wolverhampton**	11.8

*The former borough of Warley refers to the Black Country, including Smethwick.

Source: *Race Relations Board Newsletter*, May 1969 (Manchester Central Library, Muhamad Iqbal Ullah research centre).

obstinately refused dispersal, and felt helpless in trying to convince the Midlands corporation. This was the major disappointment in a whole list of setbacks. In the few references to dispersal in his memoirs, Howell admits that the circular was ultimately jettisoned by demographics: "The policy we advocated had some short-term success but to my great regret it was soon overwhelmed. Other local authorities failed to take a similar approach on the establishment of multi-racial communities. If we had succeeded, who knows how much better race relations would be in our country today?"[82]

"Unpreparedness", a word used several times in this chapter, does not tell the whole story. For the introduction of dispersal owes a lot to a myopic reading of the social world in which New Commonwealth immigrants evolved. The DES's bureaucratic ethos produced some state simplifications and some "planning for abstract citizens", a phrase borrowed from James C. Scott's *Seeing like a State: How Certain Schemes to Improve the Human Condition Have Failed*. Indeed, despite the DES's flexibility in applying the "about one third" quota, it was never expected – there is no trace of this in archives – that many schools where immigrant children would be sent were far from multiracial havens of tolerance. In this sense, the state simplifications which paved the way for dispersal were tantamount to a form of racial myopia. Or, to quote Scott, "What is striking, of course, is that such subjects – like the 'unmarked citizens' of liberal theory – have, for the purposes of the planning exercise, no gender, no tastes, no history, no values, no opinions or original ideas, no traditions and no distinctive personalities to contribute to their enterprise". Similarly, for the purpose of bussing, the white children of West Yorkshire or Ealing suburban schools were supposed to have no prejudice, no hostility, no ingrained proclivity to look down upon those they actually saw as "the Pakis on the bus".

Notes

1 This is according to Education Department inspector Alan James, as quoted in *Guardian*, 30.5.1972.
2 H.E.R. Townsend, *Immigrant Pupils in England: The L.E.A Response*, Slough: National Foundation for Educational Research, 1971, p. 34.
3 Elizabeth Buettner, "'This is Staffordshire, not Alabama!' Racial Geographies of Commonwealth Immigration in Early 1960s Britain", *The Journal of Imperial and Commonwealth History*, vol. 42 (4), 2014, pp. 710–40.
4 Notice, for instance, the number of press articles and documentaries on what has been dubbed "Britain's racist election", or "Britain's most racist election". Among others, see *Guardian*, 15.10.2014; also the documentary *Britain's Racist Election*, broadcast on Channel Four on 15.3.2015.

5 *Guardian*, 16.4.1963.

6 Brocklebank-Fowler *et al., Commonwealth Immigration*, p. 13.

7 *Strangers Within*, London: Young Fabian Pamphlet, 1965, pp. 14–15.

8 Kirp, *Doing Good by Doing Little*, p. 44.

9 Sally Tomlinson, *Race and Education: Policy and Politics in Britain*, Maidenhead: Open University Press, 2008, p. 28.

10 E.J.B. Rose (ed.), *Colour and Citizenship, A Report on British Race Relations*, Oxford: Oxford University Press, 1969, p. 266.

11 On these three quotes, see *ibid.*, p. 267.

12 John Power, *Immigrants in School, A Survey of Administrative Policies*, London: Councils and Education Press, 1967, pp. 6–7.

13 Rose (ed.), *Colour and Citizenship*, p. 266.

14 James C. Scott, *Weapons of the Weak: Everyday Forms of Peasant Resistance*, New Haven: Yale University Press, 1985, p. 315.

15 As guaranteed by section 76 of Education Act (1944). For details, see Introduction.

16 See Fabian Society, *Strangers Within*, p. 15.

17 Department of Education and Science, *The Education of Immigrants*, London: HMSO, 1965, pp. 4–5.

18 George Padmore Institute (Finsbury Park), "The School in the Community" (BEM 1/2/3).

19 On the questionnaire and the DES answers, see Brocklebank-Fowler *et al., Commonwealth Immigration*, p. 20.

20 See Fabian Society, *Strangers Within*, p. 20.

21 See Brocklebank-Fowler *et al., Commonwealth Immigration*, p. 18.

22 *Guardian*, 25.9.1965.

23 See Hill and Issacharoff, *Community Action and Race Relations*, p. 46.

24 Brocklebank-Fowler *et al., Commonwealth Immigration*, pp. 15–19.

25 Fabian Society, *Strangers Within*, p. 29.

26 See Nenad Stojanović, *Dialogue sur les quotas: penser la représentation dans une démocratie multiculturelle*, Paris: Presses de Sciences-Po, 2013, p. 24, p. 91.

27 Patterson, *Immigration and Race Relations*, p. 259.

28 In his study, Townsend never identifies individual LEAs. Although comprehensive, his analysis is quite frustrating sometimes for that reason. See Townsend, *Immigrant Pupils in England*, pp. 19–33.

29 *Guardian*, 16.4.1963.

30 Ealing Library, Borough of Ealing Council (Education) minutes, 26.7.1966.

31 This situation already existed in 1965: see *Guardian*, 12.6.1965.

32 Ealing International Friendship Council, *The Education of the Immigrant Child in the London Borough of Ealing*, Ealing, 1968, p. 6.

33 *Ibid.*, p. 7.

34 *Middlesex County Times (Southall Edition)*, 12.5.1972.

35 Ealing archives, Borough of Ealing Council minutes, Education Committee, 27.6.1965: "education of immigrant children": "that in the case of Beaconsfield

Road infants school, the number of immigrant children to be admitted in September 1965, compared with English children, be in the ratio of three to two".
36 West Yorkshire Archives, BBD1/7/T14923, letter by T.E. Hall, 29.8.1969.
37 Ealing archives, Middlesex County Council, Education Committee minutes (April 1963 – March 1964), p. 2.
38 Power, *Immigrants in School*, p. 7.
39 Hansard, *House of Commons Debates*, 28.10.1965, vol. 718, cols 323–5.
40 Denis Howell, *Made in Birmingham: The Memoirs of Denis Howell*, London: Queen Anne Press, 1990, p. 187.
41 *Ibid.*, p. 188.
42 Myers, *Struggles for a Past*, p. 23.
43 *Ibid.*, p. 21.
44 Quoted in Patterson, *Immigration and Race Relations*, p. 254.
45 Birmingham City archives, Wolfson Centre, City of Birmingham Education Department, Letter by Mr Stickland to Mr Chapman, 6.1.1970 (copy of a letter to Mr Powell). I want to thank Christian Ydesen for providing me this specific archive.
46 For both, see Stoler, *Along the Archival Grain*, p. 3.
47 Such statistics could be: teacher/pupil ratio, size of class, type of course pursued, pupils' ages at leaving school, etc. See George Padmore Institute (Finsbury Park), "The School in the Community", BEM 1/2/3.
48 See Myers, *Struggles for a Past*, pp. 88–9.
49 Quoted in David Milner, *Children and Race*, Harmondsworth: Penguin, 1975, p. 202.
50 Power, *Immigrants in School*, p. 9.
51 Quoted in *Education*, 14.4.1967, p. 719.
52 Select Committee on Race Relations and Immigration, *Education, Vol. 2 (Evidence)*, London: HMSO, 1973, pp. 354–5.
53 Tod Porter, *Trust in Numbers: The Pursuit of Objectivity in Science and Public Life*, Princeton: Princeton University Press, 1995; Alain Desrosières, *Prouver et gouverner: une analyse politique des statistiques publiques*, Paris: La Découverte, 2014, pp. 71–4.
54 Alain Desrosières, *The Politics of Large Numbers*, Cambridge, MA: Harvard University Press, 1998.
55 Bailkin, *The Afterlife of Empire*, pp. 8–9.
56 Rose (ed.), *Colour and Citizenship*, p. 200.
57 Ruth Glass, *London's Newcomers: The West Indian Migrants*, Cambridge, MA: Harvard University Press, 1961, p. 159.
58 Kirp, *Doing Good by Doing Little*, p. 37.
59 See Fabian Society, *Strangers Within*, p. 15.
60 See Brocklebank-Fowler *et al.*, *Commonwealth Immigration*, p. 20.
61 Townsend, *Immigrant Pupils in England*, pp. 34–5.
62 Bebber, "'We Were Just Unwanted'", p. 641.
63 *Birmingham Evening Mail*, 1965, undated newscuttings, Indian Workers Association archives at Birmingham City Library, Wolfson Centre.

64 See for instance, Trevor Phillips and Mike Phillips, *Windrush: The Irresistible Rise of Multi-racial Britain*, London: Harper Collins, 1998.

65 Deakin (ed.), *Colour and the British Electorate*, p. 112.

66 Fabian Society, *Strangers Within*, p. 16.

67 Quoted in *Immigrant Children in British Schools*, p. 33.

68 Kirp, *Doing Good by Doing Little*, p. 86.

69 Bebber, "'We Were Just Unwanted'", p. 643.

70 See Rose (ed.), *Colour and Citizenship*, pp. 446–7.

71 Only think of the slogan "No Taxation Without Representation" for instance. On this interplay between taxpaying, citizenship and belonging, see the use made of Rodney Hilton's work on medieval England in Pierre Bourdieu, *On the State: Lectures at the Collège de France, 1989–1992*, London: Polity, 2015, pp. 33–4.

72 Delmont, *Why Busing Failed*, p. 222.

73 Kogan, *Dispersal in the Ealing Local Education Authority*, p. 27.

74 For all these quotes, see *Daily Express*, 17.11.1965.

75 *The Times Educational Supplement*, 3.5.1968.

76 George Padmore Institute (Finsbury Park), "The School in the Community", BEM 1/2/3.

77 Power, *Immigrants in Schools*, p. 49.

78 *Ibid.*, pp. 44–5.

79 *Ibid.*, pp. 46–7.

80 *Ibid.*, pp. 51–2.

81 *Ibid.*, p. 32.

82 See Howell, *Made in Birmingham*, p. 189.

3

"Before it gets out of hand":
the introduction of dispersal in Bradford

There were few if any vociferations, no angry white mobilisations, no ministerial visit, no frightened mention of an "irretrievably immigrant school" in the Commons: clearly, the introduction of bussing in Bradford was a very hushed affair compared with Southall. Dispersal in the West Yorkshire city was brought about by local school authorities to face an immediate crisis situation but also as a proactive measure to forestall difficulties in the near future. In this respect, Bradford did give the lead to other towns facing similar situations. This is substantiated by the fact that Bradford introduced bussing a few months before it was nationally promoted by the DES. New arrangements around dispersal came into effect as of 1 January 1965 locally, whereas 7/65 was produced on 14 June of the same year.

In Bradford, most New Commonwealth immigrants were Pakistanis, who were very often employed in the local textile mills. The majority among these were peasants from the district of Mirpur (in Azad Kashmir), many of whom had been displaced by the building of the Mangla valley dam[1] which flooded their villages. Very early on, they would make up around 80 per cent of the workers doing night shifts. Most kept a low-profile approach to their working and living environment, which was largely due to the myth of return: these people's key concern was to accumulate remittances and send at least 50 per cent of their earnings back to Pakistan to build *pakka* (solid) houses to return to in five or six years' time. Pakistanis were concentrated in the north and west of the city centre, in the Exchange and Manningham wards, and Little Horton and Listerhills respectively. In a few streets (around Lumb Lane), about 80 per cent of the residents were Pakistani immigrants. According to the 1961 census, Bradford had a population of 295,768, with 3,457 Pakistanis, 1,512 Indians, 984 West Indians and a small number of people from West Africa.[2] Among Pakistanis, 3376 were males (97.7%), a mere 81 (2.3%) females.[3] By 1964, local authorities estimated the Pakistani immigrant population at around twelve thousand, and by 1970 it had grown to around twenty-one thousand,[4] with an explosion in the number of wives and children. By then, dispersal had already been in full swing for five years.

Despite these rapidly increasing figures and the difficulties in integrating a group so markedly different from white Britons, Bradford was managing to avoid the major racial tensions which were at play in Smethwick, Birmingham or Southall. During the 1964 general elections, the move to Labour was slightly above the national average, especially in the wards which faced a real influx in New Commonwealth immigration. In the Bradford North ward Labour even grabbed the seat from the incumbent Conservative.

Several reasons have been alleged for Bradford's moderate approach to race relations in the 1960s: the general reluctance of political parties to play the race card at elections;[5] the very moderate, cautious approach taken by the local paper, *The Telegraph & Argus*,[6] read by around 90 per cent of Bradford households in the 1960s; the long tradition of immigrant groups (Irish, Jews, Poles, Germans) integrating into the city; the historical influence of the left in a place where the Independent Labour Party was born (1893); and lastly the fact that, as opposed to Birmingham and London, the housing shortage, however real, was not so severe. Maurice Spiers in his 1960s study of the city went so far as to wonder whether "race [was] likely to become a political issue in Bradford",[7] before venturing to reply in the negative.

We now know this was a foolhardy forecast. Indeed, post-industrial Bradford has repeatedly been connected with severe race-relations crises: the Ray Honeyford affair (1984–85), the public burning of *The Satanic Verses* on Centenary Square (1989) and the urban disturbances of 1995 and of 2001. For the historian, the interest lies in the fact that dispersal was ushered in when Bradford was a town where apparent racial harmony prevailed, and was terminated as massive job losses affected all districts, and as the town was more and more portrayed as a "problem city". Ray Honeyford's "ghetto school" (Drummond School in Manningham), accommodating a huge majority of Muslim children, was an immediate consequence of dispersal's abolition. In July 2001 it went ablaze with flames in scenes redolent of Brixton 1981.

"Bradford city of fear": the 1962 outbreak of smallpox

The influx of Pakistanis in the Bradford area brought about a violent, mutual culture shock: for Pakistanis that of emigrating to Britain, for some Britons that of having to adjust to migrants whose habits were so radically different from theirs, whether in the neighbourhoods, in the workplace or in the playgrounds. As educationalist Gordon Bowker put it in the late

1960s, "The transition from a rural peasant community to a school at the heart of a modern industrial community in which he is cut off from others by the language, and in which there is so much that is new, can only produce bewilderment".[8] Specific dietary requirements sometimes raised an issue and many children were unused to eating with knives and forks. Classroom adaptations were also numerous for Asian children: most would have to learn to hold a pen or pencil and were unused to sitting at a desk too. Since Urdu is written from right to left, changing to English required a difficult adjustment in terms of hand and eye co-ordination. Punjabi is written from left to right, but below and not on top of the line.[9] Predictably, school staffs argued that the younger they were when they arrived in Britain, the easier it would prove for them to adjust.

For the local Commonwealth Immigrants Advisory Council, Pakistani immigrants were "solely concerned with money and personal comfort is a secondary consideration … The sharing of a room even in a substandard house let in lodgings is a luxury as compared with the standards in the villages of Pakistan and this mental attitude to the normal way of life is very difficult to break down."[10] General improvements were promoted thanks to the Urdu-language section of the *Telegraph & Argus* (about half a page) but, since most of the Pakistani workers were illiterate, some leaflets on the use of dustbins, standards of hygiene and road safety had to be read out in factories.[11]

Added to the physical weakness of some exhausted immigrants and their difficulty in adjusting to the cold and wet climate, these circumstances were favourable to the outbreak of epidemics, and those male Pakistanis were largely associated with "TB", "smallpox" and "gonorrhoea". The outbreak of smallpox from mid-December 1961 to mid-January 1962 caused the death of twenty-five people nationally, with five people dying in Bradford alone. It was due to a Pakistani immigrant arriving by plane: much of the ensuing debate was about the government's responsibility for having health checks at entry, or whether to blame it all on the Pakistani immigrants. Locally, some irritated townspeople called the epidemic "Pakipox". The *Telegraph & Argus* received many angry letters from Bradfordians demanding more drastic immigration control and the end of "welfare generosity" for immigrants. For a short spell, it felt as if some local and national symbols proudly cherished by Bradfordians were imperilled by the weak, sick bodies of Pakistanis. Some important football, rugby and hockey games had to be postponed and the NHS was strained by the vaccination of about 250,000 Bradfordians in a few weeks. Fleet Street reported on those endless queues of Bradfordians awaiting vaccination, and some Conservative tabloids published headlines such as "Bradford City of Fear", which did hurt the sense of local pride among some white Bradfordians, a feeling already discussed for Southall in Chapter 1. Similarly, it felt as though the Pakistanis were themselves setting the clock back: in the UK, anti-smallpox vaccination had ceased to be mandatory in 1948. Names like "TB"[12] or "smallpox" associated with the Pakistani presence sounded plainly incompatible with a nation most of whose denizens had "never had it so good".

Nevertheless, Pakistan's toxic Christmas 1962 gift to the city actually caused little genuine panic. The huge local strain on the NHS also provided Britons with the chance to pride themselves on the efficacy of their cherished health system, as is evidenced by a Pathé archive video.[13] Yet, within the endless queues to get vaccination there was much grumbling against the Pakistanis' cumbersome presence. And it is against this general suspicion of and resentment towards Pakistanis that dispersal was debated, introduced and implemented.

Before it gets out of hand: the introduction of dispersal

Unlike other LEAs (such as Brent) which were reluctant or hostile to the collection of statistics on immigrant children, Bradford proved adept at compiling detailed statistics. It's fair to imagine that the outbreak of smallpox had a role to play in this. Pakistani men and their wives and children were so many bodies to be checked at entry, gauged, compartmentalised by an administration willing to produce statistics on who was sick, who was born in the UK, who was able to speak English and so on. As a consequence, the West Yorkshire and the Bradford education archives hold an impressive swathe of graphs, tables and figures evidencing the extent to which authorities wanted to implement an efficient governmentality of the territory under its jurisdiction. These sources (see Table 4), where it is not rare to come across the categories "half-Asian", "Negro", "half-Negro", are so many illustrations qualifying the claim that British legislation in the 1960s was still "the quintessence in colour-blindness".[14] No similar graphs have been found for other authorities, including Southall. That such statistics were configured as a subtle form of racial discrimination is testified by the way "Commonwealth" was defined internally in Bradford: it was recommended not to include children from Canada, Australia, New Zealand in the "Other Commonwealth countries" category, in the same way as, when Pakistan left the Commonwealth in 1971, children from there were still included as being from the Commonwealth, a word which in pragmatic terms actually meant "Black" (including "Asians").[15]

Officially, the Bradford corporation started to collect statistics on the racial composition of schools from 1 January 1965, but there is earlier evidence of statistic-gathering which testifies to the local concern around

Table 4 Number of children from the Commonwealth on Bradford school registers (23 January 1970) (total: 6052)

Country of origin	English-speaking children	Non-English–speaking children	Total
Pakistan (both parents)	1262	1003	2265
India (both parents)	1463	372	1835
West Indies (both parents)	1016	13	1029
West Africa (both parents)	82	11	93
Other Commonwealth countries (both parents)	124	17	141
Half Asian	401	12	413
Half Negro	275	1	276

Source: West Yorkshire archives, Health and Education Reports on Children of Immigrants, BBDI/7/TI4923 (1965–1970)

Table 5 Immigrant children in Bradford schools (%) (4 February 1963)

St Jude's C.E. Junior and Infant	41
All Saints' C.E. Infant	27
All Saints' C.E Junior and Senior	20
St Andrew's C.E Junior	30 (one class 45)
St Andrew's C.E Infant	37 (one class 48)
Green Lane Junior	8 (one class 25, another 17)
Green Lane Infant	10

Source: Bradford archives, City of Bradford Education Committee, Commonwealth Immigrants Advisory Council report, 4.2.1963

the extent of ethnic-minority clustering in certain areas. The report from which Table 5 derives is dated February 1963, and shows that only very few schools had above 25 per cent of immigrants, in a city nearing three hundred thousand inhabitants with some 150 schools. "Immigrant children" were not pigeonholed into specific racial or ethnic categories, and were taken as a block.

These figures also show how far the Commonwealth Immigrants Act (1962)'s government restrictions on immigration from the Commonwealth were actually having the reverse effect.[16] This was felt very keenly in Bradford, where the arrival of mothers and children brought about a severe strain on social services, primarily on schools. In 1965, the number of dependants, particularly from Pakistan, was expected to double in the

Table 6 Immigrants as a percentage of all children, Bradford LEA
(January 1965–69)

1965	3.6%
1966	5.0%
1967	6.3%
1968	8.1%
1969	9.7%

Source: West Yorkshire archives, Health and Education Reports on Children of
Immigrants, BBDI/7/TI4923 (1965–70).

next five years. But in actual fact, as shown in Table 6, the number of
immigrant children (primarily from Pakistan and India) just about tripled
between 1965 and 1970.

The Labour-controlled Bradford Council was acutely aware of the situation, which was badly aggravated in the summer of 1964. Suddenly, over
three hundred additional immigrant children presented themselves on the
school doorsteps on the first day of the autumn term. Most could not speak
English. Two schools were overwhelmed and the staff started to protest.
Overnight, these schools raised their proportions of immigrants to around
50 per cent, which included a large number of non-Anglophones.[17] Despite
the above reference to the suggestion that 10 per cent of immigrant children in a school could legitimate dispersal, no such spreading scenario had
hitherto been put forward. In February 1963, the city's schooling authorities had asserted that "the authority do not contemplate any segregation
of these children. On the other hand, there are no 'plans' to spread them
over a greater number of schools. As the schools near to their homes are,
in general, far from full it would not be possible to refuse to let a parent
exercise his choice in this matter."[18] Until the summer crisis of 1964,
Bradford was reluctant both to adopt a *laissez-faire* approach leading to
the spread of "ghetto schools" and to introduce dispersal. But the summer
crisis of 1964 forced it into a U-turn.

Pressured by this situation, a primary education sub-committee meeting
held on 23 November 1964 introduced the concept of dispersal for the first
time.[19] As in other such bodies in LEAs with a large influx of New Commonwealth immigrants, much of the debate revolved around issues of
immigrants' residential concentration, integration and assimilation as well
as deficiency in the English language. There was often a degree of overlap-
ping, if not of confusion, between these issues. The meeting started with
the reminder that in Bradford there were now 1,500 Commonwealth
immigrant children, five or six hundred of whom could not speak enough

English to participate in schools normally. From this assessment of the situation on the ground it was suggested that:

> A limit should be fixed on the proportion of immigrant children admitted to a particular school, this to be 25% in the case of primary schools, subject to this percentage being reduced in the case of large schools; for secondary schools it may be that the limit should be fixed considerably lower and each school should be dealt with in the light of its particular circumstances.[20]

From the outset, the Bradford quota was envisaged as flexible. But whatever percentage was agreed upon, transport arrangements would be necessary and some difficulties would arise, for the new policy would have to be explained to immigrants, through the printing of information in newspapers, in their own languages, and with the use of interpreters and translators if need be. The Bradford education authorities were fully aware that "the administrative problems involved would be very great".[21] They were also aware, very early on, that "these items of policy involved discrimination, something that had previously been carefully avoided". But all parties involved, of whatever political hue, voted in favour of dispersal since it was thought to provide everyone, Bradfordians and immigrants alike, "a reasonably fair deal".[22]

A few days later, Bradford's education committee further clarified the city's position towards immigrant children. Fully cognisant of their vastly increasing number, it was decided that, as of 1 January 1965:

A/ All children of Commonwealth immigrant parents should be medically examined before admission to school.

B/ All such children arriving at the age of 10 or over unable to speak English should be admitted to immigrant education centres or special classes in schools;

C/ All such children presented for admission at the age of nine or under, whether English speaking or not, should only be admitted to the school of the parents' choice if the proportion of immigrant children to the total numbers on roll were less than 25%, and similarly older children able to speak English, whether newly arrived or discharged from the immigrant education centres and special classes, should be dispersed into schools with less than 25% on roll; and

D/ to facilitate the operation of the scheme, a system of central registration should be set up.[23]

A few points are noteworthy. First, section A owed a great deal to the outbreak of smallpox in the Christmas period of 1962. In most cases, a medical examination took place just before the language test. No matter how administratively convenient it was, the juxtaposition of these two symbolised a further barrier to integration in the UK. As Brenda Mary

Thomson suggests, this was hardly "an encouraging introduction to British schooling. Conducted in the medical environment and in a clinical manner, it would seem like yet one more hurdle to surmount to be 'fit' for life in the UK."[24] Thought it may be surmised that some of these tests were conducted in a humane enough way, the general procedure testifies to a quite ruthless governmentality once again.

Point C made it clear that the 25 per cent quota in itself trumped language deficiency (with the insistence on dispersal "whether English-speaking or not"). In other words, even those who were already English-speaking would be dispersed if the school of their parents' choice had already reached the 25 per cent quota. This was despite the Bradford recommendation to set a 15 per cent quota regarding immigrant children who were not Anglophone.[25] Surely, that was an objectionable vision of integration, even for the period: it entailed that, in order to be integrated, it was seemingly more important to be schooled alongside a vast majority of white indigenous pupils than to actually speak the English language. The priority given to ascriptive identities (here, the biological fact of the children's and/or parents' place of birth, and the corollary fact of being an "immigrant") over acquisitive identities (the fact of having learnt the English or not) could whet suspicions that the (deterministic) conditions of eligibility for dispersal were nothing short of racial discrimination. As late as 1977–79, Brenda Mary Thomson gathered evidence that to have an Asian name was often used as sufficient justification for bussing. Similarly, the adviser for immigrant education and the senior registration officer acknowledged that ultimately a decision to register a child for subsequent possible allocation to a language centre and for bussing was made on skin colour.[26]

As for point D, about the need for "central registration" of immigrant children, it was a two-edged sword. From a strictly administrative standpoint, it promoted efficiency. But from the point of view of immigrant families, it was concrete evidence of parental choice denial, a parental choice nearly all Pakistanis were totally unaware of anyhow. What they did see was that the (often Asian) education welfare officers with whom they had an appointment would first check the validity of their passports, something which they had no right to do as education welfare officers.[27] Whereas most white native parents just had to walk one or two hundred yards to have their very young children registered in neighbourhood schools, immigrant children were expected to go to the City Hall, and have their children registered there, then await news of the school where they might go.[28] That contrast was experienced evidence of the denial of the neighbourhood school principle for immigrants. As these principles were being laid out, the number of schools accommodating more than 25 per cent of immigrant children swiftly increased. For early 1963, Table 5 indicates that four schools had reached the local quota. Two years later, twelve schools had at least 25 per cent of immigrants, thereby necessitating dispersal on a larger scale. These demographic difficulties did not weaken support for bussing in the Labour-controlled Bradford council. As elsewhere, it was seen as a way to avoid ghetto schools. Yet, there was little grassroots support for it. Among the (native and immigrant) parents, it was not clear that support for dispersal was very strong.[29] A few native parents complained about their children "being held back", and there were some applications for transfers to schools without a large intake of Asians. Philip Bendall, Bradford's chief education officer, merely stated in 1964 that "parents are perhaps a little less satisfied than they were"[30] before the Pakistani influx.

As for immigrant parents, most were uninformed, apathetic or simply had other pressing concerns: to make a living, to deal with poor health issues or to adjust to life in "Vilayat", in cultural, linguistic or climatic terms. Just as they had been used to mud houses without electricity in Kashmir and did not contemplate for themselves living conditions defined as "decent" by British natives, immigrants often assumed that the schooling provided for their children would, in any event, be of much better quality than back home. Yet local schooling authorities were concerned that these immigrants would produce a generation of under-achievers, as was to be illustrated by later, worrying statistics on Pakistani or Bangladeshi British children.[31] In 1965, Bernard Pickles, the Bradford headteacher of All Saints School, from which Asians would be bussed, was very blunt about these children's future prospects: "There is not the remotest possibility of any of these children entering grammar schools".[32]

In the early years of dispersal, the farthest distance travelled by bus was two miles. The system and its general framework evolved very little until 1970–71. Every six months an up-to-date report of the situation on the ground was issued for the education authorities. The Bradford administrators prided themselves on having tackled the situation before it got out of hand, and deftly avoided a Birmingham scenario. According to T.F. Davies, the city's director of education, "we caught the situation before the number of immigrant children in our schools became too high".[33] Yet Bradford's robustly proactive approach just could not cope with the increasing numbers of immigrant children. For a few years after 1965, between twenty-five and thirty of them arrived every week, thus necessitating the creation of a new school every few months or so. It is this emergency situation which prompted the Bradford visit in June 1967 of David Ennals MP,

Table 7 The growth of dispersal in the Bradford area: number of buses used (1966–77, January unless otherwise stated)

1966	2
1967	4
1968	6
1969	6
1970	10
1971	14
1972	17
1973 June	20
1974 February	19
1975	23
1976	22
1977	24

Source: compiled from documents held by City of Bradford archives/West Yorkshire archives

parliamentary under-secretary of state at the Home Office, who was faced with the very difficult task of responsibility for immigration policies as well as integration policies in the Wilson government.[34]

Although the total number of immigrants started to ebb in 1968–69, the influx of those coming from Pakistan (generally non-Anglophone immigrants) continued unabated. In such circumstances, the number of buses sending (mostly) Asians out of the inner areas of the city inexorably increased, as is shown in Table 7, which includes much of the 1970s to be discussed in a following chapter. The figures given are for primary and junior schools only, since those dispersed to middle schools would almost always travel by public transport.

Bradford's administrative efficiency in setting up and implementing dispersal won kudos with the DES as well as with some of the national media. Yet, *The Guardian* depicted the city's administrative zeal as a double-edged sword; for the newspaper, the local schooling authorities' handling of the situation constituted a form of "benevolent dictatorship".[35] It is to the extent and limits of Bradford's administrative "model" that we now turn.

A national model of sorts

In his autobiography, Denis Howell admits to having been impressed by Bradford's approach to dispersal. He pays tribute to the West Yorkshire city as well as to the town of Luton.[36] Howell's encomium rested on his realisation that Bradford managed to combine effectiveness with a humane concern about individual needs, at a remove from a coldly bureaucratic administering of schooling policies. Howell went so far as to claim that dispersal did not prevent education authorities from "discuss[ing] with the parents which was the best school for them to choose".[37]

Educationalist Gordon Bowker made a somewhat similar point in his 1968 study *The Education of Coloured Immigrants*.[38] Maurice Foley, joint under-secretary for economic affairs in the Wilson government, enthused about the Bradford approach to the issue of integration of immigrants, which he called imaginative and unorthodox. Foley was pleased with the dispersal initiative, which to him was a humanitarian approach to a real challenge. Ever eager to bolster pride in local institutions, the local press (*Telegraph & Argus*) was quick to report on such national praise.[39] The other major reason why Bradford was praised was, as has been argued already, that dispersal there was deemed a commonsense, non-ideological response to a pragmatic challenge.

Howell's and Foley's praise led *The Guardian* to surmise that Bradford's policy must have served as a model for circular 7/65.[40] Yet, just as Southall's peculiar experience could hardly inspire a nationwide policy, Bradford's situation could hardly serve as inspiration for cities which faced issues markedly different in kind and/or in degree, and whose urban dynamics bore little resemblance to the West Yorkshire city. Howell dreamed of introducing in Birmingham the very policy implemented with such apparent success in Bradford. Nevertheless, even if some specifically local elements made dispersal by consent (and without bussing) partially feasible in the second English city, it still remained the case that Birmingham had, in 1965, twenty-two schools with an immigrant children population between 16 and 70 per cent,[41] whereas Bradford had a mere five.

Another element making dispersal more likely to generate consensus in Bradford was that the city was perceived as having an alarming proportion of non-Anglophone Pakistanis making up what seemed to be a seriously isolated minority. T.F. Davies, one of the education officers dealing with immigrants, ruefully noted that he had been "surprised and disappointed to find that the vast majority of immigrant children born in England five years ago have no English when they reach school age".[42] Hence, it was more naturally felt that dispersal's muscular integrationism could only be beneficial to its Bradford target population, as was to be stipulated by chief officer of education P.T.B. Bendall in a 1976 interview: "Even those born here in England don't speak English when they become five and are supposed to enter school. We disperse for their benefit, so they will learn to speak English and also so they will be exposed to British culture and saved

Table 8 Pakistani immigrant children in some English LEAs (1970)
(towns in bold operated dispersal of immigrant children at some point
between 1963 and 1986)

Local Education Authority	Number of Pakistani immigrant children	Total number of immigrant children	Pakistani children as percentage of immigrant children
Birmingham	2614	18,172	14.4
Blackburn	**347**	**1187**	**29.2**
Bradford	**2210**	**5460**	**40.5**
Halifax	**306**	**425**	**72.0**
Huddersfield	**859**	**2794**	**30.7**
Inner London	2184	68,947	3.2
Manchester	1290	5754	22.4
Walsall	**278**	**2658**	**10.5**

Source: National Archives, compiled from ED 269/14

from the effects of living in a virtually isolated culture."[43] Bendall's integrationist rationale was bolstered by cold statistics: if both proportions and actual figures are counted, Bradford had the most substantial Pakistani community in the whole country. Birmingham was just above in terms of real numbers, and Halifax was well above in terms of proportions, but Bradford had more than seven times as many Pakistanis as Halifax, as is shown by Table 8.

Clearly then, if there was one city where dispersal could seem to make statistical sense in order to deghettoise a vastly secluded, non-Anglophone community, it was Bradford. And this seemed to make even more sense in gender terms. Decades before talk of "parallel lives" among Pakistani and Bangladeshi Muslims hit the headlines, dispersal was hailed as a policy whereby *female* students, in particular, would be made to open up to British society, and to learn the English language in the process. In other words, dispersal was seen as a potential *purdah*-killer, for without dispersal, and to quote the words of a Bradford education officer, "a girl may be much more willing to accept *purdah* as her future lot".[44]

But, to say the least, some gender statistics do not bear this out, for there was a stark unbalance between Pakistani boys and girls on roll in Bradford schools even after dispersal. Indeed, the city had, for 1970, 1647 Pakistani boys and a mere 563 girls, a ratio of more than three to one, which is slightly above the gender discrepancy found for Birmingham (1918/696), Huddersfield (553/306) and Halifax (230/76).[45] It is impossible to tell whether the threat of dispersal did deter some parents from sending their daughters to school. But it is clear that this 3/1 boy/girl ratio makes it very difficult to regard dispersal as an actual or potential *purdah*-killer.

Besides, the effect of dispersal and *purdah* was to generate ever greater isolation of dispersed children in suburban schools. Indeed, some mothers' social invisibility obviously prevented them from having any dealing with schools whatsoever. That point was raised by the Select Committee on Race Relations and Immigration in a document sent to the Yorkshire Police in 1970:

> Attention is drawn to the plight of married women, particularly those of the Muslim faith who come from rural areas of Pakistan to join their husbands who themselves have probably spent several years in this country. These women, used to the laws of *purdah*, very frequently are virtually prisoners in their home. Their husbands, even though they may have been exposed to Western influences for some years, either enforce or acquiesce in this situation. As a result, these mothers keep their young children within the house also; will not escort children of infant age to school or to a special bus, and in extreme cases find their situation so miserable that they either degenerate into apathy or return to their own countries.[46]

In the general debate on the urgent necessity for integration, that point was missed.

Bradford was also made into a model because, as has been suggested already, the town had introduced bussing without any real controversy. The absence of either (white) backlash in favour of dispersal or of (brown) backlash against in the early years delineated the contours of a broadly pragmatic initiative, as was illustrated by some of the evidence given to the House of Commons Select Committee on Race Relations in 1970: "Dispersal has never been a controversial issue in Bradford. No immigrant organisation has opposed it and many parents have welcomed it. It is certainly becoming difficult but phasing it out would lead to grave consequences."[47]

The low profile kept by Asian immigrants may account for the degree of apathy facing the introduction of bussing. A clear illustration of this apathy is provided by the fact that less than 20 per cent of the six thousand on the electoral roll voted at the 1964 general elections.[48] A few years later, whilst some individuals may have been irked by the indiscriminate way in which dispersal was imposed, they had very few channels through which to make themselves heard by local authorities. The Bradford Community Relations Committee, for one, was notoriously apathetic and had considerable difficulty in gaining the confidence of mainstream immigrant associations. The social makeup of its executive members was at a total remove from that of Pakistani immigrants in the West Riding of Yorkshire: the six

Asians on the board comprised a doctor and his wife, a solicitor, a businessman and a teacher, the wife of a university lecturer.[49] Hill and Issacharoff are very dismissive of Bradford's CRC as opposed to Birmingham's and Ealing's, the former being critical of the City Council race-relations policy from within, the latter from without. As for Bradford's CRC, it "did not even see it as within their scope to engage in any critique of local authority policies and members seemed totally unaware of any grounds for criticism of such policies".[50]

On top of this, deep rifts between Pakistanis, Indians, Bangladeshis and West Indians made a union of immigrant families wellnigh impossible, as was exemplified in 1970 when a Pakistan party failed to gain solid ground in Manningham, a very multi-ethnic area.[51] The years 1970–71, when an anti-bussing early response could have crystallised, historically coincided with the war leading to the independence of Bangladesh (December 1971), the death toll of which, though impossible to ascertain,[52] certainly brought about a worsening of tensions between Pakistanis and Bangladeshis throughout England.

Given this general backcloth, it is unsurprising that no trace of anti-dispersal backlash has been found among Pakistanis in the early years. This was despite the coldly bureaucratic way in which dispersal operated. Indeed, according to T.F. Davies, the Bradford authorities had been "quite ruthless in cutting down the percentage of immigrant children in schools, and had not taken into account family relationships", which it was their wont to do with most native children, allowing brothers and sisters to attend the same school.[53] This not only dents the view that Bradford was a dispersal model (where authorities could "discuss with the parents which was the best school for them to choose", to quote Howell again) but also typifies the Asian habit of keeping a low profile in the face of this "ruthless" humanitarian paternalism.

Upon close scrutiny, there are quite a few other reasons for taking the general praise of Bradford's exemplarity with a pinch of salt. For one thing, the introduction of dispersal was not experienced by all as a relief and a welcome easing of the pressure wrought by the large influx of non-Anglophone children. In two of the schools[54] which had some of their children dispersed, the staff bemoaned the forced transfer of large numbers of Asians, hailed as "quick, good learners, lovely, lively children", who had hitherto been accommodated in fully equipped rooms and taught by well-trained staff. Some teachers upbraided schooling authorities which to them placed an excessive focus on race, despite official claims to the contrary. One such teacher argued that "just because they are coloured doesn't mean to say they're daft, you know".[55] In one of the two schools at least ten places were left vacant in its reception class. In the other school the headmistress admitted to feeling "angry and frustrated" because she was having to "turn away immigrant parents and because the children are being sent instead to schools which do not want them and have no experience of dealing with them".[56] T.F. Davies admitted that Bradford was facing, in suburban areas, "problems of accommodation and staffing. It is no use adopting a policy of dispersal if no places are available in outlying schools."[57] Those feelings were sharpened by the fact that, until the late 1960s, most of the reception classes in Bradford were taught by mainstream teachers, not by specialist ones, as opposed to nearby Huddersfield, which had developed a real expertise in the education of (non-Anglophone) immigrant children.[58] This critique of dispersal was raised in general terms by the Select Committee on Race Relations and Immigration: in LEAs which operated bussing, "the ability to concentrate teachers especially trained or attuned to the needs of immigrant children is lessened".[59]

More worryingly, it would be simplistic to believe that, once dispersed, immigrant children were placed in situations allowing them to interact with natives, in accordance with the "contact hypothesis" as a *sine qua non* for assimilation. There were many situations where immigrant children were concentrated in special classes in schools prior to the advent of dispersal, only to be concentrated thereafter in immigrant classes within suburban, predominantly white schools. To many of these, only the urban landscape changed, not the fact of ethnic concentration. In All Saints School in November 1965, out of 174 pupils there were 95 immigrants, but 60 of these were concentrated in three special classes. After dispersal began, surplus immigrant children (to reach the 25 per cent quota) were sent to special classes in suburban schools.

Bradford's prioritising of special classes or reception centres was consistent with the large number of non-Anglophone students, most of whom could not follow mainstream courses. But the city, like Slough, Walsall and Coventry, was criticised for keeping children in reception centres for much too long a time and for isolating them from the rest of the students.[60] In so doing, Bradford strove to maintain an artificial 25 per cent quota. This meant that, even after the children had satisfied the English course requirements, they could not be reassigned to their neighbourhood schools until there was "space" for them, that is when the proportion of immigrant children allowed this return,[61] which for many was simply never.

Browns elbowing Bradfordians aside?

In the 1960s, dispersal was an initiative which, albeit in a minor mode, did fuel 'White Backlash' against Asians and immigrants more generally. As has been argued already, the general deterioration of the schooling services was accelerated by the immigrant presence, certainly not caused by it. This point was hammered time and again by schooling authorities in an effort to stave off racial hostility, such as here by T.F. Davies for Bradford: "It is easy, too, to blame immigration for our present ills of shortage of accommodation and teaching staff. This simply is not true. These difficulties are chronic and would have existed without the presence of a single immigrant."[62] Depending on their personal politics, the extent to which their families were affected by dispersal (the overwhelming majority of white families were not), their friendship circles and their personal itineraries, Bradfordians were more or less prone to accept the view that the immigrant presence was in fact a "'barium meal'"[63] highlighting the many housing and schooling deficiencies of decaying inner cities.

In the mid-1960s, as today, one way of deracialising debate and of keeping accusations of being "racialist" at arm's length was to place the focus on the sheer cost of dispersal, which indeed increased the financial burden on Bradford City Council. The issue for some, then, was not so much what or who Asians were but rather how much they cost. In areas with a strong socialist tradition like Bradford, it was felt that the profits generated by immigrants filled the pockets of profit-hungry industrialists, but also that the corollary social costs were borne by "tax-payers", a word which is so central to "White Backlash" talk. That sort of commonsense talk made it possible for some to insist on their hatred of inequality rather than their hatred of foreigners.

In general terms, the immigrant presence brought about large financial costs which were not personally felt by Bradfordians, whereas the social costs were minimal but were felt very keenly by the limited number of families affected. Regarding the former, obvious budgetary consequences of the immigrant presence could be the postponement of school-building renovating programmes or the reopening of recently closed schools to accommodate pupils. Exactly one month after Powell's speech in Birmingham, Edward Short and Alice Bacon, respectively secretary of state (education and science) and minister of state at the Department of Education, went to Bradford to reassure the local authorities about the government's commitment to take its share in the financing of immigrant education. The cost of teaching immigrant children in the city totalled £246,000 a year. It was estimated that Bradford had the largest number of Pakistani children in the country. Four language centres already existed, one more was planned. There were sixty-four full-time teachers for these, plus fourteen part-time.[64] Just as worrying was the fact that dispersal brought about some unneeded, artificial situations: it seemed difficult to incur capital expenditure to provide additional accommodation in suburban schools for dispersed immigrant children while there was, as has been seen above, some spare accommodation in some central-area schools.[65]

It was partly to alleviate such economic strains that two years earlier, in 1966, section eleven of the Local Government Act introduced special provision for areas like Bradford. Soon to be called (or vilified as) "Section 11 money", this grant was made available to towns "as a consequence of the presence within their area of substantial numbers of immigrants from the Commonwealth whose language and customs differ from those of the community". In 1967, £1.4 million was allocated, and £46 million had been given by 1981.[66] Itself a form of "affirmative action" to address the question of "racial disadvantage" (as it would called by the early 1980s), section eleven became the bane of some activists from Southall to Bradford, who were very critical of how money from this "cash cow" was so misused that ethnic minorities ended up seeing precious little of it.[67] For some whites, though, such minority-targeted policies confirmed the wrongheadedness and injustice of the "race-relations industry", a phrase already routine in the 1960s.

As opposed to the financial costs, the social costs of dispersal had a direct impact on some native whites, however few they were. It is a fact that, especially by 1968–69, some white students were refused places in schools to which Asians from areas further away were dispersed.[68] This inconvenienced some native parents, and indirectly accelerated the (white) move outside Bradford's inner districts. On 19 June 1969 for instance, the Bradford Educational Services Committee made a recommendation that "in order to make room in certain schools where there are no immigrants or relatively few, the number of English children to be admitted at the age of five or later be limited to a figure which will allow the admission of substantial numbers of immigrants". Ten days later, a second meeting of the same authority changed this recommendation into "in order to fulfil this policy [of dispersal], the number of schools admitting immigrant children be increased".[69] Such a U-turn, as was exposed by some Conservatives (Councillor Merrick) in the City Council, evidences the authorities' embarrassment when faced with this demographic dilemma, and the political risk was really high if such school placement reorganisations became routine or reported in the papers. The same Jim Merrick was very prompt to point out the way in which such moves were generally "hushed up".[70]

It is no coincidence that Enoch Powell himself exposed this kind of situation through his so-called "Rivers of Blood" speech, in an excerpt quoted in the introduction to this book.[71] And some Bradfordians were also quick to mention their own city as a place where such unacceptable elbowing aside of whites was "routine". One letter to the editor of the *Telegraph & Argus*, very critical of the paper's supposed spinelessness in race-relations issues, stipulated that "in some towns it may not happen, but in Bradford it does. Many white children are denied the schools of their choice because the places are filled with the immigrant quota."[72] To refer to "many white children" was no doubt a gross exaggeration, but it bears repeating that such cases did occur. The problem was raised in hushed tones in 1967, as the pressure on school places by Asian families mounted: "In one or two cases English children who become five during a term have had to be refused admission so as to make room for immigrants who are already of compulsory school ages".[73] News of even a very limited number of such issues was likely to spread like political dynamite around the town, and confirm the "White Backlash" perception that ethnic minorities got preferential treatment at the expense of native English folks. If some whites could spread the wildest, unauthenticated stories about Pakistanis (think of those Pakistanis swarming in the attics of houses in Blackburn and Birmingham, in interviews conducted by Jeremy Seabrook in the late 1960s),[74] the very same people would inevitably clutch at stories which were *true* in order to substantiate the "fact" that they were being sneakily elbowed aside by Asian peaceful penetration. And that perception was only bolstered by the revelation that, in some cases, native whites had to pay bus fares to school whereas dispersed Asians travelled free of charge.[75] As will be seen in the next chapters, dispersal was to reinforce feelings of a double injustice across racial boundaries: whites were irked that some Asians elbowed their children aside and travelled for free whilst Asians, 15 per cent of whose children were dispersed in Bradford,[76] would complain more and more often about being denied the right to neighbourhood schools and to parental choice which whites naturally enjoyed.

For some, the sole fact of adapting the bureaucratic apparatus to make way for immigrant children was in itself preferential treatment. That that situation was unprecedented in the history of immigration to the UK was taken as evidence of gross privilege. One Madeleine Walsh, even before the advent of dispersal, wrote to Audrey Firth, chairman of Bradford Health Committee:

> Why it has become necessary to establish a class to teach these Indians and Pakistanis English when Poles, Lithuanians, Latvians, Chinese, Russians, Estonians, Hungarians and Germans have all succeeded in learning the language without such aid by the education authority. It is not equality some people want, it is preferential treatment.[77]

Of course, most of the nationalities mentioned here had arrived in Britain before the emergence of a modern Welfare State and before the Butler Act (1944), so that such parallels were anachronistic. What matters more, probably, is that this "White Backlash" talk feeds on a nostalgic view of a bygone (imperial) Britain when foreign people knew their place. In some way then, this kind of discourse reads like a *racialised* variation on the

1960s talk about "permissive society"; it adumbrated Powellite discourse in a clear way. As Bill Schwarz put it, "Powellism ... created Powell".[78]

Still, the extent of this native backlash against immigrants ought not to be exaggerated. The perceptions of unfair treatment were still inchoate in the 1960s, and would only surface uninhibitedly in the wake of what Simon Heffer called Enoch Powell's "detonation".[79] For instance, there is no real trace of a native reaction against the presence of Asians in schools where they were dispersed. In this respect, the following exchange between Peter Evans, a *Times* journalist specialising in race relations, and T.F. Davies is itself illuminating, in a discussion on the general question of the internalisation of racial prejudice among children:

> Evans: Do you think the attitude of the parents might influence them?
> Davies: It might do. This is one of the dangers of the policy of dispersal. We are going to send children in the very near future into the best districts of Bradford and we may get some reaction. Up to the present, even in a fairly good district, there has been no adverse reaction at all.[80]

In order to cultivate this broad acceptance, and also to cultivate the absence of a real Pakistani and Indian resistance, it was felt that some issues had better be hushed or toned down. This is another reason why Bradford's approach could be regarded as a "model" one, notwithstanding the shortcomings studied in this chapter. For instance, as early as 1968–69 some councillors did start to fret about the discriminatory nature of dispersal. In the event that the newly formed Race Relations Board started investigating the issue, what would be the City of Bradford's reaction? it was asked. Some councillors tried to circumvent the accusation of racial foul play by invoking "positive discrimination" or "positive action" based on social, not racial or immigrant, needs.[81] To that end, the recently published Plowden Report (1967) proved quite timely. That kind of argument was both disingenuous and half-hearted. But more interesting for the purpose of this chapter is that there had already been some anticipation of litigation, even before the Race Relations Act (1968) provided some solid grounds for it, and precisely at a time, 1965, when the very first Race Relations Bill was being discussed in the Commons. This is, to be sure, one more illustration of how Bradford's approach was conceived by its makers as being a "model" one.

Notes

1 The building of the dam lasted from 1961 to 1967.
2 On all these points, see Badr Dahya, "The Nature of Pakistani Ethnicity in Industrial Cities in Britain", in Abner Cohen (ed.), *Urban Ethnicities*, London: Tavistock, 1974, pp. 78–80.

3 Humayun Ansari, *The Infidel Within: The History of Muslims in Britain, 1800 to the Present*, London: Hurst & Co., 2004, p. 254.
4 Dahya, "The Nature of Pakistani Ethnicity", p. 70, p. 80.
5 Maurice Spiers, "Bradford", in Deakin (ed.), *Colour and the British Electorate*, p. 154.
6 The Leeds-based *Yorkshire Post* was less cautious and more confrontational.
7 Deakin (ed.), *Colour and the British Electorate*, p. 156.
8 Gordon Bowker, *The Education of Coloured Immigrants*, London: Longman, 1968, p. 61.
9 *Ibid.*, p. 62.
10 West Yorkshire archives, Commonwealth Immigrants Advisory Council, "Report on Houses in Multiple Occupation", BBDI/7/79771 (1965).
11 Eric Butterworth, John Goodall and Bryan Hartley, *Immigrants in West Yorkshire, Social Conditions and the Lives of Pakistanis, Indians and West Indians*, London: Institute of Race Relations, 1967.
12 Tuberculosis among Bradford Pakistanis was thirty times higher than among the British population at large (see West Yorkshire archives, 28D94/1, health report dated 18.5.1962).
13 See www.britishpathe.com/video/smallpox-menace-aka-small-pox (accessed 27.12.2016).
14 Rose (ed.), *Colour and Citizenship*, p. 200.
15 Thomson, *Asian-named Minority Groups*, pp. 182–3.
16 *Guardian*, 19.10.1965.
17 T.F. Davies, "Educational Problems in Bradford", in Race Relations Committee of the Society of Friends, *Report on the Immigrant Child and the Teacher*, London: Society of Friends, 1966, p. 94.
18 Bradford archives, City of Bradford Education Committee, Commonwealth Immigrants Advisory Council report, 4.2.1963.
19 Bradford archives, Bradford Council minutes, Educational Services Committee, minutes of meeting held on 20.10.1970.
20 Bradford archives, Bradford Council minutes, Educational Services Committee, minutes of meeting held on 27.11.1964.
21 *Ibid.*
22 Davies, "Educational Problems in Bradford", p. 95.
23 West Yorkshire archives, "City of Bradford Educational Services Committee, the education of children of commonwealth immigrants", Report issued in June 1969.
24 See Thomson, *Asian-named Minority Groups*, p. 196.
25 Patterson, *Immigration and Race Relations*, p. 257; John Lenton, Nicholas Budgen and Kenneth Clarke, *Immigration, Race and Politics: A Birmingham view*, London: Bow Group pamphlets, 1966, pp. 17–18.
26 Thomson, *Asian-named Minority Groups*, p. 232.
27 *Ibid.*, p. 185.
28 West Yorkshire archives, City of Bradford Education Committee, "Report on Present Situation", February 1967, BBDI/7/TI3687.

29 *Yorkshire Post*, 25.2.1966; Mark Halstead, *Education, Justice and Cultural Diversity: An Examination of the Honeyford Affair, 1984–5*, London: Falmer Press, 1988, p. 232.
30 *New Society*, 19.11.1964.
31 Tomlinson, *Race and Education*, pp. 101–2. By the 1990s, ethnic-minority achievement was greater than ever before, but stark contrasts still prevailed between, on the one hand, West Indians, Pakistanis and Bangladeshis and, on the other hand, Indians and Chinese, with the latter two generally hailed as "model minorities".
32 *Daily Express*, 17.11.1965.
33 *Sunday Mercury*, 13.2.1966.
34 Hill and Issacharoff see this as totally incompatible in *Community Action and Race Relations*, p. 28.
35 *Guardian*, 19.10.1965.
36 See Howell, *Made in Birmingham*, p. 188.
37 *Ibid.*, p. 188.
38 See Bowker, *The Education of Coloured Immigrants*, p. 62.
39 *Telegraph & Argus*, 10.5.1965; 21.5.1965.
40 "It was probably due to Bradford that the circular was ever sent out", *The Guardian*, 19.10.1965.
41 Sheila Allen, *New Minorities, Old Conflicts*, New York: Random House, 1971, p. 155.
42 See Davies, "Educational Problems in Bradford", p. 96.
43 Lewis Killian, "School Bussing in Britain, Policies and Perceptions", *Harvard Educational Review*, vol. 49 (2), 1979, p. 190.
44 Bradford archives, "One-day conference (on dispersal) at Margaret MacMillan college of education: November 24th 1974", P.T. Bendall paper, p. 8.
45 Figures compiled from National Archives, education files, ED 269/14.
46 West Yorkshire archives, Letter by Select Committee on Race Relations and Immigration sent to Yorkshire Police, 26.1.1970, BBDI/7/TI 4923.
47 Bradford archives, "Education in a multi-racial city: the report of the joint working party on the education of immigrants and their children, August 1976", p. 17.
48 *New Society*, 17.11.1964.
49 See Hill and Issacharoff, *Community Action and Race Relations*, p. 145.
50 *Ibid.*, p. 227.
51 *Telegraph & Argus*, 20.5.1970.
52 Estimates range from 300,000 to three million people, with widespread allegations of genocidal rape against Bangladeshi women.
53 Allen, *New Minorities*, p. 156.
54 In the *Guardian* article (19.10.1965) from which this information is retrieved, the two schools remain anonymous, but it is obvious that one is All Saints.
55 *Ibid.*
56 *Ibid.*
57 Davies, "Educational Problems in Bradford", p. 96.

58 On this contrast between the two towns, see Rose (ed.), *Colour and Citizenship*, p. 276.
59 London Metropolitan Archives, ILEA archives, 1969 Select Committee memorandum submitted to the DES, p. 6.
60 *Telegraph & Argus*, 4.3.1966.
61 Killian, "School Bussing in Britain", p. 189.
62 See Davies, "Educational Problems in Bradford", p. 98.
63 This metaphor is used by Hill and Isacharoff, *Community Action and Race Relations*, p. 289.
64 On the ministerial visit and these figures, see *Telegraph & Argus*, 20.5.1968.
65 West Yorkshire archives, "The Dispersal of Immigrants", letter by Alderman T.E. Hall, 29.08.1969, BBDI/7/TI 4923.
66 Tomlinson, *Race and Education*, p. 31.
67 Ealing was violently criticised for its misuse of this cash flow; see London Metropolitan archives, LMA/4463/B/02/01/007.
68 See Halstead, *Education, Justice and Cultural Diversity*, pp. 38–9.
69 Bradford archives, Educational Services Committee minutes, meeting (30.9.1969), pp. 67–8.
70 Bradford archives, Educational Services Committee minutes, meeting (15.7.1969), p. 32.
71 Powell claimed that some of his constituents at Wolverhampton "found their wives unable to obtain hospital beds in childbirth, their children unable to obtain school places".
72 *Telegraph & Argus*, 26.4.1968.
73 West Yorkshire archives, City of Bradford Education Committee, report on present situation (February 1967), BBDI/7/TI3687.
74 Jeremy Seabrook, *City Close-up*, Harmondsworth: Penguin, 1971, pp. 73–4.
75 This kind of inequality was also exposed in Blackburn, as will be seen in Chapter 5.
76 Halstead, *Education, Justice and Cultural Diversity*, p. 38.
77 *Telegraph & Argus*, 18.5.1962.
78 Schwarz, *Memories of Empire*, p. 18.
79 Simon Heffer, *Like the Roman: The Life of Enoch Powell*, London: Faber & Faber, 2008 [1988], p. 449.
80 Davies, "Educational Problems in Bradford", p. 101.
81 At that time in Britain, "positive discrimination" was *only* about specific social needs, it had not been translated into racial terms.

4

Reluctant cities: how London and Birmingham said no to dispersal

The respective situations of the two major British cities have already been touched upon. But London's and Birmingham's paramountcy in race-relations debates post-1945 and the fact that they accommodated the largest New Commonwealth populations in the country certainly warrant an in-depth analysis of their approaches to dispersal. More specifically, it is the complexity of the rifts within the Birmingham administration as well as the categorical rejection of dispersal in the Inner London Education Authority which are at the heart of this chapter. The 1969–70 controversy around the introduction of "banding" in the outer London borough of Haringey, frequently dismissed as a peculiar form of "dispersal", will be expanded upon, if only because some of the attitudes and discourses around "banding" obliquely shed light on dispersal in places like Southall and Bradford.

Beyond the "tipping point" in Birmingham?

Multiracial mosaic and race politics

Birmingham is the largest local government authority in England and Wales, administering about a million people in the 1960s. The West Midlands conurbation presented itself then as a "pepperpot mixture of Nineteenth and Twentieth century, with renewal and dereliction and industrial and residential areas often cheek by jowl".[1] In 1966 New Commonwealth immigrants represented 4.2 per cent of the total population of the city, concentrated in its middle ring: Aston, Handsworth, Soho, Balsall Heath, Sparkbrook, Moseley. According to 1968 DES statistics, immigrant children counted for 9.6 and 8 per cent in primary and secondary schools respectively.[2] But upon closer scrutiny specific areas had very large immigrant populations: the best-known case in educational terms was Grove Primary School in Handsworth, whose 90 per cent intake of immigrant children in the late 1960s attracted a great deal of national media attention (see Figure 4).[3]

It should therefore come as no surprise that there were cries in favour of dispersal in areas like Handsworth or Sparkbrook, both from Conservatives and Labour Party councillors or MPs, as well as, of course, from disgruntled white constituents. What will be explored here are some of the major reasons why Birmingham introduced only a moderate dose of voluntary dispersal in the late 1960s, at a time when some staunch advocates of "bussing out" immigrant children had written off Birmingham's case as hopeless.

Birmingham was mostly characterised – like some inner London boroughs – by its remarkable ethnic heterogeneity. In some areas, such as Sparkbrook, the Irish were the main immigrant group. Typically, they were often deemed *real* immigrants only in so far as they embodied public policy issues. In the words of two headmasters, the "tinker Irish" who "pose[d] really serious problems and educational difficulties" ought to be pigeonholed as immigrants, whereas the bulk of them merely "trying to adjust" should not.[4] This hybridity should hardly seem surprising for, as Kevin Myers puts it, "The Irish inhabited their own distinct community of Britishness which managed to combine widespread prejudice with a sense that they somehow belonged to, or could be tolerated in, British society".[5]

Birmingham's officialdom had no such qualms about West Indians. According to a 1965 consultative document entitled "A First Report on the Educational and Social Problems of the Coloured Immigrants", West Indian children were described as speakers of a wholly debased form of English, which was "a positive handicap to normal language development appropriate to a literate society". These children were "something of a behaviour problem"; they were "physically robust but mentally lethargic, often alternating between sullen withdrawal and ebullient high spirits"[6] West Indians were much more numerous in Birmingham than in Ealing or Bradford, in both numerical and proportional terms. There were, in January 1970, 9232 West Indian children for 4418 Indian children enrolled in Birmingham schools, whereas the same figures for Ealing as a whole were 4155 Indians for 2527 West Indians.[7] This stark contrast made the circumstances for the introduction of dispersal in each urban milieu markedly different, unless, of course, one saw (coloured) "immigrant children" as a cohesive, problematic whole whose sole presence was experienced as a strain. A cursory reading of the local press and archives confirms this impression, since the fact that approximately half of immigrants were West Indians (9232 out of 18172 for January 1970) was never taken into account to make sense of the legitimacy of dispersal plans. Indeed, though

Figure 4: Students at Grove School in Handsworth

speakers of a type of English frowned upon in the job market, these West Indians were still Anglophones. Wake-up calls in favour of dispersal from among both major political parties just seem never to have taken that fact into consideration, thereby conforming to the racial bias (rather than the linguistic concern) connected to dispersal. In Birmingham too, and although forced bussing failed to materialise, colour and the fear of "being swamped" in "ghetto schools" trumped actual linguistic deficiency.

Education on the agenda

Much as in Southall, tensions around schooling and immigration really started to intensify by 1962. In December of that year, a two-day conference was held by the Birmingham LEA on the theme "What can we do to give immigrant children and their schools special help?" The chief education officer, Sir Lionel Russell, had just issued serious warnings about the city's situation, which he was afraid might be grossly simplified in the press. His view was that the sudden immigrant influx was aggravating "the problem of integration and language difficulties", thus leading to "the swamping of certain streets and neighbourhoods", and to "some schools having 'gone black' with astonishing rapidity".[8] In order to alleviate some of the pressure on already strained schools, "spreading the immigrant children" was presented as a policy option just days before the conference.[9]

As elsewhere dispersal could be envisaged only as a one-way street. For the Birmingham chief inspector, to introduce the bussing of "whites" would have been "madness" as it would have triggered an "explosion". Yet the advisability of avoiding native insurrection stumbled against certain hard facts: indeed, on account of the scarcity of school places, dispersal if introduced might well have had to be a two-way process in some very strained areas, since the places left vacant by immigrants would have had to be filled by white children, who in turn would have had to be dispersed away from their neighbourhoods.[10] Glossing over this potential stumbling block, most advocates of dispersal only contemplated the transfer of "coloured junior children to outlying schools". But even this, as elsewhere, raised difficulties: the same chief inspector acknowledged that the spreading scenario would raise "the problem of the eating habits of the Asiatics", not to mention, in their eyes, the "unreliability and lack of time sense on the part of the West Indian parents and children".[11]

The truth is that in Birmingham an at best lukewarm attitude prevailed about dispersal. During the 1962 conference, suggestions to "transport the surplus immigrant children" from immigrant areas to the outskirts ultimately garnered scant support. For one thing there might be complaints from parents in the receiving schools, but "most of all it would be educationally and socially unsound; what immigrant children need is help to put down roots in the neighbourhood in which they live; their school can probably be the most helpful of all agents in this process; but it must be a fairly local school and not one in some remote suburb".[12] So instead of dispersal, a sharp increase in the number of peripatetic English teachers was prioritised, as well as an increase of allowances for schools with a large intake of immigrant children. A majority at the Birmingham City Council held firm on the "neighbourhood school" principle as a prerequisite for immigrant integration. A few also warned that American experience of bussing in some localities ought to serve as a powerful deterrent. Nigel Cook, chairman of the education committee, stated that in those localities "the bus taking children from one area to another became known as 'the Black Bus'. It built up a hostility in the receiving areas which was not conducive to integration."[13] References to "the Pakis on the bus" in Bradford or Huddersfield make this transatlantic parallel quite germane. Such cross-city journeys would be daily reminders objectifying "immigrant children" as "problems" because they were "coloured", regardless of whether they were Anglophones. F.M. Smallwood, chairwoman of the primary education sub-committee, exposed this very same racialisation process.[14]

Dispersal's hot potato

It was on this broad basis that the Labour-controlled City Council wrote off dispersal, which it regarded as segregationist, as a policy option in July 1965 (one month after circular 7/65).[15] It was illuminating that the debate on the feasibility and legitimacy of dispersal cut across traditional party ties: some key Labour figures came out in favour (Howell, Hattersley), whilst some Conservatives (the City Council Conservative leader Frank Griffin) were unrelenting nay-sayers. To say that Denis Howell was frustrated that his native city would have none of dispersal is to put it mildly. He dismissed the policy choice as a grave incentive to "White Flight": "[I]f there is an over-concentration of immigrants in one school, then our own parents are going to move their children from that school. This movement would have nothing to do with the colour bar ... They would want to move their children to other schools where valuable time in class is not being wasted because of the language barrier." Roy Hattersley, Labour MP for Sparkbrook at the time, thought that such obduracy would make everyone a loser: "[W]e are approaching the point in Birmingham where some inner-ring schools will be totally filled with non-English speaking children. This is particularly unfair for the immigrants and it is also causing problems for the local English children."[16]

Howell and Hattersley, as well as the Conservative advocates of dispersal, had some strategic allies. Much of the local press (especially the *Birmingham Post*) was with them. The Birmingham branch of the NUT promoted the "spreading of children", although the National Association of Schoolmasters insisted on the difficulties involved for dispersed children at primary level, who were simply too young.[17] The NUT held that owing to the specific urban dynamics in Birmingham "the most badly affected schools were surrounded by other schools where there were hardly any immigrants at all".[18] Indeed, the areas where it appeared urgent to disperse were strictly limited to two narrow belts, one in the north (Handsworth, Soho, Rotton Row), the other in the south (Small Heath, Sparkbrook, Balsall Heath).[19] Howell insisted that there were schools within a mile of these areas which had virtually no immigrants, so dispersal seemed, on this basis, practically feasible. Besides Howell and the NUT, some headteachers from the schools with the largest intake of immigrant children were quite vocal in promoting dispersal. One of them, Thomas Bloxham of Golden Hillock Secondary Modern School, attracted national press attention when he refused entry to five Pakistani children in September 1966 because, in his view, there were already too many non-Anglophone students in his school.[20]

Across the city some white parents vocally agreed with this daring move. Ever since 1959–60 a perception that immigrants were the "beneficiaries of special provision", and that they were "depriving white children of resources" prevailed in some areas,[21] but the 1961–62 "beat-the-ban effect" and the subsequent increase in numbers of immigrant children proved a tipping point to many. In November 1965, about six months after circular 7/65, some angry white mothers at Grove Primary School (Handsworth) threatened to withdraw their children if the number of immigrant children entering the school was not reduced.[22] The demand, also articulated by some West Indian mothers, was for the number of immigrant schoolchildren to be curtailed by 30 per cent, in order to reach a fifty-fifty balance. At the time, fear of not reaching the required level to pass the much-dreaded eleven-plus exam was rampant, although the test itself was being more and more openly challenged by comprehensive schooling. This was precisely the point made by Joan Williams, the local parents' spokesperson: "We feel our children will be unable to pass or even reach the standard required for the eleven-plus examination".[23] That West Indians as well as some Indians[24] themselves participated in mobilisations against "ghetto schools" across the city speaks volumes about the internalised need for upward mobility and the quest for respectability among some immigrant parents whose demands chimed with those of native whites. For some among them, such local and short-lived "rainbow coalitions" were evidence enough that their campaign was anything but "racialist". More generally, it illustrated a cross-racial parental concern with the dog-eat-dog competition for the best schooling and subsequently the best jobs introduced by the "white heat" of the "technological revolution" that Harold Wilson had invoked in a well-known 1963 Scarborough speech.

Another (white) parent, one Doreen Volrath, complained that her two children had not been placed on an equal footing because her son, now at Grove Junior School, stood no chance of passing the eleven-plus, while her daughter was shining at George Dixon Grammar School, having been through Grove Junior *before* the immigrant influx. If the local headmistress dismissed such attitudes typical of parents unable to see that children have different abilities,[25] it still remains the case that the immigrant presence served as a barium meal for the inconsistencies and inequities of the class-based English school system, where the eleven-plus separated thousands of siblings across the country, lionising those who had passed as "bright" and implying that those who had failed were "thick". Positioned awkwardly on the social class divide between the haves and the have-nots, some white parents at Birmingham were irked that immigrant children hurled them, through their massive presence in their children's schools, into some inferior category: the working classes perceived as largely "unfit" to pass the eleven-plus. In this way too these white people's sense of social positionality was dangerously challenged. But, in the end, for all these parents' vehemence and the national attention this received, calls for boycotting schools were barely sustained.

Other imbalances or inequities were brought to the fore in some of these mobilisations. In Moseley for instance, an area depicted as "three-quarters coloured" in 1968, some among the board of governors and the committee of parents of local schools rallied against the nearly all-white Anglican school in the vicinity, which avoided having to "share the burden" of immigrant children. Betty Preston, from the local committee of parents, said: "Class discrimination is accepted, but colour discrimination should not be tolerated. We have protested to the minister of education that public funds are being spent on making this church school a state preparatory school for selected white children."[26] At the heart of Moseley, that school siphoned off most of the bright and white students, poised to pass the eleven-plus. Local controversies of this kind erupted throughout the country, most particularly in large conurbations. The anomaly whereby faith schools were spared from having to "share the burden" started to smack of plain discrimination after the Race Relations Act of 1968 had been passed. In South London, for instance, "Church of England schools in the Southwark Anglican Diocese [were] warned that if they refused to offer places to non-Christian immigrant children they may be accused of discrimination".[27] One deputy director of the Southwark diocese (J.H. Coombes) hazarded the suggestion that it would be a Christian act for some of these schools to accept non-Christian immigrant children.[28]

Opting for dispersal of a kind

In spring 1966, the newly elected Conservative council initiated a form of voluntary-based dispersal. Whilst it was hailed as a welcome move by most of the press and local political figures, for some this pyrrhic victory just tinkered at the edges of an issue that had become unsolvable a few years back. Mrs Wilkes, the headmistress of Grove School, had said a few months prior to the policy U-turn that dispersal "obviously could not work when a school reached the situation her own [was] in".[29] Be that as it may, F.M. Smallwood, primary education sub-committee chairwoman, stated that "a policy of friendly persuasion of parents to get immigrant children dispersed through the outer areas of the city rather than concentrated in the inner ring schools, was being actively pursued".[30] And, like most of the local press, Alderman S.E. Dawes praised the new policy, which reconciled hitherto antagonistic positions and claimed that it "seem[ed] to be working quite well".[31]

Very little is actually known about this "friendly persuasion" form of dispersal. Birmingham's education committee deliberately refrained from going public about this, convinced that "the less public debate and dispute" there was, "the more they [could] hope to achieve, quietly, by persuasion".[32] But despite the early positive vibrations and officialdom's cautiousness, it does seem that, especially among new arrivals, there was great reluctance to let their children travel further to go to school. Neighbourhood schools, for them, meant the reassurance of the local community's comfort zone. It is therefore no surprise that, writing in the late 1960s, Michael J. Hill and Ruth Issacharoff described Grove Park School in Handsworth as accommodating immigrant children as around 90 per cent of its pupils, since "[Birmingham's] Education Department does not practise a dispersal policy".[33] This highlights one of dispersal's practical and moral quandaries: if forced, dispersal faced legitimate accusations of unfairness, illegality and racial discrimination; if based on persuasion, it faced accusations of plain inefficiency.

John Rex, the professor of sociology who was also a key figure in Birmingham, inveighed against dispersal, which he saw as a "viciously racialist policy". Promoting instead, like Nicholas Deakin and Brian Cohen,[34] a voluntary form of housing dispersal, Rex could hardly "believe it is supported by people who think it is a liberal thing to do".[35] His puzzlement underscores the way the Birmingham debates brought to the fore one of the obvious dilemmas in dispersal: some of those who were against saw it as "segregationist" since it objectified double racial standards, whereas on the contrary some like A.E. Thomas, headmaster of a Handsworth school, argued that "people forget the alternative to dispersal is segregation".[36] Amidst all this, parallels with Birmingham (Alabama) or between Handsworth and Harlem abounded,[37] from both pros and cons, and polarised and muddled debate all the more. But soon enough though, Birmingham's administration became embroiled in another, related, controversy over forced housing dispersal, which operated from 1969 to 1975. This has already been developed in the introduction to this book, but it is more than likely that those who decided to push for housing racial quotas were spurred by the realisation that voluntary schooling dispersal was just a makeshift with no teeth.

London's advocacy of community schooling

Setting the scene

From its inception in 1965 until it was vengefully disbanded by Kenneth Baker and Margaret Thatcher in 1990,[38] the Inner London Education Authority comprised the following thirteen boroughs: Camden, City of London, Greenwich, Hackney, Hammersmith and Fulham, Islington, Kensington and Chelsea, Lambeth, Lewisham, Southwark, Tower Hamlets, Wandsworth and Westminster. As such the ILEA was the largest education authority in the country, and the LEA in Britain with the largest number of immigrant children in its care. With Birmingham, it was also unique in accommodating a remarkable ethnic diversity. To the usual influx of West Indians and immigrants from the Indian sub-continent were to be added Cypriots and Maltese as well as Turks, mostly in the Tower Hamlets and Hackney boroughs. Remarkably, most borough schools had an immigrant population of at least 10 per cent, as Table 9 shows. As elsewhere in the country though, the immigrant population was very unevenly distributed, and also very unevenly distributed within boroughs. In the mid-1960s, more than half of the ILEA schools had fewer than 10 per cent immigrant children, whereas many others had, in varying degrees, up to 68 per cent.[39]

Broadly, the situation was comparable with the Outer London boroughs, which also had a very significantly higher proportion of

Table 9 Immigrant children in Schools of London boroughs (%) (January 1968)

Camden	17.5
Greenwich	4.2
Hackney	23.6
Hammersmith	16.1
Islington	23.4
Kensington and Chelsea	17.9
Lambeth	19.9
Lewisham	12.3
Southwark	12.7
Tower Hamlets	9.3
Wandsworth	15.1
Westminster	17.1

Source: London Metropolitan archives, ILEA archives

immigrants than elsewhere in the country, where immigrants also were quite unevenly distributed between and within boroughs, and where Brent, Haringey (and Ealing to a lesser extent) had much greater numbers.

Despite these commonalities, the schooling situation in the ILEA was somewhat distinct from that obtaining in other markedly multiracial LEAs across the country. The teacher/pupil ratio was quite favourable,[40] 1 to 15 in secondary schools and 1 to 21 in primary schools for the year 1972–73, so much so that the ILEA avowed that "never before in this country have schools been so well staffed, numerically as they are in Inner London".[41] Moreover, there was, compared with the rest of England and Wales, a smaller proportion of children of school age in London, and all demographic projections for the next years and decades conclusively showed that school rolls would decrease, thereby alleviating strains on many local schools, and contrasting with the situation in boroughs like Ealing. In Camden for instance, it was estimated in 1968 that some catchment areas would witness a student drop of around 33 per cent (primary school population) over the next five years, and 48 per cent in the next ten years.[42] On top of this, the London school care service could rely on some 2100 voluntary workers in the late 1960s, an impressive figure by English and Welsh standards. Although this battalion of social workers officially catered to the educational needs of everybody regardless of ethnicity or race, in boroughs like Islington, Hackney or Lambeth it is clear that they spent a great deal of time addressing immigrant problems. All in all, this general situation made Michael Young, an education expert who was part of the Plowden Report team, state that the ILEA was "blessed with very large resources".[43]

London's holistic approach

It is very difficult to tell how much these elements weighed on the policy choices operated by the ILEA *vis-à-vis* immigrant children. One thing is sure, though: London was adamant in having none of dispersal, and in exposing both the policy itself and most conceptual and social representations undergirding its introduction. By and large, London's approach was summarised thus by Sir William Houghton, ILEA's education officer: "In London we are getting away from any idea of regarding immigrant children as 'one' problem. We look at each school individually, and consider its needs and difficulties as a whole, not just on the basis of the proportion of immigrant children, regarding them as all in one category."[44] In the same interview held in the mid-1960s, Houghton also made this statement: "I feel that it is no longer relevant to talk in global terms of a need for 'a policy on immigrant children'",[45] which was a very far cry from the prevalent approach in many multiracial LEAs, whether or not they introduced dispersal.

When dispersal was debated and then recommended by the DES, London's policy clearly anticipated the schooling philosophy which was ushered in by the publication of the Plowden Report (1967). The problems raised and issues experienced by immigrant children were little different in nature from those of under-privileged, native white families. As was posited by an HM Inspectorate report on the ILEA primary schools, for all the specific concerns raised by the presence of non-Anglophone immigrants, "many of the problems are the same as those of socially and culturally deprived indigenous children".[46] In particular, there was a shared child-centred focus on the difficulty in communication, among both categories of children, and, as was pointed out in the Plowden Report: "The psychological trauma of placing a child without adequate powers of communication in a new social situation can be serious".[47] These were no mere theoretical musings: in a 1968 HM Inspectorate research into fifty-two London schools with twenty-seven accommodating large numbers of immigrant children, nineteen of the latter schools reported having witnessed an overall fall in the general standards since immigrant children arrived, whereas eight did not. In general terms, "schools which find no great fall in standards tend to be those which have been for many years coping successfully with culturally-deprived native children".[48] Hence compensatory education through measures of "positive discrimination" as advocated in the same report was often welcomed as urgently desirable. But what is key here is that the ILEA, much like Brent and a few other LEAs, did in many ways anticipate the recommendation of such measures by the DES. By taking a vigorously holistic approach based on the

improvement of general resources and on the shared needs of certain
categories of children regardless of their racial identities, they both challenged the broadly consensual perception of immigrants as characterised
by some radical Otherness, and thwarted accusations that immigrant
children got preferential treatment because they received differential
treatment, two hazards that were at the heart of dispersal as introduced
in Southall and elsewhere.

Rejecting dispersal

The London schooling administration rejected wholesale the broad
assimilationist rationale behind dispersal as well as the many practical
consequences it inevitably brought about. Regarding circular 7/65 in
general terms, an ILEA report stated that "most of the suggestions made
in [it] had already been put into practice in inner London" before its publication. It went on to say:

> We do not think it practicable or desirable to have to introduce any special
> scheme for redistributing overseas children between schools; we see grave
> objection to any scheme which artificially injects into a school a large group
> of children from outside the neighbourhood, thus separating them from
> their home surroundings and local playmates and frustrating the Authori-
> ty's policy of encouraging parents to take an active part in school life –
> important for the integration of immigrant parents.[49]

The ILEA gave further justification and illustration of this refusal in a
memorandum sent to the House of Commons Select Committee on Race
Relations and Immigration, in which London was just as equally critical
of dispersal. Balancing the number of immigrant children without resorting to dispersal was a way of accepting urban geography as it was, and as
it was felt very keenly by (immigrant) children. There were often some
possibilities of evening out the number of immigrant children in specific
schools, and dispersal was not desirable because to spread those children
would be very time-consuming and because there were geographical
stumbling blocks to this: canals, busy roads, railway lines, all of which
naturally determine a school's catchment area.

In this memorandum, the issue of where exactly to disperse children is
raised, as well as the potentially explosive question of having to disperse
in return some children originally from the receiving schools:

> In areas where there is a large concentration of families from overseas
> and all the schools have a considerable proportion, it would be neces-
> sary to transfer some of these to schools a good distance away. Where
> there is general pressure on the accommodation room could be found for

transported immigrant children only by transferring local children. Such an operation would be unworkable and undesirable.[50]

Besides, such artificial social engineering could only estrange both parents and children from the dispersal schools as well as from their area of residence. What follows encapsulates very well London's approach and chimes perfectly with the vast majority of testimonies collected of formerly bussed children. For these reasons at least it is worth quoting at length:

> Primary schools should, in the main, serve and reflect the neighbourhoods in which they are situated and it is very doubtful if it is educationally and socially desirable to disturb the natural relationship between school and neighbourhood. Further, any divorce of the school from the neighbourhood would lessen children's chances of playing in their home district with school friends. The artificial injection of a large body of immigration into a primary school serving a mainly non-immigrant population (or vice versa) might cause friction in the neighbourhood if local children were thereby prevented, on a large scale, from gaining admission. The policy of encouraging the parents to take an active part in the life of the school, which is a very important part of the education of immigrant parents, in such circumstances, would be much more difficult to achieve.[51]

London's resolutely child-centred and parent-centred approach was to be expanded upon in a 1973 pamphlet, *An Education Service for the Whole Community* (see Figure 5), a programmatic document whose every page clashes with the principles vindicating dispersal, although dispersal itself is never mentioned. Sixty thousand copies of the document were printed, with one sent to each teacher. Forty whole-day conferences were scheduled throughout the London division in order to disseminate the report's key findings and ideas.

The broadly holistic philosophy is legitimated thus from the outset of the pamphlet: "We are sometimes dismayed by the way in which children are tugged apart by the divergent influences upon them: a home which has no contact with school, teachers who do not appreciate the degree of deprivation to which the child has been subjected, the leisure group, the gang, with an ethos quite different from either that of home or school".[52] In the part "Whom do we miss?", the first answer is "parents" because, for all the administration's outreaching efforts, "many parents have almost no contact with the education service unless and until a crisis arises".[53] It is no surprise the ILEA embraced wholeheartedly the concept of community school as defined thus by the Plowden Report: "A school which is open beyond the ordinary school hours for use of children, their parents, and, exceptionally, for other members of the community".[54] Too often though, this remained a rarity rather than the norm, which is why the pamphlet laid

Figure 5: "An Education Service for the Whole Community". Pamphlet published by the Inner London Education Authority, 1973

great stress on the schools which took original initiatives to reach out successfully to parents, in Lewisham, Peckham, North Islington[55] and other areas. Once again, it bears repeating that none of this has anything to do with dispersal, but that such programmes were in themselves rebuttals of the rationale behind dispersal.

A reservoir of ability rather than a strain

Instead of understanding immigrant children solely as a public policy issue to solve, instead of solely gearing this public policy to the necessity to bestow upon immigrants the English language and the British/English "way of life", the ILEA was alive to the fact that immigrant children had themselves a major contribution to make to collective life at schools, and particularly to native white children. A 1967 HM Inspectorate survey of ILEA primary schools where immigrant children made up more than one-third of the whole school population states that "it is good to read that there are many examples of the special contribution stemming from their own cultural heritage that immigrants can make to the life of schools. This is the way to share different experiences to the benefit of all."[56] Elsewhere it is claimed that, especially in under-privileged areas, the presence of immigrant children does provide "a reservoir of ability".[57] In more specific terms, immigrant children had special contributions to make in disciplines like geography (by describing their origins, their native culture etc.) or in specific parts of the curriculum (handicraft, art, sport etc.). One school stated that these pupils "must be made to feel part of a large family of nations within the school, not to feel different from the rest, but at the same time to feel proud of their heritage".[58] Some ILEA documents from the period also insist on the risk to reify the category "immigrant children" as though they were part of one single, undifferentiated whole. Instead, some parents (West Indians) wanted to assimilate to a British/English model which they had already largely internalised; others (Asians) wanted their children to be fully conversant in English to elbow their way into a ruthless job market but at the same time were adamant that some important cultural, linguistic and religious specificities must be kept; others still (Turks, Cypriots, Italians) probably felt different from both West Indians and Asians. This diversity of approaches ought to be respected, in line with Roy Jenkins's growingly influential definition of integration as not being "a flattening process of assimilation". Noticeably, these mid- and late 1960s descriptions adumbrated the multicultural approach in education which would culminate, in London as in other English cities, in the 1980s.

Nuances

To be sure though, one must not paint too rosy a picture of these policies. For one thing, the contribution of immigrant children to the culture of native children was only understood in a social context of native deprivation, as though white working-class students were cultureless, and as though upper- and middle-class native children could not benefit from interaction with immigrants. Potentially, the risk was to nourish "White Backlash" feelings among working-class white families, as would be highlighted a few decades later by Roger Hewitt in his study of the borough of Greenwich,[59] which was still overwhelmingly white in the 1960s (see Table 9). Another qualification must be that the ILEA, as has been seen, enjoyed resources which were "unmatched in most of the rest of the country",[60] and which were probably the envy of more than a few LEAs that operated dispersal.

Although this is beyond the scope of this book, the ILEA was also known for having introduced a policy of banding, and for placing a very disproportionate number of West Indian children in schools for children with special educational needs, known back then as ESN schools (schools for the educationally subnormal). In 1966 the ILEA reported that 23.3 per cent of the children in ESN day schools were of immigrant origins, a huge disproportion, which rose to 28 per cent the next year.[61] The RRB and West Indian activists such as Bernard Coard would develop an interest in that anomaly. Now, regarding banding, the ILEA was the only one in the country to operate such a system. This was carried out most discreetly, in order not to raise controversy and to forestall any resistance from among parents.[62] The London Authority introduced three broad bands: the best-performing 40 per cent, then a middle band with 35 per cent, lastly the lowest-performing 25 per cent. In their respective comprehensive schools, they tried to even out pupils from each category. Although London chose to move to comprehensive schooling as early as 1944, it still kept a large number of grammar schools, which creamed off the best pupils. London grammars had pupils only from the best 40 per cent.

The reason why the ILEA operated this system was in order to modify the older vehicle of inequality, the dreaded eleven-plus examination. By doing so, it also tried to combine three principles, often seen as mutually exclusive: first, the need to strive towards an ability mix and social mix; second, parental choice; third, the need for schools to be zoned as neighbourhood schools.[63] Like dispersal, banding was an artificially introduced disruption of the catchment areas of schools. But unlike dispersal it was not explicitly connected with the substantial presence of immigrant children. It was only when Haringey borough contemplated banding in 1969 that a link was established between academic performance and over-representation of (in this case West Indian) immigrants. The reason why this sparked a local furore was that there were suggestions of a correlation between IQ and colour.

An IQ-based dispersal in Haringey?

Bernard Coard, the Grenada-born pedagogue who published the acclaimed pamphlet *How the West Indian Child Is Made Educationally Sub-normal in the British School System: The Scandal of the Black Child in Schools in Britain* (1971), dismissed wholesale as institutional forms of racism the British state strategies towards "Black students".[64] In a piece published in *The Guardian*, he expressed the view that "a low self-image, and consequently low self-expectations in life ... are obtained through streaming, banding, bussing, ESN schools, racialist news media, and a white middle-class curriculum; by totally ignoring the black child's language, history, culture, identity".[65]

This is an important view for three reasons. First, it emphasises the various forms of emancipatory movements in the 1970s, which contrasted with the broadly low profile kept by ethnic minorities and immigrants in the previous decade. And the struggle against dispersal took its deserved place among these movements. Second, and to qualify the previous point, it highlights the way that, in the early 1970s, West Indian activists articulated more radical critiques than the bulk of Asians, by borrowing concepts such as "institutional racism" and by adopting the rhetoric and sometimes the style of Black radical activists from across the Atlantic. Third, it is very helpful in placing dispersal (here referred to as "bussing") firmly in the context of West Indian and Asian people's efforts to find their deserved place in British society. Although these have been omitted from this book for the purpose of analysing the sadly under-researched issue of dispersal, multiculturalism, ESN schools, Anglocentric school curricula redolent of the colonial age, supplementary schools and the scarcity of ethnic-minority teachers all constituted specific questions alongside which dispersal has to be considered. And the 1969–71 controversy in Haringey is but another facet of this narrative. It also illuminates certain elements pertaining to dispersal alone, which is why it is worth more than just a passing reference.

To comprehend what was at stake, a presentation of the borough of Haringey's schooling situation and of one of the key players to this scandal, Alderman A.J.F. Doulton, is in order.

First then, the borough of Haringey, often associated in British public opinion with Tottenham. As shown in Table 10, this area of North London had a larger proportion of immigrant children than even Brent, making it

Table 10 Immigrant pupils in maintained schools, Inner and Outer London boroughs (%) (January 1970)

Borough	All pupils	Immigrant pupils	Percentage
Bexley	33,917	609	1.8
Barking	28,046	545	1.9
Hounslow	30,504	3152	10.3
Waltham Forest	32,189	3526	11.0
Newham	39,423	6007	15.2
Ealing	43,480	9241	21.3
Brent	40,615	11,214	27.6
Haringey	35,715	10,249	28.7
Inner London Education Authority	405,991	68,947	17.0

Source: National Archives (Kew), compiled from ED 269/14

the LEA with the largest percentage of immigrant children in the whole of England and Wales. The situation was very badly strained in primary schools, as well as very unbalanced, with many overcrowded schools in central Hornsey, central Tottenham and Bounds Green, whereas in places like Coldfall there were isolated schools with real possibilities of further accommodation. On top of this, teacher turnover was also very high, of about 25–30 per cent a year. And, in more general terms, Haringey had a population of approximately 250,000 people in 7491 acres, a density of thirty-four persons per acre that was well in excess of all other London boroughs.[66] It was in such circumstances that in 1967 Haringey introduced comprehensive schooling.

Very much despite himself, Alderman Doulton became the infamous author of the so-called "Doulton Report", issued on 13 January 1969. He was accused by some West-Indian activists of having "created a Frankenstein"[67], a monster which it was proving a very difficult task to deal with. Doulton had become vice-chairman of education in 1968 when the Conservatives in power in Haringey realised that they lacked expertise and personnel in the field, so aldermanic vacancies were filled by him and George Cathles (chairman). Doulton, who originally had no particular tie to the Tories,[68] was also the headmaster of a large private school in the fashionable area of Highgate.[69]

The "Doulton Report" is officially entitled "Haringey Comprehensive Schools". The paragraph which was to cause the controversy is called "Immigrants" and it is inserted in a report full of coldly objective statistics, some of which are illuminating, such as the much larger proportion of immigrant children in primary than in secondary schools. In the part on immigrants, one reads: "On a rough calculation about half the immigrants will be West Indians at seven of the eleven schools,[70] the significance of this being the general recognition that their I.Q.s work out below their English contemporaries. Thus academic standards will be lower in schools where they form a large group."[71] The same idea was repeated later in the report. Immigrants were presented as a "social problem" of such magnitude in Haringey that a *laissez-faire* approach could not properly be envisaged. Nor could a head-on assault on the problem – to limit the proportion of immigrant children in any one school – be seriously considered since it would "fairly certainly produce an outcry". The best option was therefore to initiate "banding by ability", a kind of middle course already in operation in the next-door ILEA, as we have seen.

The report was agreed upon in March by the borough's education committee. It acknowledged the quandary that it was placed in, for "IF WE DO NOTHING, the probability is that some schools will become in effect 'ghetto' schools with an entirely immigrant population". However, "IF WE TAKE STEPS to spread the immigrant school population, we may be accused of discrimination". Hence, after a great deal of dithering, and in the interests of the community as a whole, it was decided that "we must take steps to integrate the immigrant population by sharing it throughout all our schools ON THE BASIS OF ACADEMIC ABILITY". The main legitimisation of the move was that only by doing this would Haringey produce a thoroughly comprehensive form of schooling.[72]

The three bands of ability were to be defined thus: the high band could be comprised of the highest-attaining 25 per cent of pupils, the middle band of 50 per cent of pupils in the middle, and the low band of the 25 per cent lowest-achieving pupils. The general distribution was therefore slightly different from that operated by the ILEA. In the tests held in June 1969, the three lowest-achieving schools were not made public.

About one month earlier, the Haringey Borough Council had given the introduction of banding the go-ahead, after perusal of recommendations made by its education committee in March. The decision was made after a twenty-one-hour debate, a lot of name-calling and after the police had had to eject some thirty people from the council building. Outside, a few hundred demonstrators were protesting, among them many West Indians and Greek parents, but also white natives, some of whom were understandably fretful about the alleged presence of NF militants. Despite the uproar, the motion in favour of banding was passed with forty-six for, twelve against, and three abstentions.[73]

The most evident parallel between banding and dispersal is a commonsense one. Both introduced an artificial redrawing of catchment areas based on certain criteria: "ability" as validated by tests in the case of banding, being an "immigrant child" (as (un-)defined by the DES) in the case of dispersal. But since the person first suggesting banding in Haringey had alleged that West Indians had lower IQs than others, it logically followed that the distinction between "ability" and being an "immigrant child" was dangerously blurred. Both dispersal and banding rested on the assumption that "immigrant children" were primarily a problem to be dealt with. And the *raison d'être* for both was a claim which was dangerously unscientific: that immigrant children were intrinsically a strain on the education of others. Quite a few West Indian parents and militants were painfully aware of the connection between dispersal and banding. In a press release by the North London West Indian Association authored by Jeff Crawford, who would become instrumental in taking the Ealing dispersal to court, banding was vilified as "a new name for dispersal".[74]

For this Black association, banding was a mere blame-the-victims ploy. In a leaflet entitled "Black Parents Fight for Your Rights", it was claimed "that Black children are being used as scapegoats in order to hide the blatant inefficiency of the L.E.A. in providing a decent school and a decent education for black children". West Indians, together with Greek parents and white natives opposed to banding, underlined the need for an unrestrained respect for parental choice as sanctified by section 76 of the Education Act (1944). To this end they worked for the setting up of legal advice centres to challenge banding decisions. They also expressed fears that dispersal would only exacerbate their children's vulnerability, especially those of them who happened not to be white: "There is the possibility that the children will have to travel some distance to the school chosen for them, and that, at these schools where they are bound to be a minority, they will be open to all kinds of vicious racism and abuse". A later claim was made in Ealing that the resources spent on dispersal ought to be funnelled back into badly needed schooling material: "The facilities available to black children in these so-called ghetto schools are a shameful scandal, and some even lack basic material such as pen, paper and ink".[75] This last point was hammered time and again by Haringey (West Indian) parents, who said in a 1969 press release immediately following the County Council decision: "We, the so-called 'immigrants', are a problem. We are an integrated part of Haringey's educational problems, problems of old buildings, poor staffing, and insufficiency of equipment among other things".[76]

Caribbean intellectual and activist John La Rose, who was so central to the political emancipation of West-Indians in the London area,[77] was to observe in 1979 that "West Indian parents are concerned parents. They are interested in their children's education but they are not always sure of what is happening in schools, or how their children are faring."[78] It was to generate knowledge and awareness from the inside that a kind of rainbow coalition of parents produced a report called "Why Our Susan? Comprehensive Schools – the Case for Parental Choice" (see Figure 6) authored by Michael Young, one of the experts working for the Plowden Commission and himself an aware parent living in Haringey.

Those opposing banding could count on some high-profile allies: John La Rose, then, as well as Stuart Hall, who together with the North-London West Indian Association managed to present a large petition of some one thousand people. Also important was the fact that in the late 1960s there had already emerged some authoritative criticisms of IQ tests, which made Alderman Doulton's claim very debatable at best, ludicrously prejudiced at worst. Summarising some of this research, notably carried out in the United States by Erik Erikson, Bernard Coard stated in 1971: "These I.Q. tests are influenced by the general state of race relations in the society at the time at which the test is conducted. These tests are not conducted in test-tubes in a laboratory." Some of the press at the time was not mistaken about Doulton's claim: *The Sunday Telegraph* dismissed it as the latest "I.Q. fallacy", following in the infamous footsteps of Lord Snow (on Jews) and of Harvard professor Arthur R. Jensen (on "Negroes").[79] A few years later, Leon J. Kamin would argue, in *The Science and Politics of I.Q.*, "There are few more soothing messages than those historically delivered by the I.Q. testers. The poor, the foreign born and racial minorities are shown to be stupid. They are shown to be born that way."[80] In both Britain and the United States, some research had established that IQ boosting was possible thanks to hard-work, better educational facilities and a greater "self-concept", not to mention the fact that there is a cultural bias in IQ tests.[81] Some openly wondered: how would British white children fare if administered an IQ test in Jamaica?

Doulton himself was at pains to prove he had been misconstrued. At a working luncheon held at the West Indian Club on 13 May 1969, he met with the high commissioners of Jamaica, Barbados, Guyana, and Trinidad and Tobago, all of whom expressed their concern that Doulton's point was very likely to produce "an entrenchment of certain preconceived ideas and attitudes about the potentialities and capabilities of West Indian children". The high commissioner for Trinidad and Tobago referred specifically to the "unreliability of and the dangers inherent in determining the I.Q. of West Indian children purely on the results of their performance on tests designed for British children". Doulton categorically denied that he had stated that West Indian were "genetically inferior in intelligence", and then went on to assure his hosts that no IQ tests would be administered to immigrant children, and that "dispersal

Figure 6: From "Why Our Susan? Comprehensive Schools – the Case for Parental Choice". Report to the Haringey Education Committee by Michael Young, 1969

[would] be applied equally to children of the immigrant and the indigenous populations".[82]

Doulton's problem was that his reference to IQ among West Indians suffered from a dangerous vagueness. He neither claimed that these children were *genetically* inferior to others nor explicitly referred to all the cultural and family tensions bearing upon the act of immigration itself, which would inevitably have an effect on IQ tests. This was exactly the point made in a summary of a Wandsworth debate following the publication of the ILEA pamphlet *An Education Service for the Whole Community*, where "the fall in the average I.Q. over the last decade" in the area was seen as concomitant with "the upsurge in immigration" and with the "great increase in emotional instability" [83] that cultural uprooting inevitably brought with it.

Doulton's highly tendentious point was banding's original sin, which really nipped it in the bud. It spawned among West Indians and others a backlash that would prove banding's demise, very soon accelerated by the victory of Labour locally. Although many teachers in the worst-performing Haringey schools were in favour of "spreading the burden", of whichever colour this burden might be, most had understood that this form of social engineering had been recommended in the most inauspicious circumstances. Mr Roberts, headmaster of Drayton School (Tottenham), confessed to being theoretically in favour of banding, but that "unfortunately, the association of banding with immigrants in early stages of discussion and the mass of ill-informed publicity have created conditions, which, to my mind, mean that a satisfactory solution to the problems of the comprehensive schools cannot now be obtained by banding".[84]

West Indian prompt and successful rallying against banding provides, on the face of it, a striking contrast with Asian acquiescence in dispersal in Southall and Bradford. Yet several elements help to make sense of this. First, the early 1960s circumstances were different from those of the later decade, not to mention that some affected white parents mobilised against banding in Haringey. Then, there was no substantial "White Backlash" pressure to implement banding in Haringey, unlike what spurred dispersal in Southall. Also, once established and developed, the policy of dispersal became quite hard to challenge, and it took much time for it to be phased out, despite years of contestation. As opposed to this, banding in Haringey was never to be introduced, therefore scrapping a project proved much easier than removing a policy involving a few thousand pupils across a whole borough. But probably much more interesting are many of the direct or oblique correspondences between the debates in Haringey and in Southall. And more important is the fact that some key players in North London (the best case being Jeff Crawford) would likewise turn against bussing west of the city a few years later. The struggle against banding galvanised the subsequent struggle against the worryingly disproportionate number of West Indians in so-called ESN schools, which the DES was forced to take seriously, and then this in turn galvanised the protracted mobilisation against bussing in both Southall and Bradford. In the three successive struggles, West Indians (in the context of banding and ESN schools) and Asians (in the context of bussing) were fighting against public authorities' deterministic readings of their children's supposed deficiencies, but also against the way the British state, through the DES and LEAs, was treating them as though their citizenship were deficient, since their children could only be sidetracked into artificial situations from which, to quote an Amrit Wilson article against reception classes, "a child can only emerge socially and academically handicapped".[85] Without buying into conspiracy theories, this could be seen as a means for those with power to regulate the quantity and type of education and use a "strategic maintenance of ignorance"[86] directed at subordinate groups expected to become a reserve array of labour in a growingly globalised economy.

Notes

1 Quoted in Hill and Issacharoff, *Community Action and Race Relations*, p. 48.
2 Grosvenor, *Assimilating Identities*, p. 97.
3 See, for instance, *Guardian*, 11.2.1967.
4 Birmingham City Library (Wolfson Centre), IWA (UK) archives, *Birmingham Post*, undated newscuttings (1966?).
5 Myers, *Struggles for a Past*, p. 22.
6 Grosvenor, *Assimilating Identities*, p. 119.
7 Compiled from National Archives (Kew), ED 269/14.
8 See Grosvenor, *Assimilating Identities*, pp. 116–17.
9 *Ibid.*, p. 123.
10 *Sunday Mercury*, 13.2.1966.
11 Grosvenor, *Assimilating Identities*, pp. 120–1.
12 *Ibid.*, pp. 123–4.
13 *Sunday Mercury*, 13.2.1966.
14 *Birmingham Post*, 19.1.1967.
15 *Birmingham Post*, 12.7.1965.
16 For these two quotes, see Grosvenor, *Assimilating Identities*, p. 125.
17 *Birmingham Mail*, 19.1.1967.
18 *Birmingham Post*, 19.1.1967.
19 *Birmingham Post*, 23.1.1967.
20 See, for instance, *Sunday Times*, 2.10.1966.
21 Grosvenor, *Assimilating Identities*, p. 115.
22 *Ibid.*, p. 124.

23 *Birmingham Post*, 10.11.1965.

24 See *Birmingham Evening Mail*, 2.5.1968.

25 *Birmingham Post*, 9.11.1965.

26 *Birmingham Post*, 10.8.1968.

27 *South London Press*, 11.3.1969.

28 *Ibid.*

29 *Birmingham Mail*, 1.11.1965.

30 *Birmingham Evening Mail*, 6.5.1966.

31 *Ibid.*

32 Quoted in Grosvenor, *Assimilating Identities*, p. 126.

33 Quoted in Hill and Issacharoff, *Community Action and Race Relations*, p. 49.

34 See Nicholas Deakin and Brian Cohen, "Dispersal and Choice: Towards a Strategy for Ethnic Minorities in Britain", *Environment and Planning*, vol. 12 (3), 1970, pp. 193–203.

35 *Birmingham Post*, 21.2.1967.

36 *Birmingham Post*, 11.12.1965.

37 See *The Times*, 27.7.1967. For background, see Buettner, "'This is Staffordshire, not Alabama!'".

38 It was the Education Act of 1988 which officially announced the abolition of the ILEA, to come into effect in 1990.

39 London Metropolitan Archives, ILEA archives, Immigrant Pupils in Schools, January 1968.

40 *Ibid.*, pp. 8–9.

41 ILEA, *An Education Service for the Whole Community*, London, 1973, p. 19.

42 London Metropolitan Archives, ILEA archives, "Report of the Education Committee", 13.11.1968.

43 Michael Young, "Why Our Susan? Comprehensive Schools – the Case for Parental Choice", London: Haringey Parents Group, 1969, p. 18.

44 Power, *Immigrants in School*, p. 44.

45 *Ibid.*, p. 43

46 London Metropolitan Archives, ILEA archives, Report of the schools sub-committee, 13.12.1967, pp. 301–2.

47 London Metropolitan Archives, ILEA archives, Immigrant Pupils in Schools, January 1968, pp. 6–7.

48 *Ibid.*, p. 12.

49 George Padmore Institute, "Joint Report of the general purposes subcommittee and the schools sub-committee (London)": "The Education of Immigrants" (BEM 1/1/2), 16.12.1965. See also *Guardian*, 25.1.1966.

50 London Metropolitan Archives, ILEA archives, Select Committee on race relations and immigration: memorandum submitted on behalf of the ILEA, undated (1968?), §11.

51 *Ibid.*, §12.

52 ILEA, *An Education Service for the Whole Community*, p. 6.

53 *Ibid.*, p. 16.

54 *Ibid.*, p. 47.

55 *Ibid.*, pp. 22–6.
56 London Metropolitan Archives, ILEA archives, Report of the schools sub-committee, 13.12.1967, p. 300.
57 Quoted in London Metropolitan Archives, "The Education of Immigrant Children in Primary Schools", p. 4.
58 *Ibid.*, p. 10.
59 The background to Hewitt's study is that of the Stephen Lawrence case; see *White Backlash and the Politics of Multiculturalism*, Cambridge: Cambridge University Press, 2005.
60 Quoted in ILEA, *An Education Service for the Whole Community*, p. 33.
61 Tomlinson, *A Sociology of Special and Inclusive Education*, pp. 36–8.
62 See Young, "Why Our Susan?", pp. 7–10.
63 *Ibid.*, pp. 1–4.
64 For Black radicals like Coard, La Rose, etc. "Black" often meant "West Indians" as well as "Asians". What they were primarily interested in was the political, emancipatory dimension of "Black" (derived from Malcolm X and the Black Panthers), as opposed to "coloured" for instance (or "Negro" in the United States).
65 *Guardian*, 4.5.1971.
66 George Padmore Institute, BEM 1/1/2: London Borough of Haringey, Education Committee, "Report of Chief Education Officer", 1.4.1968 – 31.3.1969.
67 George Padmore Institute, BEM 1/1/2.
68 *The Times*, 3.5.1969.
69 George Padmore Institute, BEM 1/2/2.
70 He is referring here to one specific area within the borough of Haringey.
71 George Padmore Institute, BEM 1/1/2: "Haringey Comprehensive Schools", by A.J.F. Doulton, 13.1.1969.
72 George Padmore Institute, BEM 1/1/2: London Borough of Haringey, "Report to the education committee on comprehensive education", March 1969.
73 *The Times*, 1.5.1969.
74 George Padmore Institute, BEM 1/2/3, North London West Indian Association, Press release, 6.5.1971.
75 George Padmore Institute, BEM 1/2/3, "Black Parents Fight for Your Rights", undated (1969?).
76 George Padmore Institute, BEM 1/1/2, North London West Indian Association, Press release, 28.4.1969.
77 Paul Warmington, *Black British Intellectuals and Education*, London: Routledge, 2014.
78 London Metropolitan Archives, "Report on supplementary schools in Hackney" (by Joseph Ramlal), 14.7.1981.
79 *Sunday Telegraph*, 4.5.1969.
80 Quoted in Tomlinson, *A Sociology of Special and Inclusive Education*, p. 9.
81 On the evolution of this general debate, see Nicholas Mackintosh, *I.Q. and Human Intelligence*, Oxford: Oxford University Press, 2011 [1998], pp. 324–59; Tomlinson, *A Sociology of Special and Inclusive Education*.

82 George Padmore Institute, BEM 1/1/2, "Report on working luncheon at West Indian Club", 13.5.1969.

83 Quoted in ILEA, *An Education Service for the Whole Community*, p. 47.

84 George Padmore Institute, BEM 1/1/2, Letter by Mr Roberts, 24.11.1969.

85 *Morning Star*, 20.10.1975.

86 This is a phrase by Margaret Archer quoted in Tomlinson, *A Sociology of Special and Inclusive Education*, p. 8.

5

Dispersing in diverse places: how the other LEAs fared

In this chapter, the aim is to provide a detailed analysis of the LEAs outside Southall and Bradford which operated bussing at some point between the 1960s and 1980s. In 1971, the DES published *The Education of Immigrants*, which insisted upon linguistic need rather than seeing "immigrant children" as a basis for dispersal. This ministerial change of policy should be kept in mind in the following analyses of LEAs over more than two decades. Piecing together information from national and local archives and newspapers hopefully provides a fairly clear picture of how dispersal operated outside Southall and Bradford. However, and as has been argued in the Introduction, tight-lipped education minutes across the country have proved an impassable barrier as far as the following questions are concerned: how many pupils were bussed in each of the LEAs discussed below? When did bussing start and end? Where did it really operate on a racial or ethnic basis, and where on a strictly linguistic deficiency one? Where did it really include some (Anglophone) West Indians and if so how many? Most of these will probably always remain unanswered.

Blackburn

A large cotton-weaving town proud of its two hundred chimneys belching out smoke, Blackburn attracted successive swathes of immigrants throughout its industrial history. Just before deindustrialisation set in, one of the last waves was made up of Gujarati Muslims, who constituted around 90 per cent of Asians locally.[1] Like Mirpuris in Bradford or Birmingham, these were non-Anglophone rural immigrants concentrated in the lowest echelons of the job market. They residentially clustered immediately to the north and east of the town centre, particularly in the Brookhouse area. By 1977, St John's ward already had a 50 per cent Asian population (see Table 11).

Table 11 Distribution of Asians by ward (%), Blackburn (1977)

St John's	49.4
Trinity	25.3
St Michael's	17.7
St Paul's	16.0
St Matthew's	13.1
St Thomas's	7.1
St Luke's	5.6
St Jude's	3.9
St Stephen's	3.5
St Silas's	3.4
St Mark's	0.9
Park	0.3
St Andrew's	0.2
St Francis's	0.1

Source: Vaughan Robinson, "The Segregation of Asians Within a British City: Theory and Practice", University of Oxford, School of Geography, Research Paper 22, 1979, p. 11.

Giving each school "a fair share of the load"

This concentration irredeemably strained educational services in the vicinity, which is why, alongside integrationist concerns, dispersal for primary school children was introduced in Blackburn. It went on until 1975, at least as far as "immigrant children" were concerned, and never seems to have involved more than 110–30 students[2] out of a primary school total of around a thousand (figures for 1972). Lancashire County Council took over Blackburn on 1 April 1974, and by 1975 its new director of education, Mr Rainbow, was of the opinion that the disadvantages of dispersal far outweighed its advantages.

Schoolchildren were bussed to ten or eleven schools in the outlying districts, mostly to the south of the town. In 1972, one year after the DES had insisted that linguistic deficiency instead of being "an immigrant child" was henceforth the one criterion legitimating dispersal, Blackburn gave the following reassurance to the ministry: "We do not operate our service on a basis of ethnic origin, but on preliminary examination of linguistic skill". Even those Asians born in Blackburn often reached the age of five without any command of the English language, being wholly brought up by their non-Anglophone mothers, since "the only English spoken is by fathers and brothers who often work long shifts in textile manufacturing and see little of the young children".[3]

Eric Hawkins (Language Teaching Centre, University of York), who was asked by the RRB to investigate the screening process leading to dispersal,[4] aired some criticisms regarding the local educational administration. His on-the-ground research led him to a conclusion gainsaying Blackburn's claim: "My discussion with the officials left me with the clear impression that the selection of infants for dispersal was made on ethnic grounds, according to the original guidance on dispersal given by D.E.S. circular 7/65". Hawkins interviewed the welfare officer responsible for deciding whether or not a child should be bussed, and it was clear that no real linguistic test was taken, that no interview really took place: "Usually he [welfare officer] sees the parents and from the information he has he states that he can safely predict the child's lack of proficiency in English because of the homogeneity of Blackburn's immigrant population". That assumption-based approach was flawed, for it failed to properly ascertain the existence, let alone the degree, of linguistic deficiency: "One of the head teachers estimated, in reply to my question, that perhaps one in five of the immigrant infants bussed to her school did not have a language handicap as to justify the bussing purely on linguistic grounds. She felt however that the bussing of these children was necessary for their 'social', not simply 'linguistic' education." All told, five out of the eleven schools which operated bussing in the Blackburn LEA admitted to accommodating students who were Anglophone immigrant children.

Eric Hawkins personally met with such a case: "While I was attempting to communicate with a five-year old Pakistani girl, one of this year's intake, she burst into tears and clung to her elder sister, aged 7+, who had come to fetch her at the end of school to return home with her on the bus. The older girl was very fluent in English and could well have attended a school near her home. But the girls could obviously not be placed in separate schools."[5] Understandably, the Blackburn authority was reluctant to part such young siblings. But the fact remains that, in an LEA which dispersed a limited number of children, no serious language examination was held, even after 1971, once the DES had jettisoned the race-based approach to focus instead on language handicap.

Blackburn's flawed policy was legitimated thus by the local director of education, in a 1972 letter to headteachers of the town's schools: "In our enthusiasm to do the right thing by immigrant pupils and, in addition, to 'protect' the education of English pupils in these schools, we may have committed a breach of the Race Relations Act". Therefore, what was recklessness, amateurism or discrimination in the eyes of the RRB was, according to local authorities, integrationist zeal and a willingness to promote harmonious "race relations" in the town. Blackburn's vindication of its own policy impressed Anthony Lester little. Disappointed with the restricted remit of Hawkins's investigation, the co-founder of the Runnymede Trust urged the York University educationalist to dig deeper, just as he hoped that, in Ealing's case, Maurice Kogan would investigate further the discriminatory nature of bussing in Southall.

National Front retaliation

The RRB developed an interest in the Blackburn situation because, in an amazing twist of irony, the NF seriously considered filing a complaint of racial discrimination towards whites against the LEA, which gave free bus passes to dispersed immigrant children whilst leaving white pupils in the cold. For this it found a willing stooge in the person of one Marjorie Parker, a mother whose son had to pay the fare to the school of her choice, and was irritated that (forcefully) dispersed Asians did not. The reason why this was a revenge by the NF was simply that the far-right movement regarded the Race Relations Act (1968) as an all-out act of war against British people on their own turf,[6] and because the Act had already justified repeated litigation against it, a few years after its implementation.[7] Since in Powellite fashion it appeared to the NF that the "black man" had now "the whip hand over the white man",[8] it seemed only fair in its eyes for white people to mobilise racial discrimination legislations whenever they felt discriminated against. Such a move by the NF was consistent with seemingly comparable forms of litigation. On BBC Radio Blackburn, Mr Martin, North-West conciliation officer for the RRB, stated that 10 per cent of the cases he had to deal with were from indigenous white people, who mostly complained against "landlords who have come from abroad".[9]

Blackburn also accommodated one of the NF's historical leaders (John Kingsley Read), and is a town where the far-right movement enjoyed a few local election successes in the mid-1970s. As in West Bromwich or Bradford, the NF was mostly white working-class, and tried to cash in on perceptions of unfairness to whites. Dispersal, however limited in scope locally, was the very stuff with which to exacerbate passions. Indeed, as dispersal's last nail was hammered in Blackburn, a Conservative councillor could still cry out: "Was no thought given to the fact that there are hundreds of mothers in Blackburn alone who are taking part-time jobs in order that their children may be educated, clothed and transported to school, without relying on ratepayers' handouts?"[10]

This is one of the reasons why both the Blackburn authorities and the RRB took the NF claim of racial discrimination against whites very seriously. As Anthony Lester made clear: "It goes without saying that the fact that her [Mrs Parker's] complaint has been made by the National Front does not entitle the Board to shirk its statutory duties". Indeed, "Mrs

Parker was fully entitled to complain to the Board about the L.E.A.'s dispersal policy and its effect upon her and her son".[11]

Marjorie Parker was aided by W. Barton, the regional head of the NF who lived in the Lancashire town. The case really started on 1 November 1971, when Barton filed a complaint against the Blackburn borough council on the basis that it provided free transport to "coloured" students and none to whites, which to him constituted a violation of the Race Relations Act 1968, more specifically chapter 71 section two, entitled "Facilities for transport and travel".[12] The second complaint against the council was also connected with dispersal, the effect of which was to remove "from certain schools in the Blackburn area white schoolchildren for the purpose of introducing coloured schoolchildren into the schools compulsorily vacated by white children", itself, it was claimed, a "direct and flagrant violation" of the same act (sub-section two part one, entitled "Education and training").[13]

Leaving aside some legal intricacies beyond the scope of this book, Anthony Lester and the RRB maintained that the claim of discrimination was very flimsy. The RRB general committee made the following reminder which would serve to clarify matters with the plaintiffs, Mrs Parker and Mr Barton. For the purpose of this case, there were currently three categories of pupils: first, coloured primary school children who were bussed at public expense; second, white children (and coloured children not covered by the first category) who were unable to attend schools of their parents' choice and who had to travel a certain distance and did so at public expense (regulations[14] provided that a child under eight must not be required to walk more than two miles to school, and a child over that age more than three miles); third, children who were not dispersed but who went to schools of their parents' choice, and who as a consequence did not receive any help. Mrs Parker's six-year-old son, David, went to Longshaw Infant School at his parents' request and was not sent there by the LEA, therefore he did not receive any help.[15] For the record, Longshaw was one of the schools that immigrant children were bussed to.

Because she "feared reprisals against her children", Marjorie Parker was very reluctant to go public about this issue, and clearly wanted her name out of the public gaze.[16] This and the very flimsiness of the case meant that it was not proceeded with and a local controversy was nipped in the bud, much to the reassurance of all those who strove to preserve racial harmony and probably much to the chagrin of the National Front. Cecil Fudge, chief conciliation officer for the RRB, stated in a letter to his colleague John Lyttle: "The last thing we want to bring about is the introduction of 'bussing' as a local election issue and that might well come about if we were to suggest to Blackburn that what they are doing appears to be unlawful".[17] In this respect at least, both the town and the RRB had common interests.

But, as has already been argued in the case of Bradford, merely anecdotal evidence of differential treatment could look like, or be interpreted as, systemic illustration of preferential treatment, or institutional "anti-white racism". Twice on the local radio, the NF inveighed against a sort of English Jim Crow in reverse: "A 75-seater bus was provided to take about fifteen immigrant children to the Everton School in Blackburn, and ... white children weren't allowed to ride on it". On top of this, "One private bus contractor has said that he has an agreement with the Blackburn Education Department to carry coloured children only".[18] On both occasions the Blackburn Education Authority refused to comment. One can only imagine the myriad backlash anecdotes inspired by such busses passing by white pupils drearily walking to school on rainy or snowy Lancashire mornings. In such circumstances, it was no surprise that the town authorities were strongly urged to do away with a policy which smacked of discrimination simultaneously against coloured immigrants and against whites.[19]

Unchristian unbalance

Another illuminating peculiarity about the Blackburn case is the disproportionate number of voluntary-aided schools, often geographically clustered in areas of large New Commonwealth immigration. Many of these were Church of England schools, such as St Matthew's, St Paul's and St John's. There seems to have been a kind of gentleman's agreement whereby these schools would admit immigrant children up to 10 per cent of their roll regardless of their families' faiths. The real dilemma was: how could a LEA allow religious foundations to enjoy aided status in order to operate their own admission procedure and still ensure that immigrant children were admitted to schools near their home, given the peculiar geographical dynamics of migration into the town? Asked for further details about its admission policies by the RRB, the Lancashire County Council dismissed the potentiality of racial discrimination in this specific instance by claiming that this was a long-standing tradition among those schools and that "the discrimination is based on religious grounds which apply as strongly against Baptists, Methodists, members of the Salvation Army and agnostics as they do against Muslims or Sikhs of Indian origins".[20] Anthony Lester lamented that Eric Hawkins's investigation into the Blackburn situation did not cover faith schools. To him, on strictly arithmetical grounds, dispersal did operate in Blackburn solely because voluntary-aided schools did not accommodate a full share of immigrant children: "The dispersal system is intimately linked with the quota system operated by the aided schools at the infant and junior level, and there also appears to be a smaller quota or complete exclusion at the secondary level".[21]

Shortage of places in state schools (coterminous with the availability of places in faith schools) meant that a few years after it had been scrapped as a policy option (1975), bussing had to be reintroduced, but this time around it had nothing to do with linguistic deficiency or immigrant integration. There is even no evidence at all that it affected only ethnic-minority pupils. In 1985, a school construction programme was announced in the town centre area: there, some as young as four years old had to be bussed as far as six miles away (from Brookhouse to Livesey or Feniscowles) because of overcrowded conditions.[22] As a result, some 445 pupils from Church of England schools and state schools had to be bussed out. Simultaneously, it was revealed that the nine Roman Catholic schools in the town had some eight hundred vacant places. St Alban's Primary School, in the Brook-house area, with 311 registered pupils in January 1985, had a capacity of 490.[23] The diocese of Salford in whose jurisdiction Blackburn RC schools were situated baulked at accommodating all those (non-Catholic) pupils, whether their names be Campbell or Khan. Although the discrepancy discussed here is still a very topical issue today given the confessionalisation of multiculturalism in schools and the critiques regularly made of admission policies in faith schools, it still remains that the Blackburn situation in the mid-1980s reaches beyond an analysis of the dispersal policy as it applied to immigrant children and ethnic minorities.

Huddersfield

An exemplary experiment

Social scientists dealing with race, education and immigration associate Huddersfield with Spring Grove School, which in the late 1950s and early 1960s served as a national laboratory for the education of immigrant children. Whether the experiment spearheaded by Trevor Burgin[24] was labelled "school within a school" or "segregation for integration", it was unquestionably the most publicised and successful attempt at addressing the issue of concentrated non-Anglophone immigrant children in England, hailed by politicians, media and academia alike.[25] Burgin's policy consisted of keeping the non-Anglophone Asians in withdrawal classes within Spring Grove, until their English became solid enough for them to join mainstream classes. His success was all the more remarkable as he had no experience in the field when he was appointed headteacher in 1958. The

Fabian Society was quick to point out that Burgin's strategy was "a converse to the dispersal approach, bringing the non-English speakers together for a specific practical purpose as opposed to the spreading of all immigrants for its own sake".[26]

Burgin's success depended a great deal on his independence and on the mediatisation of Spring Grove, which acted as a powerful magnet for a specific type of teacher. Nearly sixty years later, Trevor Burgin recalls:

> We were very lucky in being able to establish an island, a real school within the school, for that we had very committed staff, knowhow (June Derrick, from Leeds University, came to Spring Grove regularly) and a lot of available space. The children would always communicate with each other. We had two things: available space, and freedom to use that space. We also quickly acquired a reputation: multicultural, liberal teachers wanting to do things differently tried to come to Spring Grove to teach.[27]

But with the increase in the number of leaving white families and the growing number of immigrants, the system eventually burst its banks. In 1963, Spring Grove was already an Asian majority school. The next year (and a few months before circular 7/65), the Huddersfield Education Department made public its intention to disperse by suggesting that "the number of immigrant pupils in each school should be kept within 20% of the total roll".[28] In 1965, Trevor Burgin was awarded a Page Scholarship from the English Speaking Union of the Commonwealth to spend two months in the United States and learn from the education of immigrant children there.[29] After his visit to New York, Boston and Miami, Burgin learnt that dispersal had become national policy during his absence. His function was henceforth to see to it that it operated efficiently.

What differential treatment?

Like other LEAs such as West Bromwich, Huddersfield dispersed non-Anglophone Asians as well as Anglophone West Indians. That is important in a town which in 1967 had some six thousand West Indians, one thousand Indians and five thousand Pakistanis, who taken together comprised 9 per cent of the local population (see Table 12).[30] G.H. Grattan-Guinness, Huddersfield's deputy education officer, justified dispersal in 1966 as "sheer commonsense", before asking: "Do we want ghettoes of dark-skinned families, be their origins Asiatic or West Indian or both? And if, for a time, it is impracticable to avoid something of this nature until these people gradually find solutions to their accommodation problems throughout our communities, can we afford, on social and educational grounds, to let similar conditions grow up in any of our schools?"

Table 12 West Yorkshire towns and immigrant children (1965–67) (towns in bold operated dispersal at some point between 1963 and 1986)

	Number in 1965	1966	1967	Increase in %	Immigrant children as % general school population
Batley	132	150	445	237	3.3
Bradford	1739	2449	3100	78	6.4
Dewsbury	175	240	346	98	3.7
Halifax	45	97	241	436	1.6
Huddersfield	600	885	1419	136	7.5
Keighley	30	45	83	176	0.9
Leeds	2024	2300	2846	41	3.5

Source: Eric Butterworth, John Goodhall and Bryan Hartley, *Immigrants in West Yorkshire: Social Conditions and the Lives of Pakistanis, Indians and West Indians*, London: Institute of Race Relations, 1967, p. 20

He went on to conclude: "In the interests of all colours, customs and cultures, as even a dispersal as can be devised seems imperative, and all the Authority's plan are to this end".[31]

The reason for including West Indians in the scheme was, in the words of Huddersfield's authority, their "educational retardation". Special language centres not being strictly necessary for them, it remained that "their admission to schools should be so controlled that no school receives more than a small proportion of West Indians". And, although it followed that "the problems of Asiatic and West Indian pupils should be treated separately",[32] both groups still fell under the dispersal policy probably in an effort to ward off white native hostility in areas of ethnic minority clustering to the north and south of the town centre.

Archives and the local press do not refer to this white native hostility, the focus being primarily on linguistic handicap and the need to introduce the children to "English ways of life".[33] Nevertheless Trevor Burgin does recollect that "it was a very controversial issue, we had to sell it to local people. Very fortunately, we had developed a very good relationship with the parents, and I take some pride in that." Schools which received dispersed children also took some convincing: "We offered a teacher on the understanding that a school would take fifteen Asian kids. There were peripatetic teachers and remedial classes, in order for bussing to be accepted politically."[34]

Asians in towns like Huddersfield, Blackburn or Halifax were very reluctant to draw attention to themselves, maybe even more so than in Bradford, where they were much more numerous. In Huddersfield middle-class Asians were prompt to refer to the self-enclosed world the bulk of their fellow-countrymen grew up in. John Goodall, a local academic, stated that "the values involved in the English idea of assimilation put forward by the small number of middle-class Pakistani *literate* in the town, edu-cationalists and so on, are scarcely conceived of in the 'stay-as-you-are' tradition of illiterate Punjabi villagers"[35] whilst Nasim Hasnie, from the Huddersfield Community Relations Council, described a "community [which] operates its own self-imposed apartheid".[36] This is quoted from a 1977 survey of Asian youths, with five hundred interviews. The pages dealing with education never raise the issue of dispersal. Prominent in the education debate was, instead, the virtual absence of Asian teachers, of a multicultural curriculum and of single-sex schools (for a more religiously minded minority within the minority).[37]

All in all, it is impossible to tell whether dispersal had any effect what-soever on a community that was closed in upon itself. Joe Hopkinson, a postgraduate student at Huddersfield University who did his dissertation on bussing locally, states: "I began this research after a family member spoke about the arrival of 'The Paki Bus', and the barrage of stones, or ice balls in the winter, that would fly at the disembarking children".[38] Parents interviewed for the 1977 survey of Asian youths felt it important that "their children should be able to meet and make friends with English youngsters of the same age, and they respond[ed] to the calls for single-sex schools with surprising apathy". In Huddersfield as elsewhere, the objec-tification of racial difference embodied in the special buses did probably exacerbate the internalisation of a symbolical barrier, reinforcing the bonding social capital of "Asians toughing it out together" and weakening the bridging social capital with white English natives. And there as else-where the paucity of sources makes it impossible to go any further than that tentative conclusion.

Halifax

Five miles to the north-west of Huddersfield, the town of Halifax presented on the face of it a fairly classic case of dispersal. Except that in the Calderdale LEA (which includes Halifax), dispersal was introduced at a late stage, in 1976–77,[39] and went on until at least 1986, five years after it had been phased out in Ealing and Bradford.

In a 1970s context of growing mobilisations against "bussing", Calderdale had to step very gingerly to initiate dispersal plans. At that time, American backlash against "forced bussing" had cast a slur on the word, and promoters of dispersal had to sound reassuring by laying emphasis on the liberal dimension this would locally take: "The use of the word 'bussing' should not be correlated with the American practice, for within the working party's recommendations the movement represents no more than the introduction of a measure of choice to immigrant families and not an exercise in direction".[40] "Choice" around dispersal was also trumpeted because it would provide, in the long run, a wider choice of opportunities on the job market to non-Anglophone Asians after they had been durably placed in an Anglophone environment by the mid-1970s, a time when the oil shock had started to destroy thousands of jobs.[41]

For all the smooth talk, dispersal in Halifax was doomed to be anachronistic from the outset. A growing body of research dominated by the influential work of Josie Levine[42] laid stress on how preferable it was to integrate those pupils in mainstream classes rather than to establish separate classes. Such research logically permeated official reports on education. The Bullock Committee Report was issued in 1975, as dispersal was to be introduced in Halifax, and it argued: "Common sense would suggest that the best arrangement is usually one where the immigrant children are not cut off from the social and educational life of a normal school".[43] Ten years later, and as dispersal in the Calderdale LEA was growingly challenged, the influential Swann Report hammered the point that "We are wholly in favour of a move away from ESL provision being made on a withdrawal basis".[44] But despite the proffering of these recommendations, by 1983 around 75 per cent of pupils learning ESL were still taught outside mainstream schools,[45] a proportion which qualifies how really anomalous the Calderdale situation was.

The CRE, which had grown out of the defunct RRB since the implementation of the Race Relations Act (1976), developed an interest in Calderdale dispersal in the early 1980s.[46] It became increasingly convinced that the LEA's dispersal amounted to a system of indirect discrimination[47] towards non-Anglophone Asians, whether intentional or not. The CRE produced a 1986 report called *Teaching English as a Second Language: Report of a Formal Investigation in Calderdale Local Education Authority*. This detailed study of the operation of ESL courses in the town appraised methods of assessment, allocations of places and "the segregation of Asian children from mainstream schooling if they are considered to need special language tuition".[48]

Among the potential cases of indirect discrimination pinpointed by the CRE were: first, the absence of (Asian) parental choice, which Calderdale argued was legitimate since the English Language Teaching Service was already a special education provision, therefore it claimed that the concept of parental choice as reiterated by the 1981 Education Act did not hold in the present case; second, the largely deficient provision of education in certain disciplines (science, craft subjects); third, the material conditions of the rooms and buildings, well below those of mainstream schools; fourth, the many pragmatic difficulties caused by bussing; fifth, the difficulty to adapt to mainstream classes after having been in segregated classrooms, which more often than not brought about a regression among pupils; and sixth, the impossibility for Asian parents to elect or stand as school governors of the language centres their children were sent to, which ran afoul of the Education Act (1980).

Bussing was but one of the various facets of this unfair treatment, facets which it would have been unthinkable to expose in the early years of dispersal. The CRE calculated that in Halifax in January 1985 approximately three hundred pupils were still bussed, half of whom were infants. The shortest round-trip travelling time was twenty-five minutes a day, the longest seventy-five minutes; the average time was forty-one minutes. Many sometimes missed out on part of the day, even if it was only fifteen minutes. It was only by resorting to bussing that Halifax managed to cope with the growing number of pupils in the town centre area, and as a consequence no new school was built. Besides, as has been seen elsewhere, "this has produced a situation in Central West Halifax in which white children in the primary age range who live in the area can receive all their education in a neighbourhood school whereas many primary age Asian children cannot".[49] Although written in a largely conciliatory manner, the CRE report did call upon the government to seriously monitor the situation and upon Calderdale to abide by the law. It was probably reassured that "Calderdale [had] already made a public commitment to changing its system".[50] By 1986, it only sounded like plain common sense that "children who feel threatened by their surroundings because their peers use language to abuse them racially are going to be less motivated to learn the language than those who feel secure. In other words, the atmosphere of the school and the attitude of teachers are as important for language acquisition as the content of lessons."[51] For over a generation many thousand immigrant children in various LEAs had endured analogous situations, and this is also how the Calderdale anachronism ought to be understood.

Leicester

As has been evidenced by the interview of its director for education (Dr Elfed Thomas) quoted in Chapter 2, Leicester was opposed to dispersal, but the sudden influx of Ugandan Asians in 1972–73 just about overwhelmed the Midlands town. In total eighty thousand people – most of them fairly prosperous educated middle-class – were expelled by dictator Idi Amin, who gave them ninety days to leave on 4 August 1972. Twenty-nine thousand came to Britain, and Inner and Outer London, Leicestershire, Birmingham, Coventry and Preston were the regions where these refugees clustered.[52]

It was probably inevitable that the arrival of Ugandan Asians caught both local and national authorities off-guard. This was despite the creation, made public on 18 August 1972, of the Uganda Resettlement Board (URB), whose task was to "make contingency plans for the smooth and orderly reception of those who need to come to Britain and for their dispersal as widely as possible throughout the country".[53] The URB was an intermediary body, for the Edward Heath government was hell-bent on distancing itself from any policy that seemed too generous with coloured immigrants, a mere four years after Powell's so-called "Rivers of Blood" speech.[54] Through the URB, it strove to channel the refugees away from strained areas in terms of housing (known as "red areas") and move them towards "green areas" on a voluntary basis.[55] But ultimately many of the Ugandan refugees to Britain opted straight for "red areas", where many already had relatives and friends. In Leicester, their number was hard to ascertain, especially in the early months, so much so that, whilst the URB had estimated 2307 for early 1973, the medical officer of health's records indicated a total of 4133, which increased difficulties in the provision of social services (including education) to that population.[56]

That the British Cabinet's help was little more than "formulaic"[57] is illustrated by Leicester's desperate attempt to get extra financial help for the 30 per cent or so of refugees who were of school age. Dorothy Davis, chairwoman of the City of Leicester Education Committee, sent a letter to *The Times* to expose Margaret Thatcher's (secretary of education under Heath) and the DES's apathy in the matter. She paid tribute to her town's heartening voluntarism so far ("Leicester has for years handled an influx of around a thousand immigrant children a year, not without strain, but certainly without fuss") and warned of the many achievements which were imperilled by the current crisis. From 1 August to 25 October 516 Ugandan children had arrived seeking places in already nearly full schools, to whom had to be added 240 new immigrants from other parts of Africa and Asia.[58] Leicester had already absorbed around five hundred Kenyan Asian children in 1968 but this new influx necessitated the renovation of old buildings as well as the erection of new ones.

The Leicester authority made it clear that dispersal would be opted for only as a last resort, because of a geographical mismatch: "We have been absorbing about a hundred immigrant children a month and have very little spare capacity. What there is is some distance from the areas in which the Asians would live. Bussing would be an answer, but that is not suitable for very young children."[59] On top of this, dispersal was frowned upon because Leicester's schooling situation was too strained already and in some areas the extreme-right presence made the arrival of Asian children unsafe. In a House of Commons meeting about the city's worrisome situation, it was claimed that "dispersal of the immigrant children was impracticable because of accommodation problems in the city schools generally. Racial tensions in the area were rising and the Authority feared an explosion."[60] Highfields (south-east of the city centre) [61] already had two secondary schools with 70–80 per cent non-indigenous children, and eleven of the twelve primary schools there had a majority of immigrant children. Wisely, two schools in housing estates at the periphery of Leicester were written off the list of dispersal schools "because of overt racial prejudice" there.[62] This concern was never officially raised in Bradford (for Eccleshill) or Ealing (for Northolt or Perivale).

Some Ugandan Asians were bussed to two new schools which, according to Valerie Marrett, became "success stories"[63] for the community locally: Hugh Latimer (Primary School) and Wakerley Secondary, which until 1975 catered to Ugandan Asian pupils only. This *de facto* segregation caused a furore among the radical left, which lambasted it as "apartheid" education, whilst the NF came out strongly in favour of it. In another baffling twist of irony, the RRB investigated Wakerley, only to find no issue at all with it, which in its turn the NF publicly saluted: "It will be a relief to English parents whose children are at schools where they are so numerically overwhelmed by immigrants to see the Race Relations Board go along with us on the policy of racial segregation as at Wakerley school".[64]

Leicester's dispersal was entirely due to exceptional circumstances linked with the sudden Ugandan Asian influx, was decided upon by a reluctant administration,[65] and could not – and indeed was never to – be justified on grounds of linguistic deficiency since the great bulk of East African Asians were already Anglophones. What was also exceptional was that, at a time when in Southall and Bradford Asians were growingly irked by "bussing", in Leicester most Ugandan Asian parents seem have embraced it willingly. There were obvious psychological reasons for this: having just been expelled, being recent refugees, having often been through camps, they were thankful for *any* education being provided for their children. In the emergency situation which was theirs, "the more abstract debate about the desirability of ethnic mixing and contact with the 'host' culture in suburban schools was never mentioned".[66] Some were also thankful for the fact that this education, unlike in Kenya or Uganda,[67] was provided free of charge. They also tended to place confidence in the local education authorities. Indeed, Leicester's avowed aim was to restrict the volume of dispersal of children, and the director of education always emphasised that it was not just immigrant children who were bussed, but "white children have to fight for places in the neighbourhood schools".[68] This confidence was bolstered locally by the active involvement of Asians in the running of education: there were in the mid-1970s nineteen headteachers of primary schools from ethnic minorities, and four of these had lived in East Africa. The fact that East African Asians were largely Anglophones did of course further their integration into the local administration, which contrasts dramatically with Bradford, Huddersfield, Blackburn or Halifax.

West Midlands towns

Fertile backlash terrain

As dispersal got under way, the industrial West Midlands towns were, with Southall, the major English hotbed of white resentment against the influx of New Commonwealth immigrants. Already notoriously deficient, local public services were heavily strained by what was seen by some as a coloured invasion. Perusal of the West Bromwich, Wolverhampton, Walsall and Smethwick local press time and again adumbrates, in the years 1962 to 1968, exactly the ingredients which would make Enoch Powell's speech in April 1968 appear plausible. For instance, Smethwick's English Rights Association was complaining of hospital beds being given to immigrant mothers allegedly at the expense of indigenous white mothers.[69] Similarly, the 1965 inauguration of Grove School in the very heart of Powell's Wolverhampton constituency soon led to autochthonous cries of immigrant takeover, since out of its original 239 children a mere 40 were white.[70] Three years later, the school had gone 90 per cent coloured, and some irritated mothers rallied around the slogan "Segregate our children!", demanding that separate classes be introduced.[71] Analogous demands in Smethwick a few years earlier had led Labour councillor E. Lowry to cry out: "This is Staffordshire, not Alabama!"[72]

This heady racial brew, which crystallised with Powell's speech and Peter Griffiths's infamous Smethwick campaign of 1964 ("If you want a nigger for a neighbour, vote Labour") as well as Malcolm X's visit to the town in February 1965, was instrumental in polarising political debate locally, and in generating bad blood between political authorities, race-relations liaison actors and the immigrants themselves. The Labour Party, typically, was placed in a political quandary, sweet-talking immigrants whose votes they needed whilst trying not to alienate the indigenous working classes. Maurice Foley was MP for West Bromwich from 1963 to 1973 as well as junior minister at the Home Office from 1966 to 1967, with special responsibility for immigration. According to one constituent, his tough task was to "foist the coloured immigrant explosion on to the backs of the original inhabitants of the Black Country towns".[73] As a matter of principle, Foley refused to meet with Don Finney, the chair of the English Rights Association, during his visit to the town; this was bitterly resented by the Association, according to which Finney had a fifteen-year experience of "dealing with immigrants".[74] Everywhere in England (including Tory-dominated constituencies) local authorities participated in events organised by race relations liaison committees, such as the International Friendship Committees which furthered the integration of immigrants; the only national exception was Smethwick,[75] which speaks volumes about racial resentment locally.

Smethwick

When George Betts School reached about 20 per cent of Asians on its roll in 1963, the education authorities of the town decided to take action, first by declaring the school full for any pupil unable to pass a test in English, and then by asking parents to send their offspring to three nearby schools.[76] In the next few years, Smethwick only reluctantly introduced a limited measure of dispersal when it appeared to be its sole possible option. Its local education officer, C.E. Robin, kept insisting that, no matter how handicapped many Punjabi children might be in their knowledge of English, most of them did really well at maths. He was also adamant that those who ranted about white children being held back found difficulty in proving their claim: "I can state quite categorically that there is no evidence available to show that any child is being held back and I am still interested in finding out whether anyone can produce it".[77]

West Bromwich

As opposed to nearby Smethwick, West Bromwich was an early promoter of dispersal. The town, like Bradford and Southall, did not wait until the implementation of circular 7/65 in June 1965 and initiated the transfer of some immigrant children away from their neighbourhood schools as early as January 1964. Although West Bromwich's percentage of immigrant children was lower than in nearby Wolverhampton and Warley (the LEA which included Smethwick),[78] the stark concentration of Asian and West Indian pupils in the Beeches Road area,[79] to the east of the town centre, led public authorities to take a proactive approach in terms of dispersal.

Table 13 New Commonwealth immigrant children in Walsall, West Bromwich, Wolverhampton (January 1970)

City	Indians	Pakistanis	West Indians	City's general population
Walsall	1525	278	610	184,430
West Bromwich	787	83	843	173,010
Wolverhampton	3297	231	2775	263,580

Source: National Archives (Kew), ED 269/14

Originally, the scheme did not include actual bussing, but the soaring number of children involved meant that soon enough double-decker buses would be operated to take some two hundred children to the outskirts of the town.[80] The major criticism made of the working of dispersal in West Bromwich was that it affected mostly infants, who were much more able to pick up English rapidly, and who were much too young to be sent two and a half or three miles away from their homes. Just as worryingly, and because of general overcrowding, (Anglophone) West Indians were dispersed just as much as (non-Anglophone) Asians, a language-blind approach which was all the more striking as, first, the number of West Indian immigrants was almost identical to that of Indians and Pakistanis combined (see Table 13) and, second, Maurice Foley himself was local MP for West Bromwich.

Walsall

Dispersal in Walsall was a very low-key business. In 1972 the general cost of bussing was £102,000 in Ealing, £10,000 in Huddersfield[81] and a paltry £500 for Walsall the preceding year.[82] At any given time between the mid-1960s and the late 1970s dispersal cannot have affected more than a few dozen immigrant children, most of whom were taken to an "induction centre", where these mostly Asian children followed "concentrated courses in English language and [were] introduced to the way of living in this country".[83] Inaugurated in December 1968, this induction centre operated until July 1975, from which time equal provision of education was to be available in the various schools where those children would now be dispersed.[84] Despite the very small number of pupils involved, when the RRB commenced its investigations into the allegedly discriminatory nature of dispersal, they found that the Walsall authorities were resolutely opaque about the policy. In 1976, Edward Ratnaraja, a conciliation officer for the RRB in the West Midlands, had been contacting the Walsall Council for three years to gain access to specific information but none had been forthcoming, and it was only when the London RRB headquarters started to sound more menacing that Walsall reluctantly started to oblige them.[85] It was small wonder that Walsall should have been so grudging, especially at a stage, 1972–73, when dispersal was more and more overtly criticised. It also speaks volumes about the RRB's conciliatory approach and actual lack of teeth, just before it morphed into the more powerful CRE in 1976.

Wolverhampton

As in other towns such as Leicester, the education authorities in Wolverhampton were averse to dispersal until the soaring number of non-Anglophone pupils seemed in their eyes to give them little choice. G.W.R. Lines, the town's director of education, dismissed circular 7/65 from the day of its inception by referring to an "arbitrary maximum of 30 per cent", before stating that dispersal did "amount, if I may say so, to discrimination both against the immigrants and the native population".[86]

The annual increase in the intake of immigrant children was around five hundred from 1962, growing to one thousand by 1967. These circumstances are crucial to make sense of the local background to Powell's speech, and also to understand the introduction of dispersal locally. Interviewed by the Select Committee on Race Relations and Immigration, the education authorities acknowledged that in the town's inner cities "schools … are unable to cope and dispersal is inevitable. At the present time (May 1968) thirteen buses daily distribute 550 children to about forty schools where accommodation is possible".[87] There is no indication that West Indians were not dispersed, for the situation seems to have been comparable to that obtaining in West Bromwich. With dispersal, only 20 per cent of the local schools exceeded the DES quota of 30 per cent immigrant pupils.

It bears mentioning that dispersal in Wolverhampton and West Bromwich never met with sustained resistance, as opposed to Bradford and Ealing. For instance, in the 1974 evidence given to the Select Committee, the Wolverhampton Indian Workers Association inveighed against discrimination in broad terms, claiming that "Jesus coloured immigrants are discriminated against in every walk of life",[88] but their memorandum is devoid of any reference to dispersal. Similarly, an October 1975 report of a Wolverhampton IWA education meeting articulated fourteen specific claims, none of which had to do with dispersal in Powell's town.[89] It can only be surmised that, unlike in Bradford and Ealing, bussing in

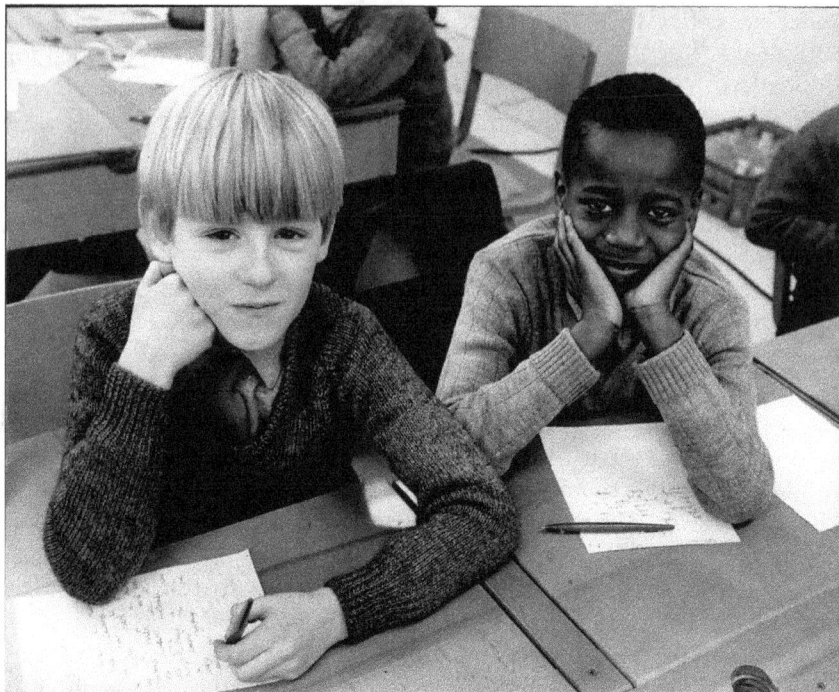

Figure 7: Two boys at Grove Primary School, Wolverhampton, 1968

Wolverhampton and other towns was too marginal a practice to ever generate any form of resistance, so apparent compliance with it was the rule.

The other LEAs

The mention of *Bristol* in this book is both surprising and undeserved. The city was very well known for its comprehensive schooling system, and enjoyed "a high reputation for administrative efficiency".[90] Many of its newly built comprehensive schools were located in the outskirts of the city (schools such as Lawrence Weston, Henbury, Withwood, Brislington, Hengrove, Hartcliffe, Bedminster Down). As one Bristol official testified to the Select Committee: "The secondary schools in Bristol are in a ring round the city centre, so that children who live in the centre – including most immigrant children – usually have a two or three mile bus journey to school. Immigrant children of secondary age are to be found in many schools, often in small numbers. This, in effect, is dispersal."[91] Therefore, regardless of whether they were immigrants, dispersal went on for geographical reasons. This was a place-based, rather than language-based or race-based, policy, thereby obliquely pointing to the irrelevance of circular 7/65's assimilationist rationale.

In *Luton*, dispersal was initiated when there was a sudden influx of Asians in one single area. The specific way in which the dispersal programme was devised by education director I.D. Macmullen and achieved by "guided choice" seems to have impressed Denis Howell.[92] In *Hounslow*, just south of Southall, precious little is known about dispersal locally, apart from the fact that it seems to have been "less whole-hearted than elsewhere and a good deal of discretion [was] left to the junior and secondary schools concerned".[93] It does also appear that there was dispersal in the *Croydon* LEA, but in this case too it operated on a voluntary basis; immigrant parents were advised to have their children dispersed if it appeared to be advisable, "to take full advantage of the educational opportunities offered to their children".[94] Lastly, as will be seen in Chapter 7, the West-Yorkshire town of *Dewsbury* also introduced a measure of dispersal, through a specific case which briefly caught the attention of some national media.

Notes

1 Blackburn archives, Report by "Asian Household Survey Team", "Some Basic Characteristics of Blackburn's Asian population", 1977.

2 Anthony Lester, on the basis of data made available to him at the RRB, was left with the impression that this was undoubtedly an underestimate. See National Archives (Kew), CK 2/515, Letter by Anthony Lester to G. Mayall (Blackburn's director of education), 3.7.1972.

3 National Archives (Kew), CK 2/515, letter to J.R. Jameson (Department of Education and Science) by G. Mayall (Blackburn director of education), 15.6.1972.

4 On the general circumstances leading to this investigation, see Kirp, *Doing Good by Doing Little*, pp. 96–7.

5 For all these quotes, see National Archives (Kew), CK 2/515, memorandum by Eric Hawkins to the RRB, "The Dispersal of Immigrant Children in Blackburn", 9.10.1972.

6 Nigel Fielding, *The National Front*, London: Routledge, 1981; for similar declarations by John Kingsley Read and Commander Andrew Fountayne, see Commission for Racial Equality Archives, Muhamad Iqbal Ullah Research Centre, Manchester Central Library, BBC Radio Blackburn script, 11.2.1975.

7 This is a fact that both Blackburn and the RRB were cognisant of: according to the director of education G. Mayall: "It appears that this organisation is perhaps to even the score as the Race Relations Board has pursued action against the National Front itself for alleged breaches of the Act" (quoted in National Archives (Kew), CK 2/515).

8 The so-called "Rivers of Blood" speech (April 1968) has "In this country in 15 or 20 years' time the black man will have the whip hand over the white

man". See full script of the speech at www.telegraph.co.uk/comment/ 3643823/ Enoch-Powells-Rivers-of-Blood-speech.html (accessed 31.3.2017).

9 Commission for Racial Equality Archives, Muhamad Iqbal Ullah Research Centre, Manchester Central Library, BBC radio script, 29.10.1975.

10 *The Lancashire Evening Telegraph*, 18.9.1975.

11 National Archives (Kew), CK 2/515, Anthony Lester, "The Dispersal of 'Immigrant' Children in Local Education Authorities", undated (1972?).

12 This part states that "for the purpose of this act a person discriminates against another if on the ground of race, colour, or ethnic or national origins he treats that other, in any situation to which section 2, 3, 4, 5 applies, less favourably than he treats or would treat other persons".

13 On all these points, see National Archives (Kew), CK 2/515.

14 See section 39 of the Education Act (1944) and its definition of the expression "within walking distance".

15 National Archives (Kew), CK 2/515.

16 National Archives (Kew), CK 2/515, Radio Blackburn Spotlight script, 17.11.1971.

17 National Archives (Kew), CK 2/515, letter dated 20.3.1972.

18 National Archives (Kew), CK 2/515, Radio Blackburn Spotlight scripts, 17.11.1971; 18.11.1971.

19 National Archives (Kew), CK 2/515.

20 National Archives (Kew), CK 2/515, Lancashire County Council letter to Usha Prashar, Race Relations Board (London), 27.6.1974.

21 National Archives (Kew), CK 2/515.

22 *Lancashire Evening Telegraph*, 5.9.1985.

23 *Lancashire Evening Telegraph*, 3.9.1985.

24 Trevor Burgin and Patricia Edson, *Spring Grove: The Education of Immigrant Children*, Oxford: Oxford University Press, 1967.

25 See Hawkes, *Immigrant Children*, pp. 28–9; Fabian Society, *Strangers Within*, pp. 17–18; Rose (ed.), *Colour and Citizenship*, p. 271; Hansard, *House of Lords Debates*, 16.12.1969, vol. 306, cols 1014–15; *Huddersfield Weekly Examiner*, 10.6.1961.

26 Quoted in Fabian Society, *Strangers Within*, p. 17.

27 Interview (Huddersfield), 27.4.2016.

28 Huddersfield archives, Huddersfield Education Department minutes, 1964–65, p. 146; *Huddersfield Weekly Examiner*, 2.1.1965.

29 Huddersfield archives, Huddersfield Education Department minutes, 1964–65, p. 230.

30 See Butterworth *et al.*, *Immigrants in West Yorkshire*, p. 45.

31 Power, *Immigrants in School*, pp. 42–3.

32 Huddersfield archives, Huddersfield Education Department minutes, 1964–65, pp. 129–30; see also House of Commons Select Committee on Race Relations and Immigration, *The Problems of Coloured School Leavers*, London: HMSO, 1968–69, pp. 659–60.

33 *Ibid.*, p. 80.

34 Interview, 27.4.2016.
35 Quoted in Butterworth *et al.*, *Immigrants in West Yorkshire*, p. 46.
36 Nasim Hasnie, "The Way Ahead: A Survey of Asian Youth in Huddersfield", Kirklees Metropolitan Council, 1977, p. 2.
37 *Ibid.*, pp. 5–6, p. 20, pp. 24–5.
38 Interview (Huddersfield), 27.4.2016.
39 *Halifax Evening Courier*, 22.9.1976.
40 *Halifax Evening Courier*, 23.9.1973.
41 *Ibid.*
42 See her articles "Going Back to the Mainstream", *Issues in Race and Education*, vol. 39 (summer), 1983; "Developing Pedagogies for Multilingual Classes", *English in Education*, vol. 5 (3), 1981.
43 See *The Bullock Report: A Language for Life*, London: HMSO, 1975, p. 289.
44 *Education for All (The Swann Report)*, London: HMSO, 1985, p. 392.
45 Commission for Racial Equality, *Teaching English as a Second Language: Report of a formal investigation in Calderdale Local Education Authority*, London: HMSO, 1986, p. 28.
46 See Paul Gardner, *Teaching and Learning in Multicultural Classrooms*, London: Routledge, 2012, p. 9.
47 This was defined by section 40 to Part VI of the 1976 Act, under "indirect access to benefits". This was broadly imported from the US Civil Rights Act (1964). For details about this, see Bob Hepple, "The European Legacy of Brown vs Board of Education", *University of Illinois Law Review*, 2006, pp. 605–24.
48 Commission for Racial Equality, *Teaching English as a Second Language*, p. 2.
49 *Ibid.*, p. 27.
50 *Ibid.*, p. 34.
51 *Ibid.*, p. 38.
52 National Archives (Kew), ED 233/11.
53 Sir Charles Cunningham, "The Work of the Uganda Resettlement Board", *Journal of Ethnic and Migration Studies*, vol. 2 (3), 1973, p. 261.
54 Vaughan Robinson, Roger Andersson and Sako Musterd, *Spreading the Burden? A Review of Policies to Disperse Asylum-Seekers and Refugees*, Bristol: Policy Press, 2003, p. 111.
55 This was on a voluntary basis (National Archives (Kew), ED 269/15).
56 Valerie Marrett, *Immigrants Settling in the City, Ugandan Asians in Leicester*, Leicester: Leicester University Press, 1989, p. 121.
57 This is the word used by Robinson *et al.* in *Spreading the Burden?*, p. 112. See also Marrett, *Immigrants Settling in the City*, pp. 119–21.
58 *The Times*, 30.10.1972.
59 National Archives (Kew), ED 269/14.
60 *Ibid.*
61 For a good presentation of the area, see Joanna Herbert, *Negotiating Boundaries in the City: Migration, Ethnicity and Gender in Britain*, Aldershot: Ashgate, 2008.
62 Marrett, *Immigrants Settling in the City*, p. 127.

63 *Ibid.*, p. 122.

64 *Ibid.*, p. 124.

65 See *Guardian*, 23.4.1973.

66 Marrett, *Immigrants Settling in the City*, p. 126.

67 It was not uncommon there for families living in the more remote areas to have to pay boarding fees.

68 Marrett, *Immigrants Settling in the City*, p. 126.

69 *Smethwick Telephone and Warley Courier*, 8.7.1965.

70 *Wolverhampton Express and Star*, 9.7.1965.

71 *Birmingham Post*, 6.9.1968.

72 *Birmingham Post*, 25.7.1965. See also Buettner, "'This is Staffordshire, not Alabama!'".

73 *Wolverhampton Express and Star*, 9.7.1965.

74 *Ibid.*

75 Foot, *Immigration and Race*, p. 225.

76 Ealing archives, Education minutes 1963–64, Smethwick letter sent to C.T. Miller, 2.10.1963.

77 *Birmingham Planet*, 14.01.1965.

78 In January 1968, figures for West Bromwich were 5.3%, Warley 9.6%, Wolverhampton 11.8%. See Chapter 2.

79 Patterson, *Immigration and Race Relations*, p. 257.

80 *Birmingham Evening Mail*, 3.5.1966.

81 *Telegraph & Argus*, 12.10.1972.

82 Walsall archives, Walsall Education Committee minutes, 1970–71, p. 155.

83 Walsall archives, Walsall Education Committee reports, 1966–73, pp. 8–9.

84 Walsall archives, Walsall Education Committee minutes, 1973–74, p. 163.

85 *Walsall Observer*, 3.12.1976; *Birmingham Post*, 1.12.1976.

86 *Wolverhampton Express and Star*, 16.6.1965.

87 Wolverhampton archives, *Select Committee on Race Relations and Immigration: the problem of coloured school-leavers*, evidence taken at Wolverhampton, 1968–69, p. 395, p. 496.

88 Wolverhampton archives, *Select Committee on Race Relations and Immigration: Minutes of Evidence 1974 (Wolverhampton)*, p. 131.

89 National Archives (Kew), Indian Workers Association files, CK 2/339.

90 Young, "Why Our Susan?",, pp. 8–9.

91 Select Committee on Race Relations and Immigration, Session 1972–73, *Education*, London: HMSO, 1973, vol. I, p. 42.

92 Howell, *Made in Birmingham*, p. 188.

93 Power, *Immigrants in School*, p. 32.

94 West Yorkshire archives, Health and Education Reports on Children of Immigrants, BBDI/7/TI4923 (1965–70), letter to Bradford Council (31.1.1969) by Croydon Council for Community Relations.

6

Taking the bullying by the horns:
the emergence of resistance to bussing

Paradigm lost

Many British policy-makers were aware by around 1970 that uncompromising definitions of integration as assimilation were obsolete. There were still hesitations about what to call the newly emerging society: was it "multicultural", "multiracial", "pluralist"? True, some Labourites were still espousing an assimilationist discourse. For instance, during the 1968 inauguration of a new school in Wolverhampton in the presence of none other than Enoch Powell, secretary of education Edward Short declared: "This school can serve this area well. I believe it will mould the several races it contains into one unified Christian community."[1] As opposed to this, some moderate Conservatives of the Edward Boyle hue were making some gingerly multicultural noises. The situation, therefore, was hardly a monolithic one, but clearly the general dynamics of integration had changed.

More pressingly, how was it possible to combine pluralist living with equal rights before the law?[2] Numerous publications, White Papers and speeches tried to address this challenge. Even by the late 1960s educational policy documents had already endorsed a language of cultural adjustment, pluralism and equal opportunity. With such a background, dispersal clearly stumbled into the turbulent 1970s looking increasingly like an anomaly. First, the focus on equal rights highlighted the anomalous nature of dispersal. Second, the embracing of cultural diversity and of multiculturalism in education weakened the assimilationist claim which was one of bussing's *raisons d'être*. Southall and Bradford looked growingly like obstinate bastions of assimilationist dispersal whilst the world outside was treading multicultural paths. In November 1978, Bradford's IWA lamented that "on one side, Bradford Council is spending money to disperse the Asian children, so that Asian languages are lost. On the other hand, Bradford University is given a grant from the E.E.C. to develop the Asian languages and cultures."[3]

Typically, legitimisations of dispersal were more and more often couched in multicultural terms: Mike Elliott, Ealing's education director, was at pains to defend the claim that "through dispersal we have been able to create a multi-racial atmosphere in the schools". More convincing was probably the following minority viewpoint within the IWA, here articulated by Piera Khabra, who feared that "all they will know is the immigrant children and their immigrant parents. Then you will send them out into a predominantly white world and expect them to cope. It just will not be fair at all to them."[4]

Serious concern was expressed regarding the immediate future of ethnic-minority students: unlike their parents, these teenagers would not turn the other cheek but would strike for equality before the law, and would not be content with their assigned roles as a surplus population in an increasingly globalised economy.[5] Corollary to these concerns was the growing fear of a radicalisation among ethnic-minority youths. A West Midlands Asian militant argued: "In the years ahead of us, when the coloured school leavers will find themselves frustrated and unable to satisfy their legitimate aspirations, they may turn to the advocates of Black Power".[6] Not a few were firmly convinced that the political and economic elites had the dice rigged against them, and there were local illustrations aplenty to nurture the feeling. For example, in November 1971 Enoch Powell was invited to give a talk at the Southall Chamber of Commerce, a speech that Camilla Schofield discusses in her seminal book on Powell,[7] and a venue which local MP Sydney Bidwell (Labour) refused to attend, enjoying an ostentatious fish and chips a few yards from there.[8]

The new integration paradigm was reflected in ministerial approaches to dispersal itself. As we know, in July 1971 the DES published *The Education of Immigrants*, which jettisoned the notion that there might be an optimum proportion of immigrant children. Support for dispersal policies was no longer whole-hearted.[9] Two years later, the DES abandoned the collection of statistics on immigrant children, which did not prevent Bradford from compiling such statistics, although it guardedly dropped the categories "half-Asian", "half-Negro".[10]

Fully backed by education secretary Margaret Thatcher,[11] the ministerial volte-face was also owing to a fear of a litigation backlash relying on the Race Relations Act (1968) which outlawed racial discrimination. That the wind of change was blowing for dispersal was likewise evident within the Ealing CRC: in 1968 a great majority of its members still endorsed it, whereas in March 1972 a vote on it was held and nine out of twelve called for its "progressive and speedy" end.[12] Martyn Grubb was to indefatigably lead the campaign against what was increasingly called "bussing".

Obstacles to resistance

And yet, there was a whole gamut of obstacles to the emergence of a resistance movement, which is why, notwithstanding the mounting evidence of racial harassment on the playground and immediately outside the dispersal schools, it took some time before Asian parents and bodies like the Ealing CRC or the IWA took up the cudgels against it. Southall and Bradford were the two places where dispersal was actively resisted, for no trace of a sustained movement against it has been found elsewhere, either in archives or in the local press.

Making ends meet

The most obvious of these obstacles was what Marx aptly called "the dull compulsion of economic relations",[13] that is the necessity for eking out a living, which siphons a great amount of time and energy, particularly from subordinate groups. This problem is all the more pressing in a situation of immigration, and it is evoked by a large number of the people interviewed for this book. Anjuna Kalsi, who suffered a great deal of racism from both pupils and the administration in Northolt High where she was bussed, recollects: "I actually never told my parents, because they clearly had their own challenges".[14] Rather frequently, interviewees added individual, dysfunctional elements which made it all the more difficult to speak publicly about certain questions: one interviewee's father was an alcoholic because he had not been able to cope with immigration and living in England, another's father had been killed in Uganda just before her departure and she was living alone with her grieving mother. Maurice Kogan himself, in his report for the RRB, was surprised that many of the children seemed to have been one-parent children, mostly because of the accidents of immigration policy.[15]

At a remove

In such circumstances a substantial number of parents were simply not cognisant of their children's problems. Therefore, it was not only that Asians were one of these "forgotten groups" of "those who suffer in silence" identified by Mancur Olson,[16] it was rather that a great deal of information was either unshared by children or uncollected by parents. For instance, Tariq Mehdood in Bradford, who would become a leader of the Bradford Twelve a few years later, was bussed to a faraway school on the outskirts of the city but neither he nor the uncle and grandfather who raised him in Bradford saw this as a problem, nobody knowing what the normal, established norm of schooling was supposed to be.[17]

Asian parents and the dispersal schools seemed to evolve in different spheres altogether. In fact, even within the comfort zone of a place like Southall, it proved difficult for a school like Beaconsfield Primary to establish contacts with Asian parents.[18] Some attributed this distance to the parents' mindset: Maurice Kogan noticed in his report that "Asian parents are shy of the school"[19] whilst recognising that "schools were so far away that some parents did not even know the name of the school their children attended".[20] Others laid the blame unambiguously on the nature of bussing itself and the way it operated. According to Martyn Grubb, "A lot of immigrant parents have not the vaguest idea which school their children go to. It is an artificial division."[21] Ample evidence of this is provided in interviews carried out for this book, as well as in interviews held in 2005–6 for the South-Asian Oral History Project (Gunnersbury Museum, Hounslow)[22] and in the Bradford oral history project on dispersal launched by Shabina Aslam,[23] as well as in Brenda Mary Thomson's PhD dissertation on Bradford. For instance, Vivienne Townsend, who worked as a teaching assistant in Acton and West Ealing from 1974 to 1981, always in dispersal schools, recollects that "very obviously, we didn't have any contact with the Asian parents, never".[24] On the side of formerly bussed pupils, Sukhwant Sandher says, quite typically, that there was "no contact between schools and parents: that was always missing in my education. There was a complete disconnect between the school and our parents, this was absolute."[25] Some children had developed a survival strategy whereby they kept silent to the parents about verbal abuse (as a norm), whereas cases of physical abuse were more likely to be complained about: "The name-calling was predominant, but it was something we took for granted. We never did mention it to our parents. As long as we were not bodily harmed, as long as we learnt something" (Kishore Taylor).[26] All of this clashes with a realisation, within the DES, of the need for greater contacts to be established between schools and parents, as was to be expressed in a Green Paper on education in 1977.[27]

Keeping a low profile

On the face of it, it is staggering that thousands of children could have borne such situations without a massive parental backlash. But the absence of complaint by Asians about racism and living conditions in England has to be nuanced, for it is too often naturalised or exaggerated altogether. First, there was in the 1960s and 1970s a tolerance of physical violence which has considerably decreased since then: school corporal punishment (in the notorious form of 'caning') went on until the 1980s, and in former parts of the British Empire (such as the West Indies) it was very much an established norm. In no way does this mean that castigatory violence administered by authorities might have led to condoning racist violence administered by fellow students, but the point is clearly that those 1960s–70s situations ought not to be interpreted from a twenty-first century standpoint.

Second, the more recently immigrants had arrived, the less willing they were to challenge the racism their children were faced with. This fact is crucial, as bussing tended to affect recently arrived immigrants rather than longer-established ones, probably in a public authority attempt to avoid unnecessary difficulties. This situation was all the more difficult to bear for those who could read into certain situations because of their individual training. Gurbax Sooch, whose son was bussed to Northolt in 1970 immediately after arrival from the Punjab, states that "I was aware of that quickly because I had been given a visa as a teacher, I had been a teacher in India [...] We were a bit frightened then but clearly if it happened now I would make a terrible fuss."[28] Such compliance must also be connected with memories of the education systems in places like India, Pakistan, Kenya or Uganda. Ravinder Vedi, whose father had just died in Uganda, recalls that "my mum didn't understand the education system at all; also, the fact that we got a *free* education (as opposed to Uganda) meant that this was something to be appreciated [...] My family wasn't really aware of this institutional racism."[29]

Also powerfully fuelling Asian reticence were parental dreams of upward mobility for their children. Quite often depicted as "unrealistic", these very high expectations of academic achievement were frequently corollary to a lack of opportunity to use their skills which the act of immigration had brought with it, especially to Asians from Uganda and Kenya. The same Ravinder Vedi says: "My mum was working in a factory after having a very middle-class life in Uganda". Anjuna Kalsi echoes: "My dad worked in the district commission of police in Kenya, but had to work for Hoover in Southall as a factory worker. My mum was a social worker in Kenya, but worked for the United Biscuit factory in Southall."[30] Such inability to use their skills and imagining the best for their children were often tightly connected in immigrant parents' testimonies. One Indian man said "I came to England to give my children better prospects for the future. I left a very good job in Calcutta, but Indian education will never match up with the English one, and I wanted to give my family the best".[31] With hindsight, "giving the best" at individual level is connected with the community's impressive achievements. Viney Jung, a solicitor and judge after being bussed from the age of four to eleven, remembers that "for most of our families the focus was on education, education, education, which is one reason why the Punjabi community has done quite well".[32] Others, whilst nuancing the proverbial rags-to-riches narrative by exposing the way schools operated as factories of under-achievement for Asians, certainly do not negate the general focus on education: "There was a huge pressure from our parents, for us to do well. Our parents wanted us to be doctors; but the teachers would think this was a joke" (Balraj Purewal). A certain number of Asian children contrasted this interiorised necessity to perform well at school with the under-achievement of working-class whites, some of whom evolved in a world where "to be bookish" was frowned upon or was to wear a stigma of effeminacy (not unlike certain racial stereotypes attached to Asians)[33] as, in their respective ways, Paul Willis evidenced in his ethnography *Learning to Labour*,[34] and as Maurice Kogan was to suggest in his report on dispersal in Ealing.[35] Lastly, there were cases when factory-working immigrants were pressuring their children to work hard in anticipation of a deindustrialisation which was starting to rear its ugly head by the 1960s: "My mum who worked in a biscuit-making factory would say, 'make sure you work extra hard because by the time you finish school there won't be any factory left'" (Rita Nath).[36]

Increasingly opaque bureaucracy

Post-1945 Britain was characterised by increasingly vertical relationships in a vastly changing society. Clearly, the processes of urbanisation, industrialisation and bureaucratisation increased interdependence whilst they decreased local autonomy. In their analysis of CRC, Ruth Issacharoff and Michael Hill noticed that "the fate of a local area is determined increasingly by changes in the urban infrastructure at the macro level".[37] Most Asian parents, despite the expertise and experience of the IWA, were ill-equipped to challenge the policy of bussing in an administrative galaxy they found unfathomable. Once again, it would be a mistake to read into this any deterministic appreciation of the low profile that many Asians kept. In very general terms, the *Community Attitudes Survey* published in 1969 concluded that "the highly involved informant on the scale relating to interest in local affairs is by contrast more likely to be older, of a higher or secondary level of education, and of a higher socio-economic status".[38] Not to mention the linguistic deficiencies affecting many, Asian parents in Southall as elsewhere were young and working-class, and the great majority lacked a university education.

Other campaigns

It is unclear whether this sub-part should be classified among "obstacles to resistance". In general terms, one of the challenges to the sociological study of collective action is to apprehend *when* exactly what Doug McAdam calls "insurgent consciousness"[39] actually emerges. In that respect the many political struggles Asians in Southall and elsewhere were engaged in may well have siphoned off needed energy to combat dispersal, but at the same time these pressing questions may have generated a growing consciousness of unequal treatment and served as a spur for action against bussing. For the historian, this catalyst/deterrent dialectic is one that is particularly difficult to elucidate.

The IWA actively campaigned against the Commonwealth Immigrants Act of 1962, then that of 1968, the latter being routinely dismissed by the anti-racist left as the "Kenyan Asian Act".[40] In 1971, the Immigration Bill was vilified by Councillor S.S. Gill, Southall's vice-chairman of the Campaign Against Racism and Discrimination, as "the most flagrant violation of all that is sensible, fair and just in British society".[41] Ajit Rai, local leader of the IWA, made a clear parallel between the discriminatory character of the 1971 legislation and that of dispersal itself,[42] thus inviting members of his community to think outside the box of single-question campaigns in order to take issue with institutional racism as a whole. In the late 1970s, the IWA was also actively involved in mobilising against the virginity tests imposed on Indian women arriving at Heathrow.[43] Broadly speaking, then, problems dealing with immigration continued to be uppermost in the IWA's minds. Making sure that family reunions were possible and dealing with immigration rights, visas and passports were very time-consuming and may have deflected attention away from other concerns. Although dispersal was very far from perfect, the dispersed children were part of a family that was *there*, unlike the siblings, wives, uncles or cousins who were still in India.

Besides immigration issues, the IWA's political muscle was also geared towards labour disputes. That tallied with a deindustrialisation which had started before the oil shock in English industrial belts such as Southall.[44] Strikes at Woolf's Rubber Factory, Rockware Glass Company and Chignalls Bakery were frowned upon by established and overwhelmingly white unions (such as the TGWU), which served as an ethnic catalyst for the IWA. Once again, this ethnicisation of labour disputes could then exacerbate an ethnic sense of Asianness to foment opposition against dispersal, but it can just as well be argued that what time and energy were mobilised on the assembly line deflected attention away from the playgrounds, school gates and pick-up points.

The long and complex enumeration of hurdles to resistance is, it seems to me, instrumental in explaining what appears to be a major paradox: the Sikhs (in Southall) who mobilised so impressively to be allowed to wear turbans in circumstances not recognised originally by British law or labour regulations (as police officers, motorcycle riders, bus drivers for instance),[45] were the very same people who did not, until a late stage, campaign to put an end to a half-baked educational policy for which many of their children had to suffer. Beyond the obvious fact that not all bussed pupils were Sikhs, it is not at all that Sikhs loved their turbans more than their children, it is rather that, as has been hopefully shown, a wide range of parameters was obscuring their view.

Race-relations busybodies

Key players

The IWA, the RRB and the Ealing CRC were pivotal players in the mobilisation against dispersal, and liaised quite efficiently together. For, unlike the wholly independent IWA (Southall), its counterparts across the country, in particular in Birmingham, refused to have any dealing with CRCs on principle, considering them to be "the product of a racialist document", that is the 1965 White Paper analysed in Chapter 2.[46]

The three bodies' respective functions and positions on the political chessboard are congruent with the general typology of social movements by resource mobilisation theorists. For instance, the IWA provided what James C. Scott called a "sequestered social site" for contest, a physical and metaphorical place where "the unspoken riposte, stifled anger and bitten tongues created by relations of domination find a vehement, full-throated expression".[47] If Scott analysed the alehouse of early modern England as a site of contest and of popular culture expression, in a migratory and post-colonial context the IWA, at least in Southall, did furnish such a location for the deploying of insurgent consciousness, until, by 1976, its moral and political authority started to be growingly challenged by younger generations from the Southall Youth Movement (SYM). It also guaranteed a free space in which members or sympathisers could develop counter-hegemonic ideas and oppositional identities, themselves resting on the Punjabi identity of the IWA (Southall) and the strong feeling of belonging in a "minoritised space" such as Southall. That collective identity interweaving the region of origin (Punjab) and the neighbourhood of immigration (Southall) is decisive in making sense of the IWA's clout, as is suggested by a whole body of literature on the sociology of collective action, which, for better and sometimes for worse [48], underlines the crucial role of a cohesive collective identity as a condition for oppositional politics to emerge.

As for the RRB and the Ealing CRC, their role was that of the government-sponsored (RRB) and local authority-sponsored (Ealing CRC)[49] third parties, or outside forces which John McCarthy and Mayer Zald called, after Michael Harrington, the "conscience constituents", that is direct and often decisive supporters of a social movement organisation who, nevertheless, "do not stand to benefit directly from its success in goal accomplishment".[50] The role of the "conscience constituents" has often been deemed all the more pivotal in circumstances when the aggrieved group is made up of members of a subordinate class,[51] in the present case immigrant, largely non-Anglophone communities.

The RRB and Usha Prashar

As we already know, the RRB took the issue of bussing very seriously. Anthony Lester, Usha Prashar (who acted as a conciliation officer for the RRB from January 1972 to January 1976 before moving on to lead the Runnymede Trust) and many of their staff were appalled that such a policy as dispersal could even exist. In the early 1970s, Usha Prashar's difficulty lay in obtaining some parental testimonies against bussing. The now Baronness Prashar recalls:

> Once we in the RRB knew about bussing, we thought "what can we do to bring this down?" I came down to Ealing in 1971, I was horrified by bussing. But it was very difficult to get an individual complaint ... What I did was that I walked the streets off the Broadway in Southall. I kicked at every door, gathering evidence. These people could relate to me, because I could speak Punjabi. ... It was more bewilderment on their part. No one wanted to be seen as creating problems. I had to reassure them, that this was being done in their interest. No one really knew how the system worked.[52]

Apart from the disagreement and moral aversion that dispersal stoked among the RRB, the educational policy was strategically harnessed by the institution as a litmus test for its political efficacy, since only very rarely did the RRB threaten legal action. Anthony Lester was irked by what he saw as the RRB's lameness and slowness in conducting cases, and exposed the institution's "manifest weaknesses" over the Ealing and to a lesser extent Blackburn cases. He bemoaned "the unjustifiable delays in conducting the investigations and a marked reluctance even to investigate matters of a complex and controversial nature. The board has not thus far been prevented from ascertaining the relevant facts in either case by the absence of statutory powers, but rather by self-imposed restraints."[53] The upshot was that, as Brett Better pithily puts it, the RRB badly "needed a win".[54] Sandwiched between the integrationist right which dismissed it as a bunch of busybody do-gooders and increasingly influential anti-racist organisations such as Ambalaver Sivanandan's Institute of Race Relations which

shrugged off the authority's conciliatory approach as ineffectual, the fledg-
ling RRB "hoped to establish itself as an agency with teeth".[55] Nevertheless,
much as it aimed at challenging what it saw as a blatantly discriminatory
policy, the RRB was keenly aware that there was political dynamite in
exploiting the bussing issue to legal ends, since other LEAs outside Southall also bussed, and there was a risk that "the matter would then become
a live political issue, resulting in a hardening of attitudes".[56]

The Race Relations Act (1968), apart from making dispersal illegal if it
rested on ethnic or racial grounds and not on grounds of linguistic deficiency, also facilitated the anti-racist challenging of dispersal, particularly
through its section eighteen. This stated that the RRB could appoint as
assessors any person having "special knowledge and experience" of a specific situation of discrimination, following "any complaint or other
matter".[57] The consequence of this reference to "other matter" besides "any
complaint" was that, according to Baroness Prashar, "we could start off an
investigation without a formal complaint, which was very encouraging".[58]
It is only with these legal circumstances in mind that the 1974 appointment of Maurice Kogan to conduct an investigation into dispersal may be
understood.

The Kogan Report

Maurice Kogan, as we already know, was a professor at Brunel University
and an expert in public policy who had served as a secretary for the
Plowden Report (1967). His name was suggested by Anthony Lester
himself.[59] In a December 1974 letter to Ealing's chief of education R.J.
Hartles, he defined the task assigned to him by the RRB as making "an
impartial assessment of the dispersal policy in terms of its objectives and
intentions, and in terms of the actual impact that it makes on the children
who are subject to it".[60] His goal was to ascertain whether or not the Ealing
authority, its registration centre, assessment centres and reception classes
were discriminatory in promoting or operating the dispersal policy; also
whether or not dispersal was discriminatory in its effects. What about the
various impacts of distance? Was the education they received less good
than they would have got had they remained in their own neighbourhood,
or had they gone to a school of their choice?

With hindsight, this report of 28 pages (not including the four appendices) appears as an essential document on the operation of dispersal
in Ealing as well as a disappointingly limited analysis of its ramifica-
tions. For instance, outside the radar of Kogan's scrutiny was the parental
and children's appreciation of the situation, a fact which was recognised
by the author himself,[61] who more broadly acknowledged that his own

"judgements on the dispersal scheme ... are based on necessarily frugal information. I spent the equivalent of four and a half days in the local authority schools",[62] during which time he went to fourteen schools, met with fourteen headteachers or heads of centres, and had discussions with twice as many teachers. This lack of scope [63] is to be regretted, and was surely regretted by Anthony Lester, who had recommended in his correspondence that Kogan "would need a full-time staff".[64] However, it was the very existence of the investigation and the report which mattered rather than its specific contents, as Baroness Prashar recalls: "It was unusual for the RRB to commission someone as an expert. So it was not so much the result or the report itself, but the process of investigation itself which changes behaviour."[65]

In January 1975, the time of Kogan's investigation, bussing in Ealing was at its peak: affecting 2989 children of primary age, with a further 1800 of secondary school age who made their own way to dispersal schools across Ealing (and including Shepherd's Bush in Hammersmith). At that stage of bussing, the number of Southall students being educated outside the area was larger than the number of those who went to school locally. The Ealing authority owned six radio-controlled coaches and used, on contract from private companies, fifty-eight buses and six minibuses. Fifty-three coaches could each take up to seventy-three children, and there were sixty-eight pick-up points all across the borough, with five main pick-up points in Southall, the biggest of which was Featherstone Avenue.

Kogan's report was mostly conciliatory in its conclusions. General registration conditions, conditions at language centres and reception classes were all quite, if not very satisfactory.[66] The question of whether West Indians were bussed too was key, since if it were the case then it followed that dispersal was discriminatory. Kogan, though, was assured that since the Select Committee had raised the question the preceding year, dispersal of West Indians did not occur any more unless by parental choice.[67] Kogan never seriously raised the question of bussing Anglophone Asians, which is all the more striking as his investigation took place after the arrival of Ugandan and Kenyan Asians, many of whom were indeed Anglophones. He was content to hint at the issue in the report's last page and then move on.[68]

According to Kogan, despite the major practical and financial drawbacks of dispersal, the policy itself was a form of "positive discrimination" (a phrase itself borrowed from the Plowden Report he had worked on a few years before) rather than racially discriminatory in nature. His conclusion on this point was unambiguous: dispersal, "far from being negatively discriminatory is an exemplary attempt to help children assimilate successfully into British education and society".[69] The main reason was that education conditions in dispersal schools were much better than conditions in Southall: "In terms of general environment (in contrast to teacher skill about which no judgement can be made), the dispersal schools are clearly and definitely better".[70] All in all then, Ealing had therefore little to fear from Kogan's report, all the more so as the author, in his correspondence, reassured Ealing's education director R.J. Hartles that the RRB would probably mobilise his own research in a conciliation effort rather than for litigation purposes. Kogan also committed to sending his draft report to Hartles and was very willing to hear suggestions before drafting its final version.[71]

Once again, it bears remembering Usha Prashar's point that the sole existence of the report and of the investigation probably mattered more than its contents and conclusions. Still according to her, "there was some emergency in getting the thing done",[72] which must also account for the report's limitation of scope. Having said that, it is striking that most Asian parents and children would have found very little to actually relate to in Kogan's document.

Striking for dignity and equality in difference

In the 1970s, there were more frequent critiques of the New Commonwealth (and largely Asian) exceptionalism that dispersal typified, which seemed to confirm institutional racism at local and national level: why indeed was it not seen as a problem that Poles in Balham (Wandsworth) were left to speak Polish and live among themselves in concentrated urban spaces, or that Italians were massively clustering in a town like Bedford and spoke Italian?[73] Not once was dispersal ever seriously contemplated for these two groups. In the eyes of the IWA leaders and Asian activists, this was blatant confirmation of a colour and postcolonial bias in the application of dispersal.

The day-to-day operation of dispersal, especially in the Ealing borough where it took on massive proportions at its peak in the mid-1970s, was also exposed as an insult to the human dignity of students, as is suggested in some photos by Dennis Morris (see Figures 8 and 9). Two key figures of the IWA, Ajit Rai and Virendra Sharma, make the following points:

> Our children of five, six years old were packed into the buses and taken to places where they had no friends, no house nearabouts. They were taken like slabs, human slabs, packing and bringing them back. It was so inhuman.[74]

> We campaigned against bussing because it was inhuman. There was no shelter, under the rain and the snow in the winter. That was my line, this thing about no shelter. If the coach was broken down, which happened sometimes, nobody would know, there was no mobile phone back then.[75]

Figures 8 and 9: From *Southall: A Home from Home* by Dennis Morris (London: Olympus Optical Co., 1999)

As has been pointed out already, it was the operation of dispersal as a one-way traffic protecting whites from having to be bussed out which acted as an incentive to mobilisation. For people already sharing strong pre-existing collective identities as Punjabis or Sikhs in Southall or Pakistanis or Muslims in Bradford, and more generally as Asians, dispersal as a one-way traffic further entrenched the feeling of "us" and "them" with clearly demarcated frames as "interpretive packages that activists develop[ed] to mobilise potential adherents and constituents".[76] These collective action frames are decisive for they "make a compelling case for the 'injustice' of the condition and the likely effectiveness of collective 'agency' in changing a condition"[77] which, like dispersal, is exposed as an affront to equality and human dignity.

The exposure of dispersal as a one-way traffic was configured into a real common sense (in Antonio Gramsci's sense)[78] to comprehend the lived reality of formal inequality in the education field. As a "spontaneous philosophy"[79] of the subalterns in Southall and Bradford, the exposure of unilateral bussing and the concomitant demand for two-way bussing (which authorities dismissed as unworkable in practice and unjustifiable in theory) were, as in Gramsci's conception of common sense, "not a single unique conception, identical in time and space". There were those for whom such double standards were a sign of exclusion: "I found our Asian kids and Asian parents were not treated in the same way as white parents and their children. We were just unwanted" (Swarm Singh Kang, who arrived from Pakistan in 1965).[80] For others these double standards in the aid of integration operated *de facto* as the worst type of segregation: "I believe it was a sort of apartheid, that was basically operated by a council, just to keep the white population happy" (Gurcharan Singh, a Punjabi and career civil servant in Southall).[81] Others still, especially community leaders, exploited the growing focus on multiculturalism in education to promote a two-way form of dispersal and expose what was in their eyes a gross anomaly: "Also, if multi-racial schools are important, why are white children not bussed to Southall schools?"[82] The critique was in sync with the subaltern status of multicultural education, which was admittedly spreading in multiracial LEAs but remained totally absent in the majority of LEAs in England, that is those which were overwhelmingly white.[83] Similarly, other community leaders harnessed two-way bussing in an effort to tackle racism and racial stereotypes, and exposed bussing as a form of discrimination in demonstrations involving dispersed children themselves (see Figure 10). Muhamad Ajeeb in Bradford, a fierce opponent of dispersal, argues: "It was difficult to introduce, a two-way traffic, but it was a political principle ... I wanted white pupils in the inner-city areas to learn about Asian culture. Many Asians were exposed to such racist

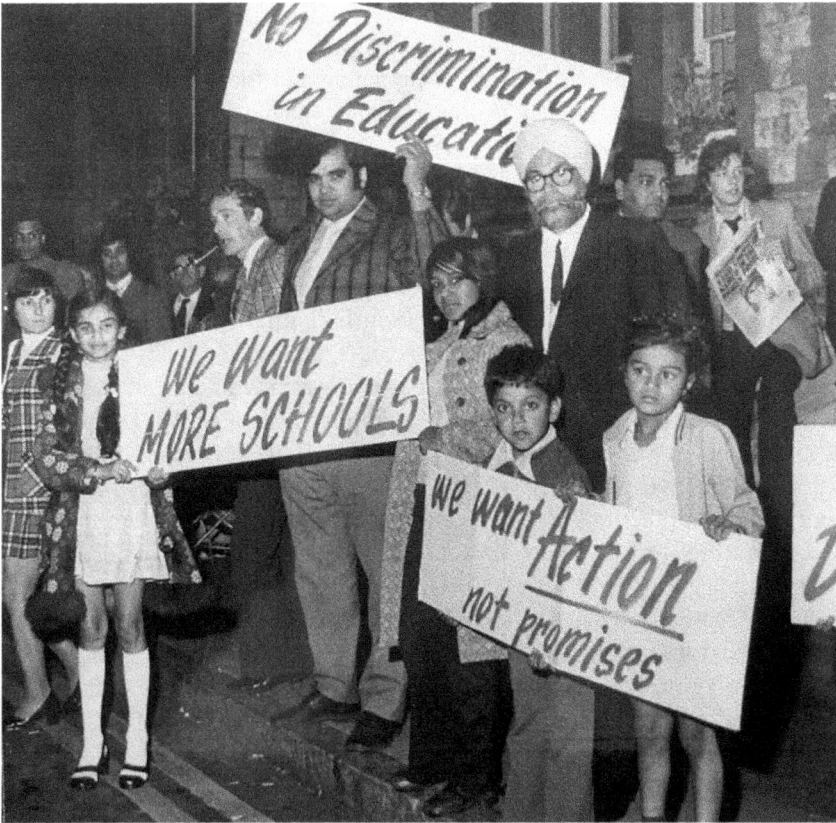

Figure 10: A protest against dispersal, Southall, 1978

name-calling."[84] As a multi-faceted narrative, this common sense had varying degrees of intensity in Southall and in Bradford. In the latter, the focus on double standards for whites and "coloureds" was probably stronger than anywhere else, notably because some inner-city schools still had free places which could have accommodated pupils – Asian or white. This led Peter Evans, a journalist for *The Times* specialising in race-relations issues, to expose the "ludicrous consequences" of bussing in Bradford.[85] Moreover, in the West Yorkshire city two-way bussing would have proved more workable in practice, for reasons of distance and traffic congestion, than in the Ealing borough:

> Much of the debate [in Bradford] was about the local schools, because some places were available there but we had to be bussed far away. (Raza Khan)[86]

I was denied a place in a school that was 5 minutes away from my home, and which was not full. Instead I had to walk to a bus collection point approximately one mile away from my home and then was bussed to a school four miles away from my home. (Noorzaman Rashid)[87]

Bigger and smaller picture

The focus on collective identity as a key condition of if not a prerequisite to collective action must be understood both in the context of the anti-bussing mobilisation at micro-level (Southall, Bradford) and in that of racism and discrimination at macro-level (England, the DES, racism as a national scourge, condoned or nourished in the media and at Westminster). This also means that dispersal (as opposed to racism) at the national level or inter-micro level was not made into an issue: it is a fact indeed that almost none of the archives on the struggle against bussing in Bradford and in Southall actually refers to each other. No trace has been found of IWA (Southall) visits to its West Yorkshire counterparts or vice versa. With hindsight, it is also noteworthy that very few of the actors in each struggle seemed to develop an interest in what was taking place in the other locus of resistance. This political isolation contrasted starkly with the many contacts between LEAs that were facing massive influxes of immigrant children and trying to devise the best means of addressing what they saw as a shared problem.

It does sometimes appear as though Bradford Asians and Southall Asians were evolving in distinct contentious spheres. There are anecdotal pieces of evidence of this which are quite telling. In November 1978 for instance, at a Bradford Trades Council conference which gathered most of the associations against dispersal, one organiser, Sue Strutt, argued that Bradford remained the only LEA still obdurately operating bussing, despite the fact that Ealing was still doing so.[88] The leader of Bradford Teachers Against the Nazis and a Bradford Labour Party leader against dispersal made exactly the same erroneous point.[89] That the Bradford (and indeed Southall) local leaders against bussing were barely cognisant of other loci of resistance is to be explained in both cases by their predominantly grass-roots focus as well as the fact that the IWA (Southall) evolved as a totally independent body. Besides, the struggle against bussing was historically placed between the horror of the Indian partition (Punjab 1947) and the emergence of Islamophobia in the late 1980s (the *Satanic Verses* crisis). If Sikhs (Southall) and Muslims (Bradford) did indeed share experiences of common discrimination in Britain, they were also divided by memories of conflict and bloodshed brought over from the Indian subcontinent, which would soon reinvent themselves with the spread of Islamophobic discourses among non-Muslim Asians.[90]

Racist murders and radicalisation

By 1972–73, many ethnic-minority associations were very vocal against dispersal. In Ealing these were the Indian Students' Association, the West Indian Student Association, the Afro-Caribbean Association and the IWA.[91] Martyn Grubb, a worker priest who had lived for many years in Southall, was the Ealing CRC leader who remained an indefatigable opponent of dispersal until the end. The local Communist Party was also actively implicated in the struggle. In Bradford, the IWA, the NUT, the Campaign Against Fascism and Racism, Bradford Teachers Against the Nazis, the local Trades Council, the Communities Relations Council under the aegis of Muhamad Ajeeb were all mobilised against bussing around the same years. With the emergence of a radical Asian youth, the IWA in both places was running the risk of appearing too moderate. As Dennis Chong has shown for the Civil Rights Movement in the United States, reputational concerns are often strong in the competition for community credibility and as an impetus for mobilisation at grassroots level when discrete agents vie for community endorsement.[92]

The radicalisation that the Southall Youth Movement embodied was due to the escalating number of racist murders in the country, of which there were forty-four from 1976 to 1981 alone,[93] mostly in the Greater London area. Two of these tragic events need detain us here. First, the murder of Muhamad Shakeel Malik on 2 October 1974, bottled to death on Greenford Broadway in Ealing. He was killed in a fight between youth gangs, just before boarding the bus on his way home. A dispersed kid who was too old to take the Ealing-operated coaches, he was going to Brent High School and, as the authors of *The Black Explosion in British Schools* (1982) pointed out, "Undoubtedly his isolation in a white community contributed to Malik's death".[94] Ravi Jain, a youth worker at the time, regretted that "many parents have reported attacks to their schools, but the reports have been ignored. The situation has become so bad that some headmasters are letting children go early to avoid clashes when other schools come out." Martyn Grubb had also asked the London Transport service to do its utmost to avoid long queues of schoolchildren at bus stops.[95]

Then, much more than this, the murder of Gurdip Singh Chaggar, on 4 June 1976, caused a real furore in Southall, and is a major chapter in the history of anti-racism not only locally but also nationally, just as the death of anti-racist teacher Blair Peach was to be three years later.

Gurdip Chaggar, from Florence Road, was an eighteen-year-old student following aero-engineering courses at Southall College of Technology. His grisly murder caused a major rift within the Southall Asian community, with the old guard of the IWA lobbying for extra motions and multiplying bureaucratic endeavours towards Whitehall, whereas most Asian youths were directly exposing racist police, promoted direct action and immediate responses against the fascist organisations that were perpetrating or condoning such acts.[96] Some within the IWA went so far as to request extra police to control rioting Asian youths outraged by police denial of any racist motive in Chaggar's stabbing by a white gang.[97] Spontaneously, an angry young crowd of some four hundred Asians demonstrated on the day of Gurdip Chaggar's funeral in Southall. This gave birth to the SYM. Dismissed as bourgeois, undemocratic and tainted with some corruption scandals,[98] the old guard was caught totally off-guard.

The generational, political and tactical rift between the IWA and the emerging SYM is also connected with issues of dispersal. Ravi Jain, a youth worker in Southall at the time, highlights the persistence of a generation gap around it: whereas after some years some of the elderly were sticking to an assimilationist embracing of bussing, many of the younger generation were appalled by bussing, not least because some of them or their siblings had had direct experience of it.[99]

Then, it is very striking that the one murder directly caused by the bussing of Asians was never made into the high-profile public issue that Gurdip Chaggar's murder was to become. The latter was not a tragedy of bussing as such. Muhamad Shakeel Malik, on the contrary, was a martyr of dispersal, but his name was very soon forgotten, and never really harnessed to the anti-bussing cause by the IWA and others. Chaggar's murder became a *cause célèbre*, but one connected with the broader issue of a racial hatred that plagued England in those years of NF upsurge. Nevertheless, the radicalisation that the Gurdip Chaggar (1976) and Blair Peach (1979) deaths generated or was concomitant with made dispersal look all the more like an anomaly. If these events took place in Southall, analogous developments were occurring in Bradford, if only a few years later: there the well-known case of the "Bradford Twelve"[100] led to the recognition that "self-defence" could be "no offence", itself a vindication of the direct action tactics of young Asians. A few months later, after a long, tiring battle, bussing there started to peter out, and multiculturalism in education and elsewhere became a pivotal element of local politics. It is probably no coincidence that Bradford and Southall became such hotbeds of Asian resistance. This, to be sure, was not solely about plain demographics. For years, indeed for nearly two decades, disgruntlement over dispersal had simmered to a point where the two places emerged into loci of struggle for the emancipation of Asians, or "Blacks" in England. Among the Bradford Twelve,[101] among the SYM, a few had been bussed themselves, but more importantly many had friends, siblings, cousins who had been bussed: bussing therefore was at the centre of these activists' symbolic repertoire, although by the time they emerged it was almost moribund. For some the very experience of bussing coincided with their racial awakening, as Noorzaman Rashid from Bradford puts it: "Bussing was the beginning of my journey to fighting discrimination, in whichever form it came".[102] He joined the local Asian Youth Movement as a teenager, not long after his bussing years.

West Indian involvement

Another irony in the struggle against dispersal was that some of its most vocal and organised enemies were West Indians living in areas where bussing did not operate. These were individual or institutional "conscience constituents", to borrow again McCarthy and Zald's apt phrase. The key player among this group was undoubtedly Barbados-born Jeff Crawford, secretary of the North London West Indian Association. Crawford, with John La Rose and Bernard Coard, was a prime mover in the Black emancipation movement around education in the 1960s and 1970s.[103] Between 1969 and 1974, he campaigned against the introduction of banding in the borough of Haringey (Chapter 4) and against the disproportionate number of West Indians in ESN schools, as well as against bussing in Ealing, which was, admittedly, the cause he devoted least energy to among the three.[104] Crawford filed a complaint against the discriminatory nature of bussing to the RRB on 19 September 1973, claiming to possess "substantial evidence" to bolster his case. Seeing that no such hard evidence materialised, Anthony Lester bitterly lamented the absence of information on the ground.[105] All in all then, Crawford's contribution lay primarily in publicising the issue of bussing outside Ealing, thereby bringing further pressure on the borough to change its policy and on the RRB to complete its investigation into the grassroots situation. Crawford probably lacked specific contacts among Southall Asians to really gain ground locally, despite the connection he had with Jim Barzey, secretary of Ealing's Afro-Caribbean association.[106] This man and West Indians in Ealing were fiercely opposed to bussing, which they regarded as an "insult".[107] In broad terms, historically situated between Bernard Coard's *How the West-Indian Child Is Made Educationally Sub-normal in the British School System* (1971) and Farrukh Dhondy, Barbara Beese and Leila Hassan's *The Black Explosion in British Schools* (1982) for Race Today Publications, Jeff Crawford's 1973–74 challenge to the institutionally racist nature of bussing, albeit

unsustained, facilitated the emergence of a broader perspective on dispersal, structurally bringing together banding, bussing and ESN schools into
a cohesive, institutionally racist package. One of the most articulate
responses to this was the creation of some supplementary schools, particularly in the London area, which guaranteed extra teaching hours to
ethnic-minority pupils (primarily West Indians) as well as courses nurtur-
ing feelings of Black agency and pride. Tellingly, the supplementary schools
that emerged as the SYM was created were the exact opposite of dispersal:
from the point of view of educational policy they served to bring ethnic-
minority children together in the absence of white autochthonous children. From the point of view of administration the schools were Black-led
and Black-run, and from the point of space distribution they were situated
in the very areas that dispersal was expected to be operated *from*, not in.[108]
In the Ealing borough alone there were two in Southall, two in Acton and
one in Ealing.[109]

Many such initiatives rested on Marxist appreciations of the Black
struggle, from mid-century "self-concept" theories as well as Frantz
Fanon's anti-colonial social psychology which underlined the colonial subjects' proclivity to internalise the colonist's gaze and value systems.[110] All
of this proved useful political grist to the SYM's mill, especially to its most
intellectually minded members.

Integration imperative or Welfare State roll-back?

The years 1977–80 saw the demise of dispersal in Southall and Bradford.
In general terms, a political system becomes vulnerable to a potential
challenge under certain conditions, which brings about an opportune time
to push through a social change, such as here the end of bussing's long
anomaly. Authors such as David Meyer and Sydney Tarrow have identified
a few of these conditions: increasing political pluralism; the decline in
repression; division within elites; increased political enfranchisement.[111]
All these four conditions, which admittedly are more appropriate in
undemocratic circumstances than under democratic ones (especially the
second, the decline in repression), applied much more to the late 1970s
than to the mid-1960s, when dispersal was introduced under circular 7/65.
The growing resort to "voice" rather than "loyalty" (or "apathy") and the
plurality of ethnic minority voices after 1975 certainly were key factors.
Also, the division among political elites was strong. In Bradford, the
Labour whip was withdrawn from Councillor Rhodes in 1976 because he
was opposing bussing, and Councillor Hussain still stated in 1978 that
"the tremendous social, cultural and educational benefits" of dispersal far
outweighed the drawbacks.[112] However by September 1979 Labour voted

overwhelmingly against bussing and, whilst Conservatives still maintained that dispersal did not contravene to the 1976 Race Relations Act
since it constituted, if anything, a form of positive discrimination, it was
self-evident they were waging a rearguard battle.[113] The division within
elites in Ealing was just as marked.

In March 1979, a petition with 1570 names was presented to Bradford
City Council: quite an achievement considering the numbers still bussed
and the difficulty in mobilising some parents (see Figure 11). Councillor
Stanley Arthur, chairman of the educational services committee, was at
pains to argue that, in the first four pages of the petition alone, one of the
signatories was non-Asian, fifty-one had children in local schools of their
first choice, fourteen had children who were bussed, forty-eight had no
children at all and one person was outside Bradford. This was a classic
attempt at delegitimisation of a public petition, according to which you
had to be directly affected by an issue to express disagreement. The uproar
caused at City Hall that day was strong and the room was almost evacu-
ated. A school boycott by Asians was threatened (but did not materialise).[114] At other times, tempers ran just as high when anti-bussing meetings
were interrupted by rowdy members of the NF, who argued that the anti-
racist left (mobilised against bussing) kept interrupting *their* own meetings.[115] In Southall, there was regular picketing by Asian parents outside
the Town Hall.

Both in Southall and Bradford the years 1977 to 1981 were marked by
frequently recurring criticisms of the authorities' deficient school-building
plans. In Bradford's case, Mark Halstead commented in hindsight that
"undoubtedly economic factors were a major consideration in the reten-
tion of 'bussing' in Bradford for so long".[116] From Maurice Kogan in Southall to *The Telegraph & Argus* (Bradford),[117] from Ealing's Communist Party
to some of the most moderate figures of the IWA, all agreed that bussing
was more and more of a smokescreen to avoid having to build badly
needed schools in inner-city areas. Already by 1974 Ealing borough had
acknowledged that it was in the children's interests to put an end to dispersal before, as Brett Bebber puts it, using "the loopholes available to
them"[118] to delay the decision to build new schools for which some sites
were available and financing could be obtained from the DES. This was a
situation that the West Middlesex Communist Party was quick to expose
in an October 1974 leaflet entitled "Stop Bussing 3000 children: Build New
Schools Throughout Ealing Borough, Use the Available £1 million" (see
Figure 12). For local communist leader John Royd, bussing was a disgrace-
ful illustration of neo-liberal politics and the Hayekian minimum state in
education. It was also a mishandling of public money by Ealing borough,
as was also typified by the controversies around the real use of the "cash

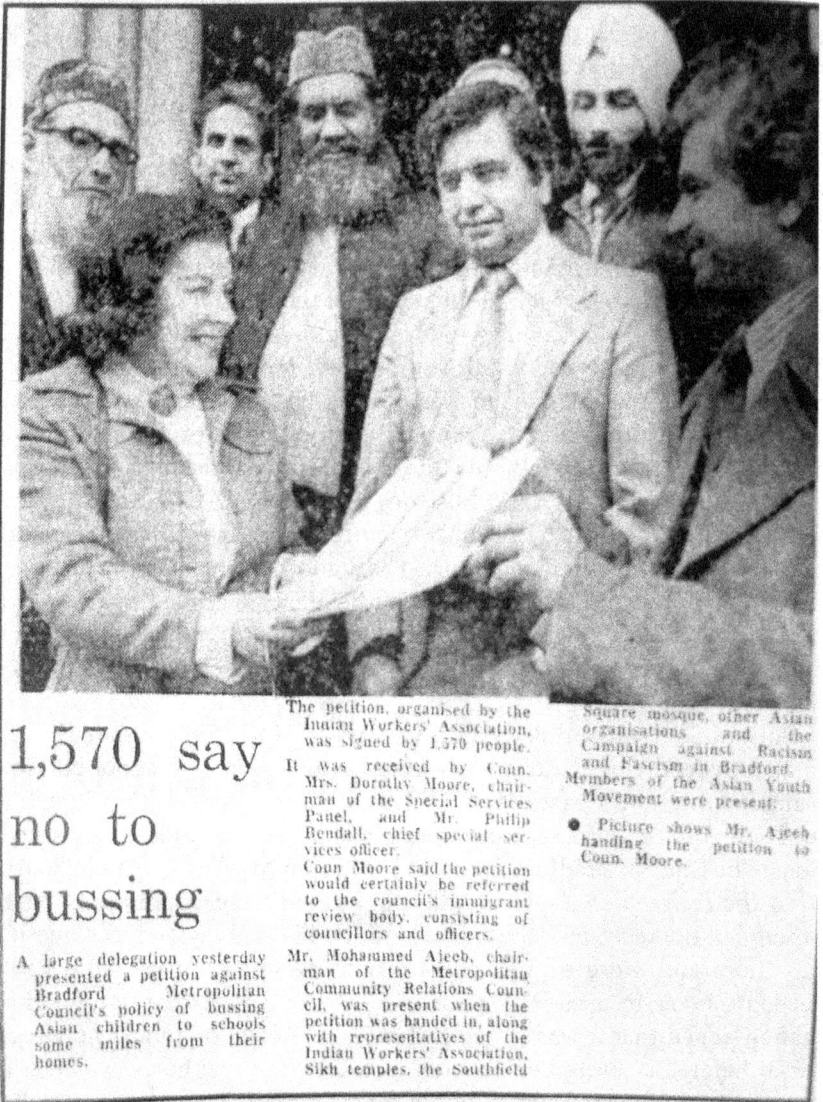

Figure 11: "1,570 say no to bussing", *Telegraph & Argus*, 6 May 1979

cow" of section eleven money (from the 1966 Local Government Act)[119] that Asians such as Balraj Purewal and Ravi Jain were to rally against vigorously.[120] To John Royd, "the sight of busloads of children, being transported about the borough twice a day ... is a constant suggestion to the entire population that there is a 'problem' of immigrant children"; he added

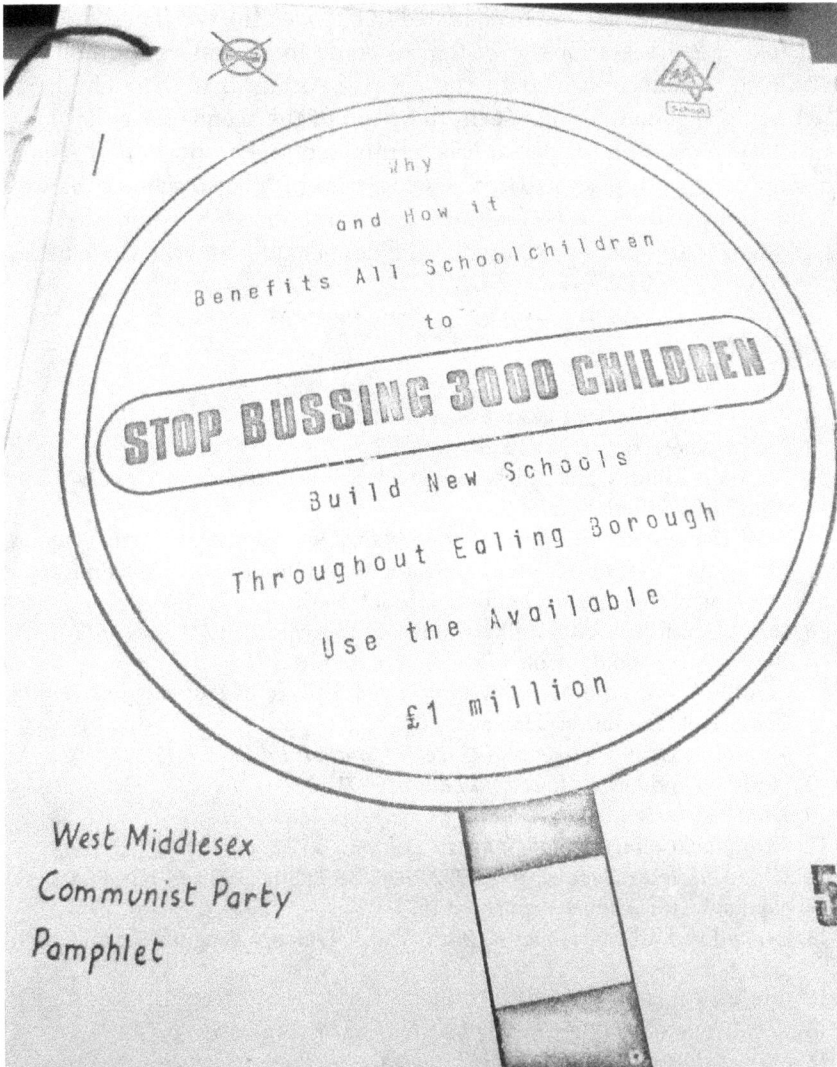

Figure 12: "Stop Bussing 3000 Children". West Middlesex Communist Party pamphlet, 1974

that "coloured children are being blamed for the Council's own short-comings".[121] By October 1974, no sites had been earmarked for any of the schools required to end bussing, and no money had been claimed by the Labour-controlled council for the purpose of ending bussing. Two months later, construction of a new school at Durdans Park was under way, and the council announced it was awaiting DES approval for two new schools.[122]

The communist leaflet had been issued in between the two dates. It would still take a few years for the system to come to an end in Southall and Bradford, which confirmed in the eyes of Asians that their children's well-being at school did not seem to be top of the agenda for either local authority. As soon as dispersal was terminated, the proportion of Asians in schools in both places soared, raising cries of "ghetto schools" as well as questions such as "Who's Afraid of ghetto schools?",[123] complex sets of issues which are further explored in the next chapter and the Conclusion.

Notes

1 *Guardian*, 11.12.1968.
2 Rose (ed.), *Colour and Citizenship*, pp. 24–5.
3 *Telegraph & Argus*, 29.11.1978.
4 For both Elliott's and Khabra's statements, see *Middlesex County Times (Southall Edition)*, 11.5.1973.
5 W.W. Daniels, *Racial Discrimination in England*, Harmondsworth: Penguin, 1969; Select Committee on Race Relations and Immigration, *The Problem of Coloured School-leavers*, London: HMSO, 1969.
6 Select Committee on Race Relations and Immigration, *Minutes of Evidence (Wolverhampton)*, London: HMSO, 1974, p. 136.
7 Camilla Schofield, *Enoch Powell and the Making of Post-colonial Britain*, Cambridge: Cambridge University Press, 2009, p. 214.
8 *Middlesex County Times and Gazette (Southall Edition)*, 5.11.1971.
9 Bindman and Lester, *Race and Law*, pp. 271–2.
10 Thomson, *Asian-named Minority Groups*, p. 183.
11 *Middlesex County Times (Southall Edition)*, 30.7.1971.
12 *West Middlesex Gazette*, 10.3.1972. See also Ealing archives, Nigel Spearing papers, ECRC Annual Report for 1971–72.
13 Quoted in Karl Marx, *Das Kapital*, Vol. 1, London: Penguin Classics, 1990 [1867], p. 738.
14 Interview (Southall), 19.10.2016.
15 Kogan, *Dispersal in the Ealing Local Education Authority*, p. 11.
16 Mancur Olson, *The Logic of Collective Action, Public Good and the Theory of Groups*, Cambridge, MA: Harvard University Press, 1971, pp. 165–7.
17 I owe this information to Anandi Ramamurthy.
18 *Middlesex County Times (Southall Edition)*, 19.5.1972.
19 Quoted in Kogan, *Dispersal in the Ealing Local Education Authority*, p. 18.
20 *Ibid.*, p. 9.
21 *West Middlesex Gazette*, 10.3.1972.
22 Much of this evidence is summarized in Bebber, "'We Were Just Unwanted'", pp. 644–50; unfortunately, these oral archives were closed during the renovation work of the museum from 2014 to 2018, which coincided with the research for this book.

23 See her website: www.bussingout.co.uk.

24 Interview (Ealing), 27.10.2016.

25 Interview (Southall), 19.10.2016.

26 Interview (Southall), 16.6.2016.

27 Tomlinson, *A Sociology of Special and Inclusive Education*, p. 129; the Green Paper notably states: "The government are of the view that parents should be given more information about schools and should be consulted more widely" (p. 5).

28 Interview, (Southall), 16.9.2015.

29 Interview, (Southall), 12.2.2017.

30 Interview, (Southall), 19.10.2016.

31 *Middlesex County Times (Southall Edition)*, 25.8.1962.

32 Interview, Southall, 25.2.2016.

33 Paul Willis, *Learning to Labour: How Working-class Kids Get Working-class Jobs*, New York: Columbia University Press, 1977, pp. 46–7.

34 *Ibid.*, p. 2.

35 See Kogan, *Dispersal in the Ealing Local Education Authority*, p. 19.

36 Interview, 6.7.2017.

37 See Hill and Issacharoff, *Community Action and Race Relations*, p. 63.

38 *Ibid.*, p. 68.

39 Doug McAdam, *Political Process and the Development of Black Insurgency, 1930–1970*, Chicago: University of Chicago Press, 1999 [1982], p. 49.

40 Ambalaver Sivanandan, *Catching History on the Wing*, London: Pluto Press, 2008, p. 111.

41 *Middlesex County Times (Southall Edition)*, 5.3.1971.

42 See Bebber, "'We Were Just Unwanted'", p. 650.

43 Helena Wray, *Regulating Marriage Migration into the U.K.: A Stranger in the Home*, London: Routledge, 2016, pp. 120–1; see also Balraj Purewal, *The Indian Workers Association (Southall): 60 years of Struggles and Achievements (1956–2016)*, London: IWA, 2016, p. 34.

44 *Middlesex County Times (Southall Edition)*, 31.3.1970 on the closing of the Tonge and Kearney biscuit factory, which made more than six hundred people redundant.

45 David Feldman, "Why the English Like Turbans: Multicultural Politics in British History", in David Feldman and Jon Lawrence, *Structures and Transformations in Modern British History*, Cambridge: Cambridge University Press, 2011, pp. 281–302.

46 Hill and Issacharoff, *Community Action and Race Relations*, p. 136.

47 James C. Scott, *Domination and the Arts of Resistance: Hidden Transcripts*, New Haven: Yale University Press, 1990, pp. 120–1.

48 For a discussion of this, see Francesca Polletta and James M. Jasper, "Collective Identity and Social Movements", *Annual Review of Sociology*, vol. 27 (2001), pp. 283–305.

49 According to the 1965 White Paper, local authorities were to provide office accommodation, secretarial staff and a partial grant to the creation of CRCs

and liaison officers. This was the case in Ealing, albeit with difficulties, since the Ealing CRC was repeatedly critical of the borough administration. On these points, see Hill and Issacharoff, *Community Action and Race Relations*, p. 16 (White Paper), pp. 209–10 (relations between Ealing borough and Ealing CRC).

50 John D. McCarthy and Mayer N. Zald, "Resource Mobilization and Social Movements: A Partial Theory", *The American Journal of Sociology*, vol. 82 (6), 1977, p. 1222.

51 Anthony Oberschall, *Social Conflicts and Social Movements*, London: Pearson Education Ltd, 1973, p. 159.

52 Interview (Westminster), 20.10.2016.

53 National Archives (Kew), CK2/515, Race Relations Board *vs* Blackburn Education Authority (1972–74), Memorandum by Anthony Lester on the Ealing situation (1974).

54 Quoted in Bebber, "'We Were Just Unwanted'", p. 653.

55 *Ibid.*

56 *Ibid.*

57 The full section has: "The Race Relations Board may appoint as assessors to assist the Board or any conciliation committee in their investigation of any complaint or other matter persons appearing to the Board to have special knowledge and experience of the circumstances in which the act to which the investigation relates is alleged to have occurred and of any other circumstances appearing to the Board to be relevant" (the full text is available at: www.legislation.gov.uk/ukpga/1968/71/pdfs/ukpga_19680071_en.pdf) (last accessed 19.6.2018).

58 Interview (Westminster), 20.10.2016.

59 National Archives (Kew), CK2/515, Race Relations Board *vs* Blackburn Education Authority (1972–74), Memorandum by Anthony Lester on the Ealing situation (1974).

60 Kogan, *Dispersal in the Ealing Local Education Authority*, p. 1.

61 *Ibid.*, p. 3: "It was not possible within my schedule of visits, nor was it implicit in the terms of reference given to me informally by the Board's officers, that I should meet the parents of children subject to the dispersal arrangements in order to ascertain their feelings about the arrangements".

62 *Ibid.*, p. 24.

63 Already by 1970 dispersal was operated in half of the borough's 116 schools (see *Middlesex County Times (Southall Edition)*, 10.6.1970).

64 See National Archives (Kew), CK2/515, Race Relations Board *vs* Blackburn Education Authority (1972–74), Memorandum by Anthony Lester on the Ealing situation (1974).

65 Interview (Westminster), 20.10.2016.

66 Kogan, *Dispersal in the Ealing Local Education Authority*, pp. 10–13.

67 *Ibid.*, pp. 9–10.

68 *Ibid.*, p. 28: "The passage of the 1968 Act makes discriminatory the bussing of pupils who are already English-speakers; the issue is to determine how many there are".

69 *Ibid.*, p. 25.
70 *Ibid.*, p. 16.
71 Kogan, *Dispersal in the Ealing Local Education Authority*, appendix I, p. 1; see, for instance, "The area of disagreement could be reduced to the absolute minimum by discussion with you".
72 Interview (Westminster), 20.10.2016.
73 See for instance, Ahmed Iqbal Ullah Race Relations Resource Centre, Commission for Racial Equality archives, "Dispersal and Choice", June 1969 exposé by Joan Lester (Labour MP for Slough and Eton). See also *Telegraph & Argus*, 27.1.1975; 11.3.1977. On the ethnic concentration of non-Anglophone Italians in Bedford, see *The Times*, "The Delicate art of dispersal", 26.1.1971.
74 Bebber, "'We Were Just Unwanted'", p. 647.
75 Interview (Southall), 18.9.2015.
76 Polletta and Jasper, "Collective Identity and Social Movements", p. 291.
77 *Ibid.*
78 For a discussion of this definition, see Kate Crehan, *Gramsci's Common Sense, Inequality and Its Narratives*, Durham, NC: Duke University Press, 2016.
79 The definition is quoted in Scott, *Weapons of the Weak*, p. 340.
80 Bebber, "'We Were Just Unwanted'", p. 645.
81 *Ibid*, p. 647.
82 *Middlesex County Times (Southall Edition)*, 12.5.1972.
83 Tomlinson, *Race and Education*, pp. 64–5.
84 Interview (Bradford), 20.10.2015.
85 *The Times*, "Integration by Bus", 28.7.1970.
86 Interview (Bradford), 10.10.2015.
87 Interview, 3.2.2016. Exactly the same point is expressed in Bradford archives, oral history collection, C0055.
88 *Telegraph & Argus*, 17.11.1978.
89 *Telegraph & Argus*, 28.11.1978; 7.3.1979.
90 For instances of Islamophobic discourses among Sikhs in the mid-1980s, see Dervla Murphy, *A Tale from Two Cities: Travels of Another Sort*, London: J. Murray, 1987, pp. 80–1.
91 Bebber, "'We Were Just Unwanted'", p. 650.
92 Dennis Chong, *Collective Action and the Civil Rights Movement*, Chicago: University of Chicago Press, 1991.
93 Ambalaver Sivanandan, *Catching History*, pp. 129–30.
94 Farrukh Dhondy, Barbara Beese and Leila Hassan, *The Black Explosion in British Schools*, London: Race Today Publications, 1982, pp. 36–7.
95 *Acton Gazette*, 24.10.1974.
96 Khalbir Shukra, *The Changing Pattern of Black Politics in Britain*, London: Pluto Press, 1998, pp. 46–7; Gurharpal Singh and Darshan Singh Tatla, *Sikhs in Britain: The Making of a Community*, London: Zed Books, 2006, pp. 98–9.
97 Adam Lent, *British Social Movements since 1945: Sex, Colour, Peace and Power*, London: Palgrave Macmillan, 2001, p. 120.

98 Ealing archives, "Media and the Asian Leadership", minutes of The National Association for Asian Youth Conference, 3–5 September 1976 (Sheffield University), pp. 3–4.

99 Interview (Southall), 21.10.2015.

100 Anandi Ramamurthy, "The Politics of Britain's Asian Youth Movements", *Race & Class*, vol. 48 (2), 2006, pp. 53–5.

101 The great majority of these hailed from Shipley and Frizinghall, not Manningham and other Bradford inner city areas; therefore they were not bussed, but were appalled at the policy and consequences of bussing. I owe this information to Noorzaman Rashid.

102 Quoted in bussingout.co.uk.

103 Warmington, *Black British Intellectuals*, pp. 47–9.

104 It is probably not accidental that *The Guardian*'s obituary of Jeff Crawford (published 10.1.2004) doesn't mention his involvement against bussing.

105 National Archives (Kew), CK2/515, Race Relations Board *vs* Blackburn Education Authority (1972–74), Memorandum by Anthony Lester on the Ealing situation (1974).

106 *Middlesex County Times (Southall Edition)*, 12.5.1972.

107 Ealing archives, Nigel Spearing papers, ECRC News, April 1972.

108 Kehinde Andrews, *Resisting Racism: Race, Inequality and the Black Supplementary School Movement*, Stoke-on-Trent: Trentham Books, 2013.

109 London Metropolitan Archives, Supplementary schools in Ealing, LMA/4463/D/11/02/002–006.

110 Warmington, *Black British Intellectuals*, pp. 65–7.

111 David S. Meyer, "Protest and Political Opportunities", *Annual Review of Sociology*, vol. 30 (2004), pp. 126–32; Sydney Tarrow, *Power in Movement*, Cambridge: Cambridge University Press, 1998.

112 Halstead, *Education, Justice and Cultural Diversity*, p. 38.

113 *Telegraph & Argus*, 11.9.1979.

114 *Telegraph & Argus*, 7.3.1979.

115 *Telegraph & Argus*, 30.11.1978.

116 Halstead, *Education, Justice and Cultural Diversity*, p. 39.

117 See *Telegraph & Argus*, 17.11.1978; Maurice Kogan, *Dispersal in the Ealing Local Education Authority*, p. 5.

118 Quoted in Bebber, "'We Were Just Unwanted'", p. 651.

119 Thanks to this, special provision was possible "as a consequence of the presence within their area of substantial numbers of immigrants from the Commonwealth whose language and customs differ from those of the community". See Tomlinson, *Race and Education*, p. 31, p. 85.

120 Interview (Southall), 21.10.2015; 16.9.2015. For Ealing and Hounslow, see also London Metropolitan archives, LMA/4463/B/02/01/007.

121 Bebber, "'We Were Just Unwanted'", p. 652.

122 *Acton Gazette*, 6.12.1974.

123 Dhondy *et al.*, *The Black Explosion*, p. 36.

7

Babylon by bus: the quotidian experience of being bussed

Some practical and not-so-practical issues faced by dispersed children have been studied already and these need not detain us further here. Rather, the aim in this ultimate chapter is to delve further into the lived experiences of being bussed in England. From 2015 to 2017, forty interviews were conducted, thirty-two with people who either were themselves bussed as pupils (27), or who went to school accommodating dispersed children (1) or who are parents of formerly bussed students (4), bussed away from Southall (22), Bradford (4), Huddersfield (1) or Smethwick (1). Two-thirds of these interviews were held face to face in England, one-third were phone or Skype interviews. Added to these were eight interviews with former anti-bussing activists (5), or former members of the administration involved in the operation of bussing (3): one bus driver, a teaching assistant in Acton, and Trevor Burgin, whose job was to organise bussing in the Huddersfield area. Three-quarters have a quite or very negative view of bussing, nearly all for racist bullying reasons.

Managing to find these individuals proved a major challenge, compounded by the fact that I live in France and that length of residence in areas like Southall and Bradford is generally (much) shorter than in more affluent towns, making it more arduous to trace back people aged fifty or so who were bussed some decades back. Social networks have been useful at times, but it has primarily been a makeshift solution. In the same way, the snowballing sampling technique has rarely proved fruitful: naturally, most interviewees had lost sight of former classmates from primary or middle school. The overall result therefore leaves something to be desired, in both quantitative and qualitative terms. Indeed, whilst the sample arrived at could have been larger, the representativeness of the interviewed actors is also in question. For it is a fact that the bulk of these are the low-hanging fruits of dispersal, by which I mean that they are often the most publicly visible and the most reachable people among a cohort of many thousand individuals across a two-decade span. Indeed, some are prosperous and have quite public jobs (solicitors, entrepreneurs, executive directors for major firms); others who have been upwardly mobile have decided to serve their community (race-relations advisers, social workers), and only a few have remained part of the working-class precariat. It is noteworthy that two interviewees were themselves keenly aware of how unrepresentative they are. This they connected with the way dispersal as an educational policy produced, among other things, some low-attainers unable to climb the social ladder. Anjuna Kalsi says, for instance: "Many of my 'bussed' friends buckled under the abuse ... and very few emerged from the darkness, scarred for life".[1] She also refers to a gendered contrast, which cannot be evidenced, let alone quantified: "There was a real gender gap in this racism and bussing thing. Many guys have just faded away, they couldn't cope with the racism and sometimes the physical racism which they were the first victims of. Many of them really haven't excelled with their lives. A huge lot have just dissolved into mainstream life." Another interviewee, Gurbax Sooch, whose children were dispersed, refers to her son thus: "Now he's forty-six years old, a successful businessman. But it's very clear that some personalities were destroyed."[2] Raj Samra, from Huddersfield, insists on how being bussed simply broke his education: "I was segregated; it had a profound effect on me. I was taken out of our residential area to go to another area, that stifled my integration to a great extent. I lost interest in education."[3]

It is wellnigh impossible to tell how much of a career-shaper dispersal proved to be among those who were indeed scarred by the racism endured, and it is how the Cormac McCarthy epigraph to this book ought to be construed: "In history there are no control groups. There is no one to tell us what might have been". Most of these are the silent voices of bussing, unreachable given this book's purview.

In this respect, it is probably no coincidence that about half of the interviewees are Ugandan or Kenyan Asians, whose parents could mobilise a social and linguistic capital that was greater than the majority of Sikh Punjabis (Southall) or Mirpuri (Bradford) or Gujarati (Blackburn) Muslims. To be sure, that general background distribution is not representative of the dispersed cohorts of students, despite the absence of specific background statistics.

For all this, it remains true that the memories and experiences shared here are without any doubt indicative of the general working of dispersal as an administrative machinery. They raise an impressive list of pragmatic issues enough in themselves to cast doubt on the necessity for bussing: issues such as racist behaviour becoming a real norm accepted as an expected part of life for many young Asians and the production of a real, symbolic or imagined segregation rather than integration of the children. It is for all these reasons that the testimonies analysed weave a cohesive narrative of dispersal as such, despite their obvious shortcomings.[4] It is also for these reasons that the "private troubles" experienced by these interviewees help to make sense of their structural causes, that is the "public issue" of special education for immigrant children in the 1960s and 1970s, to borrow Charles W. Mills's classic dialectic on the general function of sociology.[5]

One word on the general methodology of the interviews. These were unstructured discussions with the use of a loosely structured questionnaire: respondents were therefore very much encouraged to talk freely about what aspects of bussing they found germane. Interviews were from twenty minutes to one hour, and respondents never asked explicitly to remain anonymous, which illustrates the extent to which this dispersed past is to them an old history, however formative, and the way many wanted to personally commit to a felt testimony. The most politically minded among them, from Southall Black Sisters staff to race-relations advisers, kept underlining how important the book project was in their eyes.

Bussing routine: physical feelings

Memories of the bussing routine are fraught with physical feelings, interviewees referring to the cold, the dark, the wait, the tiredness, the noise of a large crowd, especially at the two major pick-up points on Featherstone Avenue (see Figure 13) for Southall and Green Lane (Manningham) for Bradford. At the former some six hundred children were rounded up every morning around the mid-1970s. This was a notoriously cramped space with many buses channelled by marshals and coach ladies, most of whom were white: "The first memory I have is how impressive it was. There were hundreds of kids every age. We started crying, we were shouted a number ... There was an assistant, called a coach lady. She would hold up a number, we would be waiting in the canteen till we were called; what you did was you waited in the canteen" (Viney Jung). This general description meshes well with recollections of Bradford's main pick-up point on Green Lane, which Noorzaman Rashid remembers as "the most amazing scene, really",[6] with always ten to twelve buses, hundreds of children being crammed into buses, and no apparent order.

Together with references to the sound of the crowds are descriptions of the cold in winter: "The emotional experience was hard, especially in the winter" (Minnie Dogra)[7] and Raza Khan from Bradford, who from the age of eight was bussed out: "I had to walk one and a half miles to catch the bus to go to St James school on Nelson Street. I remember one morning, the wind was so strong and cold I couldn't breathe. My dad would work

Figure 13: Bussing pick-up point on Featherstone Avenue, Ealing

from seven am to seven pm. There was no money for public transport back then."[8] What was also to leave a deep imprint was how dark it all felt: "The most striking thing about it was the darkness. For a large portion of the year it was dark in the morning. My pick-up point was Oswald Street, we lived four streets away. It was a bit like going through a twilight zone" (Manjeet Singh).[9]

Tiredness, caused by young age and the necessity to wake earlier to be bussed out one to seven miles away, was recurrently referred to. This was a major incentive in the investigation into bussing by the RRB, according to Usha Prashar: "What it was like for the kids: it was about tiredness. The general impact of this was huge upon the children," Minnie Dogra echoes this general point: "I always had to get up extra early. It seemed such a long journey, as a young child, I'd always be very sleepy." This generated certain risks, sometimes wreaking panic among some families. As a mother of bussed children Gorbax Sooch states: "When they were coming back sometimes, they were so young and the coach trip so long that they would fall asleep on the buses, twice they remained asleep after the pick-up point, we didn't find them until 7 pm, we thought they had disappeared, we were so afraid". Kesar Singh Bhatti was a bus driver who faced that issue repeatedly: "Many times the coach lady would find the kids at the end of the bus, sleeping, it did happen many times. It was very unfair to these poor children."[10]

Getting up early was a heavy strain, especially for the youngest. Another strain (in the form of pressure and fear) was linked to missing the bus: "It was essential to be on time so we all arrived early" (Sukhwant Sandher); "We would also share a packet of biscuits, which we ate on the way to the pick-up point if we were late. We had to wait for about thirty minutes, we were always worried about missing the bus" (Manjeet Singh). One major practical shortcoming of bussing was that the late-comers would have to remain outside all day or go to the local school instead, to be looked after for a day. The irony was that it was only by being found at fault (missing the bus) that these children could enjoy the privilege of a neighbourhood school, if only for a day. For Minnie Dogra, this meant getting the opportunity to be schooled alongside her siblings, since she was the only child who was dispersed in her family: "If I missed the bus I would go to my sister and brother's school, and would be kept there, and stay all day". This short-lived, positive turn of events was despite the fact that so-called "stragglers were given a very hard time indeed" (Parminder Grewal), echoed by Viney Jung's recollection, "If you were late you got into serious trouble, because the bus had left and the local school had to take care of you". Beyond the obvious fact that the bulk of bussed children would arrive late in their dispersal schools in the morning and leave earlier than others to get back to their neighbourhoods at a reasonable time, there was the aggravating factor that, in occasional instances, pupils would be left out all day: "Another disadvantage was that I had an eye-situation; I had to go to the eye-specialist quite often, so one appointment at any time of the day would make me miss the whole day at school, since I couldn't possibly catch the bus" (Parminder Grewal). There were also frequent mechanical problems as buses were not "checked for roadworthiness and very often coaches broke down", according to a former bus escort lady. In Southall in particular, there was a network of private companies operating the system, with Foxes (of Hayes) being the major one. There were also smaller operators from Slough, Hounslow and Brentford, and there was also Ralf's near Heathrow; not all of these liaised efficiently with Ealing Council to run the machinery of dispersal daily.

Brenda Mary Thomson reveals some Bradford statistics which are quite illuminating about the absenteeism of bussed Asians. In the years 1977–79, they were absent 12 per cent of the time, which was significantly higher than expected and more than their Asians peers who were not bussed and schooled in inner cities. One example is quite telling: on 13 July 1977, one thousand children from Bradford were transported to Elland Road stadium in Leeds for the celebration of the silver jubilee of the Queen. On that day, dispersed Asian pupils were told there would be no bus service. In order for mostly white children to rally around Queen and country, Asians were on that day reminded of their deficient citizenship, still officially in aid of their smoother integration.[11]

The sheer separation from the neighbourhood was a baffling, confusing experience for most. This may have been positively apprehended, at least at the beginning: "In the early days I quite enjoyed the views of outer Bradford that I had never experienced before" (Noorzaman Rashid). But before long the same interviewee became aware that this was "an extraordinarily long journey, the bus would not take the most direct route, since there were plenty of schools on the way". Minnie Dogra's memories are valuable for a different set of reasons. Unlike nearly three-quarters of the interviewees she is adamant that she "didn't experience racism really, being an emotional person I would remember it". And yet her view on bussing remains a largely negative one. Her general focus is on childhood feelings of geographical distance, on emotional secureness and on how the profound imprint of apparently innocuous events was to shape her general mindset:

> I now realise it was a short trip, but back then it seemed very long. It was a ten-minute drive (fifteen-minute if there was a lot of traffic) to Norwood Drive, but it really felt like an hour. In Norwood Green there were open fields, horses, I had to go into the countryside, from an urban setting; it felt like I had to go very far away. The impact on me was huge for the rest of my life, because of that I developed a huge sense of security, which I've always kept.

Racism as unchallenged norm

Until about 1972–73 there was virtually no recorded reference to racism in the playground among dispersed children, or to racist bullying or violence on the way to schools, especially for those in middle schools who had to take public transport on their own and were not sent by coach directly to the schools. Evidence of all this started to accumulate by 1973, especially in the Ealing CRC newsletter through recounted anecdotes which in public meetings "provoked great interest".[12] Some of these were also reproduced in local newspapers, such as is shown in Figure 14. As has been noted by analysts of community-organising in the United States, the influence of individual story-telling and of moving personal anecdotes is pivotal for people to rally around a particular cause: narratives of injustice and undeserved harm generate intra-group solidarity and help to convince fence-sitters to mobilise, all the more so in the present case as these stories are about or by children.[13]

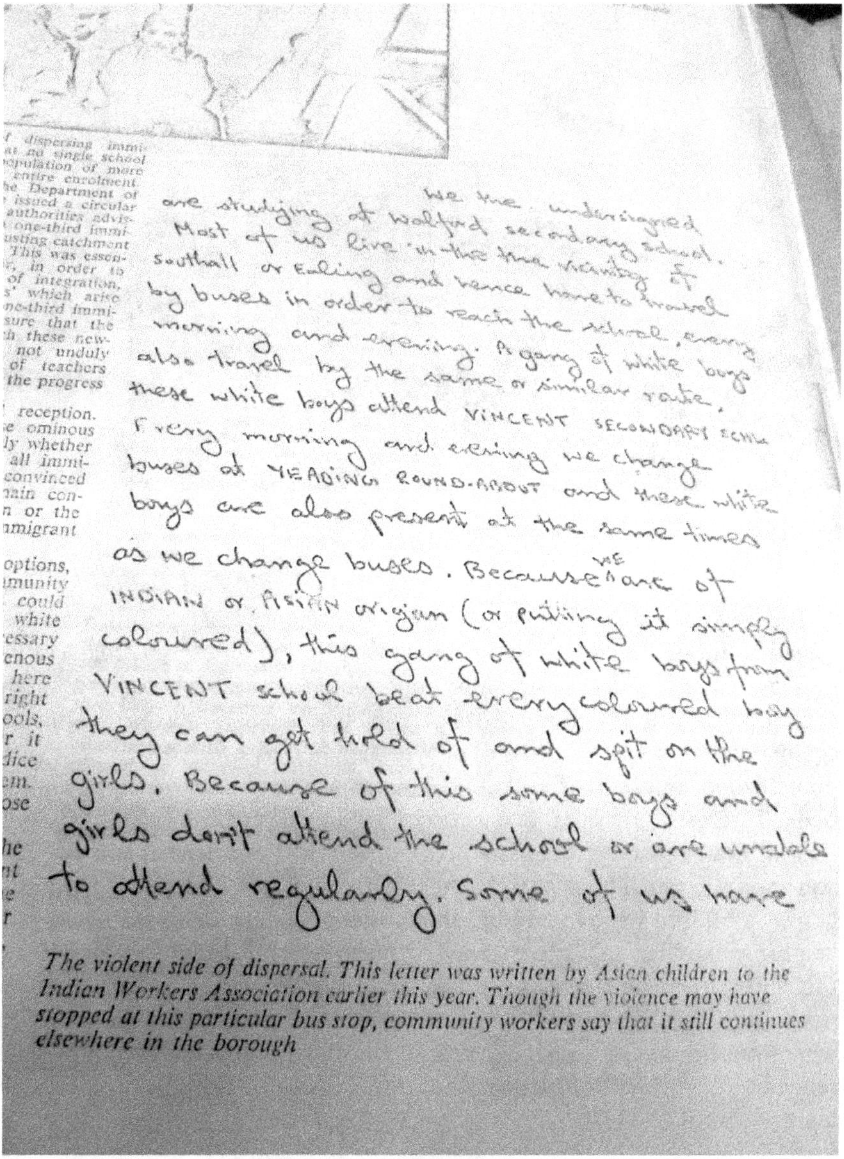

We the undersigned are studying at Walford secondary school. Most of us live in the the vicinity of Southall or Ealing and hence have to travel by buses in order to reach the school, every morning and evening. A gang of white boys also travel by the same or similar route, these white boys attend VINCENT SECONDARY SCHL. Every morning and evening we change buses at YEADING ROUND-ABOUT and these white boys are also present at the same times as we change buses. Because we are of INDIAN or ASIAN origin (or putting it simply coloured), this gang of white boys from VINCENT school beat every coloured boy they can get hold of and spit on the girls. Because of this some boys and girls don't attend the school or are unable to attend regularly. Some of us have

The violent side of dispersal. This letter was written by Asian children to the Indian Workers Association earlier this year. Though the violence may have stopped at this particular bus stop, community workers say that it still continues elsewhere in the borough

Figure 14: Letter from bussed students to the Indian Workers Association, *Inside London*, 18 October 1973

Figure 15: BBC footage of children on a coach, Bradford area, c.1975

The weight of mounting (anecdotal) evidence notwithstanding, Maurice Kogan could still maintain in his report that "unhappiness and coach sickness quickly go and it is virtually impossible to assess whether any psychological damage or lasting sense of being labelled or being discriminated against remains with the child, or whether he has ever perceived it",[14] a point which no doubt would stoke the ire of many interviewees for this book. Interestingly, on the few times when television covered bussing issues,[15] journalists showed the pick-up points at Southall and Bradford, and then the journey on the coaches; as in quite a few newspaper photographs, children were invariably shown sleepy (Figure 15) or smiling and laughing together as a group, waving merrily at a journalist who breaks their humdrum routine (Figure 16). That type of limited coverage, which never got into the schools[16] or immediately outside the dispersal schools where racism was rife, also permeated the articles or television clips that tended to be critical of bussing, but without ever referring to racism, at least not until 1975–76.

Broader picture

Racist bullying and violence against bussed children were only one chapter in the history of racial violence in British schools, which the CRE was to expose in its seminal report *Learning in Terror* (1988), published after Ahmad Iqbal Ullah's murder in a Manchester (Burnage) school. This account of dispersal is totally in sync with the broader narrative: in

ALL SMILES as immigrant children board one of the school buses at Southall—but their parents frown on the idea of bussing.

Picture : |

Figure 16: Bussed children, *Middlesex County Times (Southall Edition)*, 12 November 1972

Learning in Terror it was argued for instance that racism was very much a way of life for many Black and Asian children across the country (including Scotland and Wales) and that for too long school administrations had done too little, harbouring the feeling that "name-calling and bullying are part of the normal workings of a community and merely reflect what is to be expected of the outside world".[17] Anti-racist activist Amrit Wilson quoted a headteacher in 1978: "Asking them to say thank you and please and asking them not to swear is one thing but asking them not to say 'nigger' or 'wog' or 'black people stink' is quite another. A discussion of these things would only make the atmosphere worse."[18] Therefore, racism in the dispersal environments (around and at the school rather than before and during the journey on coach) was an unchallenged norm both because the question had barely been considered by public authorities and also because it reflected a much broader issue. In this sense, the vast panoply of anecdotes recorded for this research have without doubt a real, not infrequently painful, resonance with Asians and West Indians who were *not* bussed.

It may even be argued that for the bussed children the coaches' self-enclosed spaces temporarily symbolised a travelling continuation of the home neighbourhood's comfort zone where links of intra-ethnic friendships could be freely deployed. That was sometimes felt keenly by Asians in dispersal schools who themselves were from the area around and consequently were not bussed: "I was never bussed, being from Northolt, but I remember the bussed children; to me they had some safety in the sense that they were driven to the school, whereas we all had to walk in what was a very dangerous area for us. They definitely did get some safety, that was a good thing" (Shakila Maan).[19]

Too young

For the bussed pupils, racism was an unchallenged norm primarily because their primary school age made them unaware of the most basic, sandpit-level political realities around racism. They had no word to refer to, let alone challenge, racial hostility: "At that age you're just too young to feel racism, but not too young to really feel different" (Rita Nath). What the second part of this sentence typifies is that their sense of racial difference was naturalised through constant reminders in the daily routine of dispersal, whether through their skin colour, the fact that unlike others they arrived as ethnic clusters by bus, the fact that they arrived late and left early, and the fact that many of them had dietary requirements which were often not respected at the canteen table, and which set them further apart. In some way, this internalised sense of racialisation among children reflected the broader, bureaucratic racialisation of these "immigrant children" by authorities.

Some (Muslim) pupils in the Bradford area were force-fed sausages,[20] and in Southall it was not uncommon for Hindus as well as Sikhs to improvise spontaneous avoidance strategies with regard to beef or meat: "We would tell the staff 'we don't eat that because it's beef'. And we were forced to eat it. So we would always shove the beef from our mouths into the desks, unseen"[21] (Swarn Shoor). To be sure, these anecdotal instances of institutional racism were not the monopoly of bussed children at the time. Other instances were more specific to dispersal as, for example, the "hutted accommodation" reserved for dispersed pupils across the borough of Ealing, which in the mid-1970s "welcomed" some dispersed pupils in more than fifty per cent of its schools. Those "things like P.O.W, sheds", to quote Balraj Purewal's phrase, contrast bafflingly with Kogan's sanguine descriptions of dispersal reception schools which were predominantly "delightful", "pleasant and effective", "positively lavish in space", "extremely

happy", "on excellent sites", "with exceptional dynamic and charm", as
opposed to Southall's "cramped sites", "distinctly tight", "old building"
schools with "constant teacher turnover".[22] Of these contrasts neither children nor parents were aware.

Another structural form of institutional racism which pupils were
sometimes unaware of until they had become adults was that many of the
dispersal schools accommodated children in reception classes or confined
them to the lowest streams whether they had deficiencies in English or
not. This has been all the more keenly expressed in the case of this research,
because of the disproportionately large number of Ugandan or Kenyan
Asians who were growing up in clearly Anglophone families. Balvinder
Vedhany was one of the few who opposed this: "I was sent to a special
class, but I spoke English, with a different accent ... I spoke out against
special classes, they thought I had no English because I was Asian, and
finally I got sent to another class ... They didn't want us to study." Anjuna
Kalsi's memory is little different: "You were also put into the lower streams
because you were Asian. I was put in a remedial class although I was
Anglophone. Early you were stereotyped into this under-achieving category." Clearly, dispersal as a pipeline to integration was often experienced
as a manufacturing of low-attainers. This phrase is barely an exaggeration,
specifically because the under-achievement of bussed pupils was often
explained away by resorting to a general, blanket assumption, such as:
"they arrive late (by bus), therefore they are failing". In Bradford, for
instance, they were often moved from one class to another several times
a year, being placed where they were well below the average level, or in
order to fill empty places in suburban schools and so on. In contrast to
this, Brenda Mary Thomson recalls that struggling non-Asian pupils were
always seen as fully fledged individuals with individual reasons to under-
achieve, such as illness, absence or home background.[23] The state simplifications mentioned in another chapter were therefore configured here as
bureaucratic generalisations by individual members of staff.

Balraj Purewal remembers the number of Asian pupils whose perfor-
mances in mathematics were outstanding: "In maths I was brilliant. Many
Indians were, because the education we got in the villages was very strong
on maths. Back there we had to shout out our tables up to twenty, even
though we were very young. But because of my English I was dumped into
reception classes, we all were, although many of us were very good at
maths." All of this illustrates some of the broader shortcomings of British
education for ethnic-minority or immigrant children, as exposed by
Bernard Coard in the case of ESN schools. Also, this low-expectation
schooling environment is an implicit tribute to the individual agency and
resilience of many among the interviewed sample who exemplify upward
mobility.

Table 14 Distribution of dispersed pupils in Ealing borough (1971–72)

	Number of dispersed pupils (approx.)	Dispersed children as % of places provided	Temporary and hired accommodation as % of all places
Northolt	450	12.7	25.60
Yeading	420	16.2	3.08
Perivale	200	10.3	23.00
Hanwell	200	11.3	21.80
North Ealing	200	8.9	25.10
North Acton	150	4.6	11.50
South Acton	120	4.1	3.79
Greenford	120	3.7	22.10
West Twyford	96	27	22.20
South Ealing	75	2.1	11.60
Southall (North)	–	–	15.90
Southall (South)	–	–	4.90

Source: The Select Committee on Race Relations and Immigration, Education, vol. 2, London: HMSO, 1973, pp. 406–7

Most children were faced with the day-to-day exposure to racist bullying, regardless of building or administrative distinctions. In Ealing, interviewees insist on distinctions to be made between the almost wholly white, "danger zones" of Northolt and Perivale and already mixed districts such as Acton. Table 14 shows that Northolt was the area where the largest cohort of dispersed pupils were sent; slightly more than half the interviewees for this book were bussed there. It is noteworthy that, in their mobilisation against bussing, Southall Asians themselves drew maps indicating where their offspring were bussed. In Bradford, the suburb of Eccleshill to the north-east of the city was an NF stronghold in the 1970s. It was where dispersed children seem to have fared worse, as Zulfi Hussain recounts: "Essentially, we were like lambs to the slaughter. As early as the first few days, it was very tough."[24] In such areas the racism felt obliterated differences between inside and outside the buildings, and exacerbated the notion that racism in the playground was merely a reflection of a broader scourge to simply come to terms with: "We also used to get police escort to get to the bus back home. Especially when it came around holiday time, the tension was escalating. It wasn't necessarily the white kids at the school we were at, it was a bunch of skinheads, NF activists and fascists who came deliberately to give us hell" (Zulfi Hussain).

It is clear therefore that racism as a norm was played out both in the immediate vicinity of the school and inside the buildings, especially in areas like the playground, which were both sites of potential bridging social capital and areas where administration control was weaker. Below are a few testimonies that summarise quite well the general appreciations of interviewees:

> There was a lot of racist banter, racist terminology, being called a "wog", a "Paki", that was the norm. I can't remember any really vicious thing, though. At football we used to play football against whites, the racist language was definitely there. (Sukhwant Sandher)

> My children were sent to Northolt, they were bussed there, they were called "Pakis" all the time at school. My son loved playing football, he absolutely loved it, but finally stopped because there was too much bullying at the school he went. Name-calling was constant, like a way of life. (Amrit Kaur)

> In secondary school we were spat at, our hair pulled, it was standard practice, we were called "Pakis" even by girls in Northolt. (Anjuna Kalsi)

> You inevitably felt odd, the other kids would say "stinky", "Paki", "gollywog". You never forgot you were Asian, you never just thought you were a kid. Your Asianness just stood out constantly. (Manjeet Singh)

> Some of the teachers were OK. At the beginning it was "in your face" all the time, the racism was raw, they would sing nasty songs, they would beat you up ... I just thought that was it; racism as a concept never occurred to me, I never put two and two together. I just got on with it. (Mel Jung)

> In the playground there was one side with Asian kids, the other side with white kids, and it was pure tribalism: taunts, fights, name-calling, etc. We would charge at each other, day in day out, the staff had no problem with that. It was routine, it was a daily thing. (Swarn Shoor)

> In those years, at the beginning especially, this name-calling didn't register. The teachers were great. The name-calling was predominant, but it was something we took for granted. (Kishore Taylor)

The overfocus on a stigmatised racial or ethnic identity acted, at least for some, as an identity obliterator, which tended to deprive these pupils of their identity's key element, their childhood ("you never thought you were a kid"), a feeling nurtured by the fact that many had busy parents working shifts in factories and also had to take care of their siblings, whether or not these were bussed as well. That denial of childhood ran parallel to a better known denial of individual identity, as Paul Willis had already shown: "racial identity for the [white] 'lads' supplants individual identity so that stories to friends concern not 'this kid' but 'this wog'",[25] and as 1990s writers on multiculturalism (such as Charles Taylor) would expose through their insistence on a "politics of recognition", wherein "the with-holding of recognition can be a form of oppression".[26]

It was therefore inevitable that from this some should have developed symptoms of anxiety, with some consequences on schooling performance: "Monday morning, my son would say, typical: 'I've got a temperature, I don't want to go to school', and it was true, he would develop a temperature because he was so afraid to go to school, at primary level" (Gurbax Sooch). This is echoed in this testimony by Shakila Maan, who herself was not bussed: "Sometimes as a kid I would sit in the public toilets to avoid school, and got sick in order to avoid school".

Exceptions to the overtly racist norm did exist. But sometimes they were couched in terms which reflected, in the conceptions of white suburban pupils, *both* a bluntly ethnocentric or racist worldview (probably echoing the parents') and an appreciation of common humanity as experienced in the day-to-day routine of a suburban school which happened to accom-modate some Asians. "Pakis are just the same as people",[27] one of the epi-graphs to this book, no doubt makes one smile, beyond being a reflection on the failure of bussing to nurture a genuine bridging capital between inner-city Asians and outer-city whites. What this innocently childish observation reveals is that learning about multiracial England for some suburban children did not go much beyond the dismayed realisation that Pakistani children indeed did not have three heads, three eyes, three arms.

Now, as far as the authentic exceptions go, it is probably impossible to connect the successful individual narratives of integration into dispersal schools with specific individual or family profiles. Two interviewees under-lined the gender gap in racist bullying, arguing that boys did get into trouble much more than girls. But it would be foolhardy to venture some explanations. One-tenth of the sample approximately has good memories of being bussed, and trying to account for this exceptionalism is too dif-ficult. Raza Khan, from Bradford, insists that he has "no memory of racial bullying. My brother was severely bullied but not myself." Chanan Panisar went straight into sixth form: she "was the only Asian in the class, outside the class we could get some bullying, especially on the bus, but in the school everybody was helpful". Similarly, Sunena Nath's memories are worth quoting at length: "I can't remember ever being bullied. We actually cried when we had to move to Villiers High School, in Southall. I have some very good memories of Northolt. I actually wanted to go to Walford High, not Villiers. I was invited at my friends' parties: Mark, Gillian, Donna, Vanessa; I had my first slow-dance with a white boy, Mark."[28] Unlike those of the majority of formerly bussed pupils, Sunena Nath's parents knew the education system and went to all parent–teacher meet-ings, but to hazard a connection between these two facts is risky. For one thing, Rita, Sunena's sister, has somewhat different memories to share. Lastly, it bears mentioning that some dispersed pupils established very friendly relationships with escort ladies, as is evidenced in Brett Bebber's article drawing from the 2005–6 oral history project at Gunnersbury Park Museum.[29]

Segregating not integrating

In 1964, just before dispersal was launched in Ealing, the *West Middlesex Gazette* published an article depicting the many extra-curricular activities in which Asian children were taking an active part at Beaconsfield Road Junior School. This involved the Southall festival of music, football, netball, high jump competition, swimming and also cricket. Headmistress E.A. Webster enthused about such dynamism and about how everybody together had met a challenge, despite the linguistic difficulties involved originally. This, she argued, "confounded the pessimists".[30]

As opposed to this, the bussed children in the years that followed missed out on a vast range of activities, so central to their mental development, sense of self-confidence and bridging social capital. Decades later, the segregation from such activities is recollected by a substantial proportion of bussed interviewees (one-third) with feelings of frustration, regret and bitterness verging on anger. To quote a few:

> The problem was you never did any extracurricular activity. None of the Asians were picked for plays for instance. You couldn't integrate. (Parminder Grewal)

> We never went to a birthday party. We never went to a friend's house until about the age of twelve. (Swarn Shoor)

> The problem with bussing was that we were gonna miss out on a lot of extracurricular activities, at ages nine to eleven. We missed out on music, sports, netball ... My parents would say you must stay and do the netball practice, so I had to come back alone, and that made me very vulnerable ... I never felt discriminated against by teachers, but we were never picked for music festivals, plays, etc. ... We were just the kids on the bus. (Viney Jung)

Conclusions from this are easy to draw. For Virendra Sharma, a Labour MP (Ealing Southall) who mobilised actively against bussing: "For the children, it was not integration, but rather disintegration, it was actually ghettoising the children". The raw racism experienced obviously compounded the feeling of segregation: "Their whole plan was failing really, since it wasn't integrating us at all; we grouped together to tough it out as an Asian group. Very soon we got into boxing, martial art classes, and our heroes would be Muhammad Ali and Bruce Lee" (Zulfi Hussain). The parallel lives that these children were living amounted to a process of separation implacably feeding upon itself: "If you're in the same class with Asians in a white school you develop natural friendships, so by default that segregation reinforced segregation" (Sukhwant Sandher). The learning of English, so central a justification in officialdom's discourse to legitimise bussing, was of little use here: "Once we spoke enough English, we arrived as a group of Asians in a white-dominated class; we also stuck to each other as Asians" (Sukhwant Sandher). Quite often, the few friendships that developed were with members of other immigrant groups, as was the case for Ravinder Vedi, bussed out to multiracial Acton: "The general atmosphere was that I felt stigmatised, you couldn't develop relationships with kids, I didn't have many friends outside the kids on the bus. There was, though, Melanie, who was Greek, and Helena, who was Ukrainian." Another key aspect for some was that they were bussed whereas their siblings were not, as was the case for Noorzaman Rashid and Minnie Dogra. Officially, LEAs made sure to avoid such separations, but in Bradford and Southall that promise was far from always kept. Noorzaman Rashid for one kept wondering, even at a young age, why he was made to travel far whereas his brothers and sisters went to school next to their house, a deeply confusing experience which kept him separate from his siblings during key formative years.

For bussed children and their families, the sense of difference and separateness from the norm as perceived by the autochthonous communities was acute from the very beginning of the day. In Bradford for instance, dispersal buses had big coloured signs at the front: a yellow ball, a red star, a blue square, which confirmed in the eyes of non-Asians that these children's parents were "thick" and could not read numbers, etc. Mollie, an English language tutor in Pakistani houses interviewed in Shabina Aslam's project, asked some pupils what schools they went to, whereupon most would answer "the ball bus" or "the star bus": "I can remember thinking 'That can't be right, they don't even know the name of the school that they go to' ... People had no concept of where they were in relation to the school, they only knew about the bus, really."[31] This person highlights the fact that these children were singled out at three strategic times of the day: first when arriving late (Shanaz: "Walking in late for assembly or for classes wasn't nice at all"),[32] then at mealtimes, when special dinners were given out (years before halal certification was part of the local political agenda), lastly when leaving early. Also, some school staff would awkwardly lay stress on these children's radical otherness: Labeeb, in Bradford, remembers that "five-ten minutes before the end of the class, the bus monitor would arrive and ask loudly, 'Can I have all the immigrants for the bus please?'" Much more subtle reminders of separateness were at play, though not all such reminders were ethnic or racial, or had directly to do with the policy of dispersal. Being from immigrant working-class families, some winced at certain questions from teachers: "I did suffer from being treated differently in many different ways. You know, like when the teacher would ask about what people did at Easter or summer I just couldn't participate, whereas most white kids go off on holiday, caravaning or camping, you know, I was at home really."[33]

Another salient aspect was that spatial arrangements within the schools as it were bodied forth the demarcation lines between autochthonous, "normal" white pupils and immigrant, allegedly non-Anglophone Asians. Aside from the number of children in temporary hutted accommodation (see Table 14), reception classes were often spatially organised in such a way as to exacerbate separateness. As a former pupil in a reception class, Sukhwant Sander recalls that his "class was at the very end of the corridor. So you could look down the corridor and see plenty of white kids. Our class was like segregated in this school, at one end, just next to the entrance, and next to the dinner hall, so we rarely ventured into this corridor full of white kids." A few hundred miles to the north, analogous feelings were expressed in Huddersfield for instance (Raj Samra). Interestingly, the spatial separateness was also felt among some school staff involved in the teaching to Asians. Vivienne Townsend, a teaching assistant in Acton in the 1970s, felt some symbolic boundaries in the staff room discussions, for her concerns were radically different from that of others: "I didn't feel we were really part of the staff. Even myself I felt quite differently from the other teaching assistants. When we started to speak about the Asians, we felt different, had other issues to deal with. There was an element of us being the poor relations in the school." That was played out in more pragmatic ways regarding the supply of schooling materials and equipment:

> I would have to ask for anything that we needed, whereas to other teaching assistants all this material would be dished out to them. I was only given an equal share when I started off as a teaching assistant working not with immigrants, so I identified straight away that I had been treated differently for several years. I generally got the feeling, at Acton, that the school saw all this as temporary, that bussed Asians were seen as temporary visitors, so let's not indulge them too much.

Teaching ghettoised children in some way produced subtle and real forms of ghettoisation among the staff themselves, which reinforced the need to deploy a missionary zeal in teaching those categories of children.

Back to neighbourhood schools

One recurrent aspect of interviews was the return to neighbourhood schools, after from two to seven or eight years of being dispersed. With hindsight the experience of being registered back in a local school is always regarded as the end of an anomaly. Nevertheless, at the time this change occurred, it was felt in varying ways, from the very positive to the quite negative. The end of racist bullying did not necessarily mean that it was all a smooth story, for certain adjustments were indeed hard to make.

Some felt the change as sheer shock, at least initially. Swarn Shoor went to Beaconsfield Road School in Southall, where he lived, after a few years in Acton. The Southall school was "really full of Asians, I was very surprised, at the start it really freaked me out. There were no other people to shout at, it was as if you went to a football game and the enemy crowd wasn't there, the other team had just disappeared!" Kishore Taylor also admits: "The fact that the school was now Asian-dominated, I found it difficult to adjust to that". In the eyes of most, though, this sea-change was soothing. Manjeet Singh went to Villiers High School (Southall) after years of being bussed: "Being with people of my own colour made a huge difference. At that time being in a majority helped." Some would wax lyrical about the back-home transfer: "Just to be able to go to a local school was so great. Coming to my local high school, which was around the corner for me, it was like the sun came out, the birds started singing. It was the best years of my life, absolutely!"[34] Through this change, others became aware of the Anglocentric, white-dominated ethos and curriculum that was prevailing in schools, and gleaned a political knowledge from this realisation which soon enough came to be translated into ethnic pride and activist politics. A few years before he became a member of the Asian Youth Movement, a Pakistani Bradfordian recollects: "It really was driven home to me then what it was all about. I'd been confined in an all-white school, where white culture, white society was being put on to me. At this school I could see that there was a lot more about school than just learning what white people wanted to teach you about white culture, white society."[35] One interviewee who had fitted happily into the mould during the years of bussing regarded the transfer to Southall with an outsider's perspective: "In Villiers High School I realised they loved being Asian. I realised you could just be Indian and love it. My teachers were also very positive" (Sunena Nath).

In terms of educational expectations, the transfer was not always a smooth passage, for some pupils who had been in reception or remedial classes could not cope with the demands of high school whereas others who had done well in such classes found that the expectations in neighbourhood schools were far too low. Reading some interviews, one sometimes feels that the transfer was between underperformance and boredom, beyond of course the reassurance that racist bullying at school was henceforth a thing of the past. Raj Samra from Huddersfield argues that "When

I arrived in high school, [...] my education had suffered a huge deal. The first time I was handed a paper, I had never seen so many red marks in my life, it showed I had got second-rate education and couldn't cope with the new expectations from school." Kishore Taylor's experience in Southall could not be more different: "I went to a high school in Southall. It was a massive change. It was in the first and second years of high school that I was wasting my time, really, doing stuff that I could almost do with my eyes closed."

Seeming compliance, calculated conformity

At the most empirical and individual level, some children were taught survival strategies to endure racism: "I grew up in a fairly political household. I grew to be aware of racism at a young age. The idea from my parents was that if people are racist you know better than them; there wasn't the West Indian idea of fighting back" (Viney Jung). Yet coping strategies were hard to apply in minority situations far from the neighbourhood: "Our parents would always say: stay out of trouble, ignore them, stay out of their way. But there were just ten Asians, it was impossible to stay out of their way, really" (Balvinder Vedhany). Others were advised to resort to more assertive ways of being streetwise, such as Zulfin Hussain in Bradford: "My parents insisted a great deal on 'education, education, education' but it was also about 'Never start a fight but make sure you finish it'".

However anecdotal or trivial they might be, these memories serve as illustrations of the *seeming* compliance of subordinate groups in history. James C. Scott in *Weapons of the Weak: Everyday Forms of Peasant Resistance* posits that "deference and conformity, though rarely cringing, continue to be the public posture of the poor. For all that, however, one can clearly make out backstage a continuous testing of limits. At the very least, one can say that there is much more here than simply consent, resignation, and deference."[36] With two further conditions of vulnerability in mind (the young age of the children and the immigrant status of the majority of Asians), general statements such as Scott's do make for compelling reading in order to make sense of certain implicitly oppositional or back-door tactics against dispersal.

One such strategy consisted in instrumentalising, whether deliberately or not, the bureaucratic ethos of ignorance of certain cultural features shared by immigrants. Sukhwant Sandher remembers:

My brother wasn't bussed and my cousin, to avoid bussing, pretended he was my brother's brother, so that he could go to Beaconsfield Road School, the school just around the corner for us. To pretend they were brothers they used the name "Singh", and everybody was "Singh" anyhow ... At the same time they were like brothers, because the concept of "extended family", among the Indian diaspora in England, was a reality. We didn't even use "cousins" ourselves, all of us in the extended family were raised as brothers, actually.[37]

There was a great deal of political agency deployed in remaining faithful to the Indian diaspora's extensive meaning of "brother" regardless of the authority's definition of the term. This was a "weapon of the weak" of a spontaneous kind whose efficacy lay in the fact that it would remain undetected by Ealing borough.

Others were more radical and had further-reaching consequences. Barrington Moore, in *Injustice: The Social Bases of Obedience and Revolt*, states that "throughout the centuries one of the common man's most frequent and effective responses to oppression has been *flight*".[38] Admittedly, "oppression" (in the situations that Moore or Scott both analyse, some of which are extreme)[39] is at best an exaggeration when applied to dispersal, introduced in the British contemporary democratic context. Still, it is noteworthy that, in certain instances, dispersal was dodged by *not* sending children to school. This type of silent resistance as apparent compliance clashed with the central focus on education among Asian parents but simultaneously chimed with some northern Pakistan cultural features, particularly but not only relative to female education.

One such case of "flight from school" was reported in 1972 in the town of Dewsbury, ten miles to the south-east of Bradford. In the district of Savile Town, a site of Asian clustering, the local authorities introduced a measure of dispersal to "desegregate" the area, which some Pakistanis disagreed with. But, to borrow Albert Hirschmann's classic triad ("exit", "voice", "loyalty"), instead of using "voice", these few families used "exit" until the schooling authorities and *The Guardian* developed an interest in the anomaly: "Last September the twelve children were due to go by bus to other schools in the town, but their parents objected and kept the children at home". Understandably, councillor Fred Fox, in charge of schooling locally, admitted to being fairly "annoyed" by the news, since "a year is a long time to go without school".[40] If such developments could occur in Dewsbury in 1972 and escape the notice of authorities for a full year, it is obvious they must have happened in Bradford a few years earlier, where the dispersal apparatus was still chaotic, when the demographic situation wrought real pressure on the bureaucracy, and when not all Asian parents were nourishing the pipe-dream that their children would become doctors or lawyers. This is undoubtedly also how the salient imbalance between female and male pupils in Bradford (with an approximately one to three ratio) must be read. As in the confusion over the name "Singh" above, these strategies of avoidance were silent, generated a breakdown of the system (at least for the families concerned) and drew heavily from Indian subcontinent cultural features brought along during the act of immigration, as well as from shirking tactics often learnt the hard way under colonial rule.[41]

One last illustration is not about compliance *per se* but rather about individual resistance which went largely unreported and therefore confirmed the general impression of community compliance and Asians keeping a low profile. Such resistance, nevertheless, struck at the dispersal system by directly challenging its legitimacy and actual arbitrariness. Two examples will suffice, one drawn from Blackburn, the other from Southall.

In the Lancashire town, one Mudassir H. Khan, a Delhi-raised Muslim, was told that his daughter Shanahz would have to travel a quarter of a mile away to school when in fact there were places available in St Thomas's School, just across the road from the Khans' house. This was owing to the "new policy of the education authorities".[42] Mr Khan met repeatedly with the education officer to challenge the decision. What follows is a reproduction of their first verbal exchange, and of the events that unfolded:

> "This way immigrant children will be able to learn the English language properly".
> I had to laugh and said: "I take it then that you think my daughter *doesn't* speak English".
> A blank expression crossed his face.
> "By the way, my wife is English and we speak English in our house".
> He insisted that my daughter would have to go to Scotland Road School, as nothing more could be done.
> In the end I got up saying, "Oh no mister, on no account can I take the risk of sending my child so far away, when there is already an adequate school on Lambeth Street. I'd rather keep her at home and teach her myself". I was determined to send Shanahz to Saint Thomas's school.
> After a week I received a letter from the education office stating that there was a place for Shanahz in Saint Thomas's school, so would I get in touch with the head-teacher there.
> She very soon became a very popular child there, and was "superstar" of the Christmas drama.[43]

An analogous, if more painful, case occurred in the borough of Ealing in 1969–70. One Punjabi immigrant living in Southall, Jaswinder Sidhu, refused the bussing of his five-year-old son Rajan to Perivale. This man was profoundly irked that "white parents only had to take their children to the local school head teacher, to register their children for the coming year, whereas Asians had to go to the Ealing Education Department".[44] He obdurately refused his son's dispersal, withdrew him from school for a full six months, went alone on hunger strike at Southall Town Hall for three days, despite the threats of the NF. Ultimately, he did get his son registered at the local school by Ealing Education Authority. He vindicates his hunger strike decades later by claiming: "I felt that the way I was treated in this country was not acceptable, I didn't want my sons to be treated the same, that's all."

Both anecdotes reveal that single individuals can successfully challenge the machinery of state authority when the authority appears unsure about the legitimacy of the policy it enforces. Both Blackburn and Ealing authorities gave in to these fathers' demands without displaying much of a resistance, especially in the case of Blackburn. Both Mudassir Khan and Jaswinder Sidhu were spurred on by individual interests relating to their children's well-being, and neither tried to initiate or even envisaged initiating a collective movement against dispersal. Mr Sidhu was also quite adept at staging his own resistance (see Figure 17). Both were Asian immigrants simultaneously demanding to be treated equally and parent consumers wishing to enjoy parental choice on the English education market. Lastly and importantly, neither of the two fitted the typically subaltern profile of the Asian immigrant: Sidhu's background was middle-class Punjabi with a few relatives who were general practitioners, whilst Khan was married to a white English woman, his daughter was Anglophone and he was one of the first Asian immigrants to have settled in that part of Lancashire back in 1956. Obliquely then, these somewhat atypical stories shed light on the general low profile kept by the mass of migrant workers. But ultimately though, it is fundamental to comprehend the way these instances are part and parcel of a multi-layered narrative of resistance against bussing, with actors not sharing the same goals, not opting for the same tactics, but eventually contributing to a weakening of a policy they dismiss as unfair, however utilitarian their motives may look. James C. Scott is once again useful here, when he exposes the "classic dichotomy between principled, selfless acts of resistance with revolutionary consequences and token, epiphenomenal activities which are individual and often opportunistic or indulgent, and have no revolutionary consequences, implying as they often do an accommodation with the system of domination".[45] To him, this dichotomy appears as "misleading, sterile, and sociologically naive".[46] He shrewdly depicts the hazardous legibility of individual choices among members of subordinate classes:

> The Southeast Asian peasant who hid his rice and possessions from the tax collector may have been protesting high taxes, but he was just as surely seeing to it that his family would have enough rice until the next harvest. The peasant conscript who deserted the army may have been a war resister, but he was just as surely saving his own skin by fleeing the front. Which of

Figure 17: "Defiant Father Reports Case to Race Board", *Southall Gazette*, 30 January 1970 (Jaswinder Sidhu)

these inextricably fused motives are we to take as paramount? Even if we *were* able to ask the actors in question, and even if they could reply candidly, it is not at all clear that they would be able to make a clear determination.[47]

Despite the obvious contrasts in the degrees of "oppression", the Khans or Sidhus who wouldn't send their children to further away schools in Blackburn and Ealing were both demanding the best for their children and making a principled statement as citizens and ratepayers striking out for equal treatment.

Toughing it out

With hindsight, about half of the interviewees regard the experience of bussing as not altogether negative. This, of course, cannot be viewed as a representative viewpoint, since most interviewees were upwardly mobile Asians, the low-hanging fruits of dispersal referred to above. The two positive aspects depicted are the mixing with non-Asian people when young and, above all, the resilience learnt the hard way by toughing it out when faced with racist bullying. Swarn Shoor encapsulates all this when saying: "We adapted much quicker, that's true. We went to uni, we were able to integrate more easily, it wasn't only negative. We toughened up at a very early age." Sukhwant Sandher also says: "I did find myself very early in an adult situation. Bussing reinforced this in a way. At the same time, the joke is almost that if it hadn't been for bussing I wouldn't have met any white kid, really." Some develop the argument that the hate-filled, dog-eat-dog atmosphere of the dispersal school playgrounds was excellent training for a ruthless job-market. Zulfi Hussain, who became a successful businessman in Bradford and Leeds, argues:

> I personally took it as you're either a victim or you're a survivor. Many of my friends and I thought we will definitely survive this. After Eccleshill, it was a real relief, everything was better than that; even when it was tough, it wasn't as tough as Eccleshill, so we coped with pretty much everything. Actually being bussed to that place has produced some of the most successful Asian entrepreneurs in Yorkshire. Very business-minded people, who are really resilient.

The irony of bussing would be, at least for these people, that the short-term segregation and stigmatisation of Asians in schools almost experienced as danger zones seem to have had long-term beneficial effects in terms of their integration into the job market. For them, it was not so much that they developed a formal knowledge of entrepreneurship as that they developed a specific mindset making them fitter to compete in a violently competitive capitalist market. This meant being able to translate race-motivated physical, verbal or symbolical violence into informal qualities of resilience and do-it-alone resourcefulness in which the question of race is irrelevant. This long-term symbolic digestion of occasionally traumatic events was also a process of deracialisation. Lastly, it was in people like Zulfi Hussain that bitterness and anger were transcended. Like Shabina Aslam in Bradford, these interviewees were much more likely than others to have come to terms with their past: she for instance does not feel any anger, simply acknowledging that "it is part of our political history, really".[48]

Benefit and disturbance of hindsight

Hindsight informs much of this chapter, for instance when considering the extent to which being bussed was a positive or negative experience. Although many of the memories shared by interviewees and reproduced in these pages are deeply individual – however much they may conform to a specific group experience in a given time and space – it must be borne in mind how in the crystallisation of memory itself it is now generally recognised, since Maurice Halbwachs's foundational work, that "it is in society that people normally acquire their memories. It is also in society that they recall, recognise, and localise their memories".[49] As an analyst of collective psychology, Halbwachs studied the development of collective memory in intermediary groups (family, social class, religious groups), to whom here ethnic minorities might be added.[50] He also lays stress on the way memory is an ever-shifting reality being reconfigured through time and by language.

For some interviewees, memories of being bussed are an ongoing process of meaning-making through time. Had they been contacted a few years earlier, certain answers, or a certain twist or shape given to answers, would unquestionably have been different. The immediate context of the populist upsurge post-Brexit, which led to the election of Donald Trump in the United States, growing Islamophobia and the polemics around the crisis of migrants in Europe have all exerted an influence on the individual shaping of recollections. Some were actually quick to evince this link. Ravinder Vedi refers to a "delayed outrage" whereby being interviewed about bussing coincided with recent news:

> I didn't think about all this until quite recently. There was a brief welcome to Britain at the very beginning and then many things made you feel unwelcome. You also understand racism quite quickly as a child. One other point is Brexit, which exacerbated certain tensions and made me think about the link between past and present. Just when you think things are progressing they no longer are; I never thought it would be that horrendous, this atmosphere.

Anjuna Kalsi interweaves her own traumatic memories of racism as a bussed student some decades back with her children's current situation at a time of growing tensions for ethnic-minority pupils, Muslims or not: "Post-Brexit, I really fear for my kids, they go to a Catholic school in Hillingdon. And because they do some physical training and fire alarm training, one was reported as an alleged Jihadi, although we are all Hindus. This racism is geared towards Asian males rather than females."

As bussing was being phased out in Southall and Bradford, Polish poet Czeslaw Milosz stated in his Nobel prize lecture (1980) that "it is possible that there is no other memory than the memory of wounds". Some of these wounds in the present case were so profound and felt at such a young age that they stifled some interviewees into memory-aphasia for years: "It's actually only now that I start talking about it ... But I never got any hatred from that, because I got involved in politics with Southall Black Sisters." Others, without highlighting the wounds of the past, do insist on the profound influence bussing has had on their identity: "It influenced a lot my personality. I'm very independent, I'm not really a mixer, I like standing back from a crowd. Also, if I have to get into a fistfight, I'll do it no problem" (Manjeet Singh, female interviewee).

Recurrently, interviewees recount their more or less recent understanding of the politics of bussing showing the way in which both they and their parents were unaware of the political and racial dynamics around dispersal. This went as far as to lack a word to refer to the experience of dispersal. Raj Bamrah acknowledges that "I don't know what the term 'bussing' actually means. All it was for us was we were going to school."[51] In much the same way, Kishore Taylor states that "it all felt like the norm. It was only in recent years that I realised the real reasons for all this." Some parents thought their children were bussed because they had registered them fairly late in the year, and there was no place available. Small wonder then that some interviewees were shocked upon discovering that the real reason why they were bussed was that they were immigrant children, not because of a lack of place, although it did become this at a late stage in Southall. There was an awkwardness in the fact that they had many vital pieces of information to communicate around dispersal without being aware themselves of the primarily racial reasons why they – or their siblings – had been bussed in the first place.

Political training and being involved in associations or participating in debates could sometimes serve as an eye-opener about the exceptional experience that bussing actually constituted: "The reason why we didn't think about it was because it was our normal lives. It was only years later, as a young adult, that I was invited to discuss this with Balraj Purewal, at Roehampton University. Talking about all this to others in the early 1980s made me realise this was indeed a special thing, because before that time this was my normality. That day in Roehampton was important since it all gained currency for me" (Sukhwant Sandher). It behoves cultural and memory entrepreneurs like Balraj Purewal in Southall or Billy Dosangh in the West Midlands[52] to facilitate a reclaiming of collective memory through community projects which are spearheaded by (former) activists and artists, and that often depend on the cash cow of national lottery funds. This in itself may be seen either as a continuation of multicultural and emancipatory politics through the back door at a time when multi-culturalism has become a boo word, or as a form of state control where national lottery money implies that public authorities enjoy the ultimate financial whip-hand on such cultural and memory projects. At a time when governments and media pressure generate suspicion of BAME communities through a revamping of assimilationist politics, this is a symbolic and historical contested terrain which is all the more crucial as it is interspersed with educational concerns at the heart of austerity agendas and with polemics on "parallel lives", whatever that means.

Notes

1 Interview (Southall), 19.10.2016.
2 Interview (Southall), 16.9.2015.
3 Interview (Huddersfield), 27.4.2016.
4 Also, quantitatively and qualitatively, these testimonies are reinforced by the Gunnersbury Park oral history project of 2005–6 (see Brett Bebber's article), by Shabina Aslam's analogous project in Bradford and by the fieldwork conducted by Brenda Mary Thomson for her PhD dissertation.
5 See Charles W. Mills, *The Sociological Imagination*, Oxford: Oxford University Press, 2000 [1959], p. 194.
6 Interview, 3.2.2016.
7 Interview (Southall), 19.8.2015.
8 Interview, 10.10.2015.
9 Interview (Southall), 19.10.2016.
10 Interview (Southall), 19.10.2016.
11 On these points, see Thomson, *Asian-named Minority Groups*, pp. 207–11.
12 Ealing archives, Nigel Spearing paper, Ealing CRC newsletter, 6.1972; Ealing CRC Annual Report, 1973–74. See also *Middlesex County Times (Southall Edition)*, 12.5.1973, evidence given by Arthur Bottomley, a member of the Select Committee.
13 See for instance Julien Talpin's work on Los Angeles: *Community Organizing: de l'émeute à l'alliance des classes populaires aux Etats-Unis*, Paris: Raisons d'Agir, 2016.
14 See Kogan, *Dispersal in the Ealing Local Education Authority*, p. 17.

15 The four known TV clips on dispersal are: ITN, "Colour in Schools" (8.11.1965); ITN, "Ealing School Bussing Problem" (27.3.1972); BBC, "Panorama" (14.8.1972); BBC, "News: School Bussing in Ealing" (9.9.1975).

16 Of course the question of permission to shoot within the school had to be raised.

17 CRE, *Learning in Terror*, p. 3.

18 In Amrit Wilson, *Finding a Voice: Asian Women in Britain*, London: Virago, 1978, p. 87.

19 Interview (Southall), 19.10.2016.

20 Ramamurthy, *Black Star*, p. 19.

21 Interview (Southall), 25.2.2016.

22 Kogan, *Dispersal in the Ealing Local Education Authority*, pp. 13–15. Not all references to Ealing dispersal schools are (very) positive, just as not all references to Southall schools are (very) negative.

23 Thomson, *Asian-named Minority Groups*, p. 231.

24 Interview (Bradford), 24.4.2017.

25 See Willis, *Learning to Labour*, p. 48.

26 Charles Taylor, *Multiculturalism and the Politics of Recognition*, Princeton, NJ: Princeton University Press, 1992, p. 36.

27 Thomson, *Asian-named Minority Groups*, p. 221.

28 Interview (Southall), 19.10.2016.

29 See Bebber, "'We Were Just Unwanted'", pp. 648–9.

30 *The West Middlesex Gazette*, 28.3.1964.

31 See https://soundcloud.com/user-358813512 (last accessed 19.6.2018).

32 https://soundcloud.com/user-358813512 (last accessed 19.6.2018).

33 Bradford archives, oral history collection, C0055.

34 See Bebber, "'We Were Just Unwanted'", p. 649.

35 Bradford archives, oral history collection, C0055.

36 Scott, *Weapons of the Weak*, p. 273.

37 Interview (Southall), 19.10.2016.

38 Barrington Moore, *Injustice: The Social Bases of Obedience and Revolt*, New York: Random House, 1978, p. 125.

39 Moore, for instance, analyses the oppression of untouchables in India and the concentration camps under Nazi rule.

40 *Guardian*, 10.8.1972.

41 The most notorious of these tactics was income-tax avoidance, which was often widespread among Asians. On this point, see Rose (ed.), *Colour and Citizenship*, pp. 446–7.

42 Mudassir H. Khan, *Still Here, After over Fifty Wonderful Years*, Blackburn: Cremer Press, 2008, p. 185.

43 *Ibid.*, pp. 186–7.

44 Interview (High Wycombe), 19.10.2016.

45 Scott, *Weapons of the Weak*, p. 292.

46 *Ibid.*, p. 295.

47 *Ibid.*, p. 291.

48 See www.bussingout.co.uk/audio.php (last accessed 19.6.2018).

49 Maurice Halbwachs, *On Collective Memory*, Chicago: University of Chicago Press, 1992 [1925], p. 38.

50 Halbwachs does touch upon this when considering the question of national memory and how non-nationals conform, or not, to this. See *ibid.*, p. 176.

51 See Bebber, "'We Were Just Unwanted'", p. 645.

52 Balraj Purewal ran two Southall projects on the history of the IWA and on the Southall Youth Movement, of which he was a key founding member. See respectively www.iwasouthall.org.uk and http://southall-inspired.com/wp-content/uploads/2014/07/Southall-Booklet-FINAL.pdf (last accessed 19.6.2018); Billy Dosanjh is an artist and documentary maker, who directed *Year Zero: Black Country* (2014), about New Commonwealth immigrants in Smethwick industries. B. Purewal's projects got national lottery financing; Billy Dosanjh's film did not, but gained in visibility via events which were partly financed by the national lottery (such as Black Country Echoes festival of 2014).

Conclusion

That the end of bussing in the years 1980–81 coincided with a multicultural U-turn in approaches to education and with the emergence of new demographic dynamics in inner-city schools is fully evidenced in Bradford's case. In 1982, a local memorandum stated that the West Yorkshire city had "a multi-racial and multi-cultural population and ... all sections of the community have an equal right to the maintenance of their distinctive identities and loyalties of culture, language, religion and custom". Race Awareness Training for teachers was also introduced.[1] Ethnic minorities, spurred by the hard-won victory against bussing, were articulating more and more specific demands. The next year, ethnic-minority parents asked for a greater accommodation of religious differences, to which the Bradford LEA responded with the publication of "Agreed Syllabus 1983: Religious Education for Living in Today's World". Some Muslim associations made an official bid to gain control of six schools, a move which the Asian Youth Movement opposed on the grounds that it would only whet racialist feelings.[2] Tellingly, the end of dispersal ushered in a new era when religion – with a special focus on Islam – emerged as a key element in debates on integration, multiculturalism and citizenship. This evolution ought to be considered in the broader perspective of the last decade of the Cold War and the emergence of a new global enemy called Islamism, Jihadism, Muslim extremism and so forth, as was manifested by the publication of Edward Said's *Covering Islam* on the American media coverage of the Iranian revolution crisis.

In terms of local demographic dynamics the changes in Southall and Bradford were quite sweeping. Dispersal had managed to maintain some artificial balance but no sooner was bussing terminated than Bradford saw a swift increase in the number of schools that were 90 per cent Asian, the most striking case being Drummond School in Manningham. There, Ray Honeyford had taken over as headteacher in 1980, just as dispersal was being jettisoned: that year the proportion of Asians (nearly all Muslims) in the school was 49 per cent, then it became 65 per cent in September

1981, 74 per cent in September 1982, 87 per cent in September 1983, and 95 per cent when Honeyford was forced into early retirement in December 1985, after a severe political crisis which had made him the *bête noire* of the anti-racist left and a national martyr in the eyes of the assimilationist right.[3] By then, throughout the city, there were at least nineteen schools with over 70 per cent of pupils from an ethnic minority.[4] A few miles to the south, in Dewsbury, Headfield School had become 85 per cent Asian in 1987. This year, some white parents averse to having their children schooled at Headfield created their own alternative school above the pub owned by one of them, Eric Haley. This shortly became another *cause célèbre* in the wake of the Honeyford affair. Ironically, Dewsbury was the town where, fifteen years earlier, some recalcitrant Asian parents had decided not to send their children to faraway schools in a context of dispersal. By 1987, the soaring number of Asian children in the Savile Town neighbourhood had made some white parents express their disagreement by opting for "leave" but this time around in a vociferous way.

Evidence-based knowledge versus state preconceptions

Few policies better epitomise the role of preconceptions in policy-making than dispersal. Already by the 1960s some argued that the existence of dispersal in an LEA was no pragmatic barometer of integration and "racial harmony", to use the period's parlance. Joan Lester, Labour MP for Eton and Slough, drew the following contrast: "In Wolverhampton there is dispersal and race relations are poor; in Slough there is no dispersal, the immigrant population is six per cent higher than Wolverhampton and race relations are far better in Slough than in Wolverhampton".[5] She went on to notice that because dispersal had been justified on the basis of better race relations one would expect real evidence of this. Likewise, the Select Committee on Race Relations and Immigration asked time and again for thorough research to be carried out into it.[6] One Midlands respondent wondered: was it so clear that the immigrant children gained linguistically from being dispersed? Did they really play with English children in the playgrounds? Or did they keep apart?[7] Similarly, as tensions were running high around bussing in Bradford, the *Telegraph & Argus* published an article entitled "Answers We Must Know", which regretted: "The only way the arguments for or against bussing can be tested is on the basis of facts. In practice, the council has no objective evidence in support of bussing, and its opponents have no objective evidence against it."[8]

Although the point made here is crucial, the truth is that there was already by the early 1960s a body of social-science research indicating that the political framework of one-way dispersal in England was itself flawed and that for it to prove successful in integrating children was a very hard bet. We have seen already that the assimilationist rationale behind it rested on the contact hypothesis, hammered time and again by local and national authorities. What was never seriously discussed, at least among policy-makers of both parties, were the conditions for the contact hypothesis to generate a substantial bridging capital conducive to integration.

Gordon Allport's *The Nature of Prejudice* (1954) is one of the largest-selling classics in the social sciences,[9] and was available in all good academic libraries across Britain when Edward Boyle visited Southall's Beaconsfield School. In it one finds clearly articulated socio-psychological provisos that can make contact fail or succeed. Four characteristics of the contact situation are deemed of vital importance. According to experiments conducted, prejudice is lessened when the two groups coming into contact "possess equal status in the situation; seek common goals; are co-operatively dependent on each other; interact with the positive support of authorities, laws or customs".[10] Needless to say, the first three conditions were utterly lacking in dispersal school interactions between white and immigrant children. At no point was this ever raised in discussions around the introduction and the legitimisation of English bussing, despite, again, the accessibility of Allport's seminal work, or the body of important research which drew extensively from Allport (such as work by Thomas Pettigrew).

Every page in Brenda Mary Thomson's detailed analysis of one Bradford inner-city school in contrast to one outer-city school (which accommodated bussed pupils) confirms this dichotomy: with poorer infrastructures overall, the Asian children in the inner-city school mixed much more freely with the substantial number of white pupils still there than those who were transplanted to the further-away suburban school, in which their integration faced all sorts of perceived or unperceived psychological, linguistic or administrative barriers.[11]

In fact, the "state simplifications" at the root of dispersal operated as though under a "spotless sky of cultures" (*le ciel pur des cultures*), to borrow Abdelmalek Sayad's phrase used to criticise the teaching of Arabic or Portuguese through flawed multicultural initiatives in French schools. Sayad was violently critical of such language teaching because it only reinforced racial stereotypes regarding ghettoised children who were taught ghetto languages, unlike, say, English, German or Spanish taught to all children: "It's as though all this were taking place under a spotless sky, under a sky where all languages, all cultures, all schools and all pedagogic systems were on an equal footing".[12] Although the policies (assimilationist dispersal versus vaguely multicultural initiatives) and the countries (England, France) involved were different, what needs to be

comprehended is that in both instances some state simplifications introduced failing systems without taking into account, let alone challenging,
the deep-seated stereotypes and prejudices at play abroad, which probably
testified to the degree of French and British administrative delusion about
their national sense of tolerance in history. This cavalier disregard had, in
the case of English bussing, some pragmatic, hard-felt consequences in the
form of racist bullying, itself the negation of the four conditions cited
above from Gordon Allport.

The mind-forged ghetto

Sloppy use of the word "ghetto" polluted British debates on integration in
the 1960s as it does today. It would be a mistake to believe that the right
has a monopoly over such usages, as is shown in John Pilger's documentary
made in 1974, *One British Family*.[13] *The Times*, in its influential series of
articles entitled "The Dark Million", wrote that "in some places, notably
Southall, it is too late to prevent a ghetto forming", six months before the
publication of circular 7/65.[14] *The Times*, as is so often the case in debates
about "ghettos" all across the political spectrum, never bothered actually
to make it clear what exactly they meant by this reference.

All too often, the general effect (or goal) has been to trigger moral
panics about ethnic minorities or immigration without borrowing seriously from the vast body of literature available on the word, most of it
coming from the United States. Indeed, absent from debates on Southall's
or Bradford's alleged ghettos are discussions on Louis Wirth (*The Ghetto*,
1928), Gunnar Myrdal (*An American Dilemma*, 1944), Horace Cayton and
St Clair Drake (the authors of *Black Metropolis*, 1945), Kenneth Clarke
(*Dark Ghetto*, 1965) or William Julius Wilson who, admittedly, was to
publish his research years after English bussing was introduced.[15] Although
drawing comparison between Bradford and Newark, or Chicago's south
side and Southall, is like comparing urban apples and oranges,[16] such readings challenge us to make sense of British situations. Because race is primarily a social construct, many of the meanings and connotations of
"ghetto" as applied to Manningham (Bradford) or Southall hinge on
whether "ghetto" is an attributed, stigmatising label from the outside or a
chosen, fully assumed one from the inside. In this sense, "ghetto" as a
"minoritized space"[17] within whose bounds a particular category of people
resides runs parallel with John Rex's distinction between "attributed ethnicity" (what minorities are called in public debate) and "chosen ethnicity"
(what minorities call themselves).[18] "Ghetto" is therefore a constantly contested terrain and urban metaphor of out-group clustering. Or, in Southall's case, the difference is between *The Times*'s depiction above and the

question defiantly asked by Farukh Dhondy in 1982, "Who is afraid of ghetto schools?" In both instances the question of government and image control is key, whether the ghetto is apprehended in negative terms as a "powerless colony" (Kenneth Clark) run by outside forces or as a "culturally vibrant place" such as was the case for Chicago's Bronzeville and Harlem in the 1940s and 1950s. The latter also typifies conflicting visions even within the ghetto, which are contested not only from the outside but also from within: just as Harlem was hailed as the Mecca of Black America by some ethnic entrepreneurs, the area was already, by the 1950s, plagued by drug problems that were tragically weakening the neighbourhood's social fabric.[19] In the same way, just as it was a site of effective Asian solidarity and cultural agency, Southall was also experiencing social, economic and health issues which naturally turned it into a welfare priority area. What this also illustrates is that, no matter how bonded together they may be by external prejudice, real or so-called ghetto-dwellers experience their daily lives in their community in very distinct ways, which are made all the more complex by inner geographical disparities *within* the "ghetto", as is witnessed by the difference between "old Southall" and "new Southall", with its rows of suburban-looking detached or semi-detached houses.

Public debate being delineated by outside forces, the pressure to manage the image control of the "ghetto" is huge, thereby leading cultural and political entrepreneurs locally to use pink rather than black when painting the area in broad strokes. Edward Boyle himself ruefully noted that in a place like Southall a 90 per cent coloured school would always be branded as a deprived school, whatever actually happened in it.[20] It was notably in order to debunk the representational vicious circle of the mind-forged ghetto that Nicholas Deakin and Brian Cohen promoted voluntary housing dispersal, which was discussed in the Introduction to this book: "The identification in the minds of the white majority between colour, poor housing conditions and a squalid environment is constantly reinforced as long as concentration in the inner city persists and even increases".[21] But beyond the stereotype-ridden images of ghetto schools there is the self-evident truth, which was not really publically acknowledged until the mid-1970s at least, that Asians in Southall and Bradford schools were broadly safe from bullying and harm in their respective "comfort zones", a point already made by Rex and Moore in their study of Sparkbrook (Birmingham), where the existence of a colony of immigrant groups was seen as a way of preventing a decline into a "state of complete demoralisation and anomie".[22]

Because circumstances were such that they reinforced ethnic-minority vulnerability and further entrenched their subordinate status, to perpetuate dispersal for years could only be counter-productive, although in hindsight many interviewees underline some positive elements about bussing, such as "toughing it out" and gaining some white acquaintances. The broad evolution of this debate runs parallel with a great thinker's intellectual itinerary in the field of education, W.E.B. Du Bois. Himself a lifelong advocate of educational integration, Du Bois started to promote voluntary separation for African-Americans upon the realisation that these were denied any form of real equality under the terms of integration.[23] That fact in Du Bois's intellectual evolution is too often neglected, and it surely helps to make sense of the debate on dispersal in England, albeit obliquely.[24]

Lastly, it seems to me that the mind-numbing recurrence of references to "ghetto" and Jim-Crow-style "segregation" in the heart of England's urban spaces evidences some contradictory features in the dominant mindset among British policy-makers and media commentators. First, there was the realisation that, as a perceived enclave of Asianness a few miles to the west of Paddington Station, Southall was a site of "'embattled Englishness'" and epitomised "a national identity configured as white, decent, orderly, and threatened", to quote Elizabeth Buettner.[25] Southall (like Bradford or some Birmingham neighbourhoods) was repugnant to a dominant majority who envisaged its national identity as "white", whiteness being imbued with a postcolonial, ethnocentric dimension associated with nostalgic reveries of being the "master race". Although Boyle was no Powell, it is with all this in mind that his 1963 speech to the Commons ought to be read: "I must regretfully tell the House that one school, Beaconsfield Road School, must be regarded now as irretrievably an immigrant school. The important thing to do is to prevent this happening elsewhere."

But very ambivalently, another reading of this speech is just as valid. For it primarily evinces a self-portrait of Britain/England as being a benevolent, tolerant nation that cannot cope with the mere idea of having witnessed the formation of a "ghetto" of sorts without doing anything about it. As has been underlined by scholars like Elizabeth Buettner, Bill Schwarz and Sonya Rose,[26] Britain/England saw itself as primarily white but, just as importantly, also as inherently tolerant. Jordanna Bailkin makes the important point that the largely US-financed Institute of Race Relations in London was, until the late 1950s, solely preoccupied with racial issues in "Alabama and South-Africa", so confident were the British of their proverbial tolerance and that "such problems would never come here".[27] This self-image of tolerance had been pitted, through history, against Nazi Germany during the Second World War but, in later decades, against Jim Crow or South African Apartheid. And it is against this self-definition as a model of liberal tolerance that headlines conflating "Smethwick", "Birmingham", "Bradford" and on the other hand "Mississippi" and "Alabama" must be read. That the urban apples of Southall (as a "ghetto" resulting mostly from ethnic clustering) had nothing to do with the urban oranges of Jim Crow (based on restrictive covenants and a systematic, historically rooted form of segregation from above) probably speaks volumes about Britain's postwar and postcolonial crises of identity.

"What kind of society do you want?"

Let me finish by saying that the debate on the desirability of policies such as dispersal is disturbingly complex and it verges on aporia. On the one hand, as Michael Merry makes clear, "Integration is not a proxy for justice. Both equality and citizenship can be cultivated and maintained under conditions of segregation", all the more so as voluntary separation "may be more likely to provide the resources necessary for self-respect for members of stigmatised minority groups",[28] a statement which chimes with many of the narratives of bullying that abound in the previous chapter. Clearly, and despite the integrationist slant in British public policies since around 2000, to have received an education in a 90 per cent Asian school does not in itself preclude integration into a mixed job market at all, and does not hamper citizenship or weaken the sense of belonging to a nation. On the other hand, there is another body of research on Northern Ireland, Nigeria, Kashmir and the Balkans which indicates that voluntary separation may reinforce ethnocentric distancing and stereotyping of outsiders.[29] Therefore, whilst dispersal was an initiative fraught with shortcomings, it is uncertain whether separation based on ethnic clustering in distinct urban geographies is itself desirable, once the smokescreens around "parallel lives" have been removed.

When Edward Boyle visited Southall in 1963, he participated in a debate on segregation and integration and was rebutted by a woman who, *vis-à-vis* the idea of segregation which was anathema to the minister, opposed dispersal by highlighting double standards in educational terms, on the grounds that England already had education segregation in the form of "Roman Catholic and private schools" for example. To her the DES's trumpeted ideal of integration stumbled against plain equality. The Eton- and Oxford-educated minister was hard-pressed to find a rational way out of this debate in order to legitimate the forceful integration of immigrants (who were also British citizens) when he and distinct faiths or social groups in British society could freely opt for segregated schooling for their children. He just shrugged: "What kind of society do you want?"[30]

In this respect, it is undeniable that the end of dispersal meant the wresting of a symbolic equality of sorts for Asians: much as Roman

Catholics, Anglicans, Jews and the upper classes could opt out of state schools and get together as a faith group or a distinct social class, Southallians and Bradfordians from certain areas could now be schooled together on a geographical-cum-ethnic basis, no matter how this education was perceived from the outside. To state the obvious, what made these different were the degrees of voluntariness in the parental choices made. A few decades later, we are only little wiser as debates on bussing rear their heads periodically to tackle class- or faith-based segregation in the English education market. This is made only more complex by strongly confessional demarcation lines, frequently deployed as a smokescreen to perpetuate social exclusivism across the country. It is with this complex present in mind that the study of dispersal's past has to be gauged, and it is why, once again, bussing does matter today.

Notes

1 On Race Awareness Training more generally, see Myers, *Struggles for a Past*, pp. 101–2.
2 On all these points and quotes, see Ramindar Singh, *The Struggle for Racial Justice: From Community Relations to Community Cohesion, The Story of Bradford 1950–2002*, Bradford: Bradford Arts, Museums and Libraries Service, 2002, pp. 129–32.
3 Halstead, *Education, Justice and Cultural Diversity*, p. 235.
4 *Ibid.*, p. 39.
5 Ahmed Iqbal Ullah Race Relations Resource Centre (Manchester), Race Relations Board archives, "Dispersal and choice", Joan Lester, June 1969.
6 Select Committee on Race Relations and Immigration: *Minutes of Evidence 1974 (Wolverhampton)*, London: HMSO, 1974, p. 137.
7 Select Committee on Race Relations and Immigration, *Education*, vol. 2, London: HMSO, 1973, p. 180.
8 *Telegraph & Argus*, 23.7.1979.
9 By the time its fourth edition went out in 1979, it had sold more than five hundred thousand copies.
10 See a discussion of Allport's conditions in Hill and Issacharoff, *Community Action and Race Relations*, pp. 287–9.
11 See Thomson, *Asian-named Minority Groups*, pp. 217–20.
12 Abdelmalek Sayad, *L'Ecole et les enfants d'immigration*, Paris: Seuil, 2014, p. 119. Translation by O.E.
13 In it Brixton and Bradford are referred to as "ghettos".
14 *The Times*, 29.1.1965.
15 For a good presentation of these scholars' view on the concept of ghetto as it applies to the United States, see Mitchell Duneier, *Ghetto, the Invention of a Place, the History of an Idea*, New York: Farrar, Strauss & Giroux, 2016.
16 The metaphor is by Loïc Wacquant, on similar conflations, but between French *banlieues* and American ghettos: see *ibid.*, p. 231.

17 The phrase is borrowed from Michel Laguerre, *Minoritized Space: An Inquiry into the Spatial Order of Things*, Oakland: University of California Press, 1999.

18 John Rex, *Key Problems of Sociological Theory*, London: Routledge and Kegan Paul, 1961.

19 Michael Javen Fortner, *Black Silent Majority: The Rockefeller Drug Law and the Politics of Punishment*, Cambridge, MA: Harvard University Press, 2015.

20 See Boyle, *Race Relations and Education*, p. 16.

21 Hill and Issacharoff, *Community Action and Race Relations*, p. 195.

22 Myers, *Struggles for a Past*, p. 29.

23 "Integration" is here understood in the American sense of "desegregation".

24 Eugene F. Provenzo, *Du Bois on Education*, Walnut Creek, CA: Altamira Press, 2002.

25 Quoted in Buettner, *Europe After Empire*, p. 261.

26 See for instance Sonya O. Rose, "Race, Empire, and British Wartime National Identity, 1939–1945", *Historical Research*, vol. 74 (2001), pp. 220–37.

27 Bailkin, *The Afterlife of Empire*, pp. 51–2.

28 See Merry, *Equality, Citizenship and Segregation*, p. 20; p. 67.

29 *Ibid.*, p. 83.

30 *Middlesex County Times (Southall Edition)*, 19.10.1963.

Bibliography

Primary sources

Ahmed Iqbal Ullah Race Relations Resource Centre (Manchester)
Race Relations Board archives
Commission for Racial Equality Archives

Birmingham archives (Wolfson Research Centre)
Indian Workers Association (UK) archives

Blackburn archives
Education Authority minutes (Blackburn)

Bradford and West Yorkshire archives
Bradford Council minutes
Education Authority minutes (Bradford)
Health and education reports on children of immigrants
Oral history collection.

Calderdale (Halifax) archives
Education Authority minutes (Halifax)

Ealing archives
Borough of Ealing minutes (1965–81)
Borough of Southall minutes (1963–65)
Education Authority minutes (Southall)
Education Authority minutes (Ealing)
Nigel Spearing papers

George Padmore Institute (Finsbury Park, London)
London borough of Haringey papers (BEM 1/1/1 to BEM 1/2/5)

Hansard (House of Commons debates archives)

Kirklees (Huddersfield) archives
Education Authority minutes (Huddersfield)

Leeds University Special Collections
Edward Boyle papers (MS 660)

London Metropolitan archives
Education Authority minutes (Inner London Education Authority)

London Community Relations Papers (ILEA/GEN/1/75)
Supplementary schools in Ealing file (LMA/4463/D/11/02/002–006)

London School of Economics special collections
Anthony Crosland papers
Fabian Pamphlets

National archives (Kew, London)
Department of Education and Science (Memorandum to Inspectors, 1977) (ED 135/37)
Department of Education and Science (Bradford mother-tongue research proposal) (ED 269/129/1)
Department of Education and Science (Education of Ugandan Asian refugees) (ED 269/14; ED 269/15; ED 233/11)
Department of Education and Science (Bradford: staffing, primary and secondary school) (ED 60/635)
Educational Facilities (Ealing) (CK 2/1468)
Race Relations Board (Blackburn and Ealing files) (CK 2/515)
Race Relations Board (Indian Workers Association) (CK 2/339)

Sandwell archives
Education Authority minutes (Smethwick, West Bromwich)

Walsall archives
Education Authority minutes (Walsall)

Wolverhampton archives
Education Authority minutes (Wolverhampton)

Newspapers

Acton Gazette
Birmingham Evening Mail
Birmingham Mail
The Birmingham Planet
Birmingham Post
The Daily Express
The Daily Mail
The Daily Telegraph
Equals (RRB Newsletter)
The Evening Standard
The Guardian
Halifax Evening Courier
The Huddersfield Weekly Examiner
Lancashire Evening Telegraph
The Middlesex County Times (Southall Edition)
Morning Star
New Society
The New Statesman

Smethwick Telephone and Warley Courrier
South London Press
Sunday Mercury
The Sunday Times
The Telegraph & Argus (Bradford)
The Times
The Times Educational Supplement
The Walsall Observer
The West Middlesex Gazette
The Wolverhampton Express and Star
Yorkshire Post

Reports and government publications

Asian Household Survey Team, "Some Basic Characteristics of Blackburn's Asian population", Town of Blackburn, 1977.

Commission for Racial Equality, *Learning in Terror: A Survey of Racial Harassment in Schools and Colleges in England, Scotland and Wales*, London: HMSO, 1988.

Commission for Racial Equality, *Teaching English as a Second Language: Report of a Formal Investigation in Calderdale Local Education Authority*, London: HMSO, 1986.

Commonwealth Immigrants Advisory Council, *2nd Report (Education)*, London: HMSO, 1964.

Department of Education and Science, *English for Immigrants*, London: HMSO, 1963.

Department of Education and Science, *The Education of Immigrants*, London: HMSO, 1965.

Department of Education and Science, *The Bullock Report: A Language for Life*, London: HMSO, 1975.

Department of Education and Science, *Education for All (The Swann Report)*, London: HMSO, 1985.

Ealing International Friendship Council, *The Education of the Immigrant Child in the London Borough of Ealing*, Ealing, 1968.

Hasnie, Nasim, *"The Way Ahead: A Survey of Asian Youth in Huddersfield"*, Huddersfield: Kirklees Metropolitan Council, 1977.

Home Office, *Immigration from the Commonwealth* (White Paper, 1965).

Inner London Education Authority, *An Education Service for the Whole Community*, London, 1973.

Kogan, Maurice, *Dispersal in the Ealing Local Education Authority Schools' System*, Report to Race Relations Board, 1976 (plus 4 appendices). Unpublished.

Race Relations Committee of the Society of Friends, *Report on the Immigrant Child and the Teacher*, London: Society of Friends, 1966.

Select Committee on Race Relations and Immigration, *The Problem of Coloured School-Leavers*, London: HMSO, 1969.

Select Committee on Race Relations and Immigration, *Education*, Volumes 1–3, London: HMSO, 1973.

Select Committee on Race Relations and Immigration, *Minutes of Evidence (Wolverhampton)*, London: HMSO, 1974.

Young, Michael, *"Why Our Susan? Comprehensive Schools – the Case for Parental Choice"*, London: Haringey Parents Group, 1969.

PhD dissertation

Thomson, Brenda Mary, *Asian-named Minority Groups in the British Schools System: A Study of the education of children of immigrants of Indian, Pakistani or Bangladeshi origins from the Indian subcontinent or East Africa in the city of Bradford*, University of Bradford, 1991.

Secondary sources

Allen, Sheila, *New Minorities, Old Conflicts*, New York: Random House, 1971.

Allport, Gordon, *The Nature of Prejudice*, New York: Basic Books, 1979 [1954].

Andrews, Kehinde, *Resisting Racism: Race, Inequality and the Black Supplementary School Movement*, Stoke-on-Trent: Trentham Books, 2013.

Ansari, Humayun, *The Infidel Within: The History of Muslims in Britain, 1800 to the Present*, London: Hurst & Co., 2004.

Bailkin, Jordanna, *The Afterlife of Empire*, Oakland: University of California Press, 2012.

Beach, Abigail, and Weight, Richard, *The Right to Belong, Citizenship and National Identity in Britain, 1930–1960*, London: I.B. Tauris, 1998.

Bebber, Brett, *"'We Were Just Unwanted', Bussing, Migrant Dispersal and South Asians in London"*, *Journal of Social History*, vol. 48 (3), 2015, pp. 635–61.

Bidwell, Sydney, *Red, White and Black: Race Relations in Britain*, London: Gordon & Cremonesi, 1976.

Bindman, Geoffrey, and Lester, Anthony, *Race and Law*, Harmondsworth: Penguin, 1972.

Bleich, Erik, *Race Politics in Britain and France: Ideas and Policy-making since the 1960s*, Cambridge: Cambridge University Press, 2003.

Bourdieu, Pierre, *On the State: Lectures at the College de France, 1989–1992*, London: Polity, 2015.

Bowker, Gordon, *The Education of Coloured Immigrants*, London: Longman, 1968.

Boyle, Edward (Sir), *Race Relations and Education*, Liverpool: Liverpool University Press, 1970.

Boyle, Edward (Sir), *The Politics of Education, Edward Boyle and Anthony Crosland in conversation with Maurice Kogan*, Harmondsworth: Penguin Books, 1971.

Brocklebank-Fowler, Christopher, Bland, Christopher, and Farmer, Tim, *Commonwealth Immigration*, London: The Bow Group, 1965.

Buettner, Elizabeth, *"'This is Staffordshire, not Alabama!', Racial Geographies of Commonwealth Immigration in Early 1960s Britain"*, *Journal of Imperial and Commonwealth History*, vol. 42 (4), 2014, pp. 710–40.

Buettner, Elizabeth, *Europe After Empire: Decolonization, Society and Culture*, Cambridge: Cambridge University Press, 2016.

Burgin, Trevor, and Edson, Patricia, *Spring Grove, The Education of Immigrant Children*, Oxford: Oxford University Press, 1967.

Burney, Elizabeth, *Housing on Trial: A Study of Immigrants and Local Government*, Oxford: Oxford University Press, 1967.

Butterworth, Eric, Goodall, John, and Hartley, Bryan, *Immigrants in West Yorkshire, Social Conditions and the Lives of Pakistanis, Indians and West Indians*, London: Institute of Race Relations, 1967.

Carter, Dan T., *The Politics of Rage: George Wallace, the Origins of the New Conservatism, and the Transformation of American Politics*, New York: Simon & Schuster, 1995.

Chong, Dennis, *Collective Action and the Civil Rights Movement*, Chicago: University of Chicago Press, 1991.

Coard, Bernard, *How the West Indian Child Is Made Educationally Sub-normal in the British School System: The Scandal of the Black Child in Schools in Britain*, London: New Beacon Books, 1971.

Cowie, Jefferson, *Stayin' Alive: The 1970s and the Last Days of the Working Class*, New York: The New Press, 2010.

Crehan, Kate, *Gramsci's Common Sense, Inequality and Its Narratives*, Durham, NC: Duke University Press, 2016.

Crosland, Susan, *Tony Crosland*, London: Jonathan Cape, 1982.

Cunningham, Charles (Sir), "The Work of the Uganda Resettlement Board", *Journal of Ethnic and Migration Studies*, vol. 2 (3), 1973, pp. 261–7.

Dahia, Badr, "Pakistanis in Britain: Transients or Settlers?", *Race & Class*, vol. 14 (3), 1973, pp. 241–77.

Dahia, Badr, "The Nature of Pakistani Ethnicity in Industrial Cities in Britain", in Abner Cohen (ed.), *Urban Ethnicities*, London: Tavistock, 1974, pp. 77–118.

Daniels, W.W., *Racial Discrimination in England*, Harmondsworth: Penguin, 1969.

Deakin, Nicholas (ed.), *Colour and the British Electorate, Six Case Studies*, London: Pall Mall Press, 1965.

Deakin, Nicholas, and Cohen, Brian, "Dispersal and Choice: Towards a Strategy for Ethnic Minorities in Britain", *Environment and Planning*, vol. 12 (3), 1970, pp. 193–203.

Delaney, Enda, *The Irish in Post-war Britain*, Oxford: Oxford University Press, 2007.

Delmont, Matthew, *Why Busing Failed: Race, Media and the National Resistance to School Desegregation*, Oakland: University of California Press, 2016.

Desrosières, Alain, *The Politics of Large Numbers*, Cambridge, MA: Harvard University Press, 1998.

Desrosières, Alain, *Prouver et gouverner: une analyse politique des statistiques publiques*, Paris: La Découverte, 2014.

DeWitt, John, *Indian Workers Associations in Britain*, Oxford: Oxford University Press, 1969.

Dhondy, Farrukh, Beese, Barbara, and Hassan, Leila, *The Black Explosion in British Schools*, London: Race Today Publications, 1982.

Duneier, Mitchell, *Ghetto, The Invention of a Place, The History of an Idea*, New York: Farrar, Strauss & Giroux, 2016.

Esteves, Olivier, *De l'invisibilité à l'islamophobie, les musulmans britanniques (1945–2010)*, Paris: Presses de Sciences-Po, 2011.

Fabian Society, *Strangers Within*, London: Young Fabian Pamphlets, 1965.

Feldman, David, "Why the English Like Turbans: Multicultural Politics in British History", in David Feldman and Jon Lawrence (eds), *Structures and Transformations in Modern British History*, Cambridge: Cambridge University Press, 2011, pp. 281–302.

Fevre, Ralph, *Cheap Labour and Racial Discrimination*, Aldershot: Gower Publishing, 1984.

Fielding, Nigel, *The National Front*, London: Routledge, 1981.

Flett, Hazel, "The Politics of Dispersal in Birmingham", Working Papers on Ethnic Relations, no. 14, Birmingham, 1981. Unpublished.

Foot, Paul, *Immigration and Race in British Politics*, Harmondsworth: Penguin, 1965.

Formisano, Ronald, *Boston Against Busing, Race, Class and Ethnicity in the 1960s and 1970s*, Chapel Hill: University of North Carolina Press, 1991.

Fortner, Michael Javen, *Black Silent Majority: The Rockefeller Drug Law and the Politics of Punishment*, Cambridge, MA: Harvard University Press, 2015.

Gardner, Paul, *Teaching and Learning in Multicultural Classrooms*, London: Routledge, 2012.

Gest, Justin, *The New Minority: White Working-class Politics in an Era of Immigration and Inequality*, Oxford: Oxford University Press, 2016.

Glass, Ruth, *London's Newcomers: The West Indian Migrants*, Boston, MA: Harvard University Press, 1961.

Grosvenor, Ian, *Assimilating Identities: Racism and Educational Policy in post 1945 Britain*, London: Lawrence & Wishart, 1997.

Halbwachs, Maurice, *On Collective Memory*, Chicago: University of Chicago Press, 1992 [1925].

Halstead, Mark, *Education, Justice and Cultural Diversity: An Examination of the Honeyford Affair, 1984–5*, London: Falmer Press, 1988.

Hammond Perry, Kennetta, "'Little Rock' in Britain: Jim Crow's Transatlantic Topographies", *Journal of British Studies*, vol. 51 (1), 2012, pp. 155–77.

Hansen, Randall, *Citizenship and Immigration in Post-war Britain: The Institutional Origins of a Multicultural Nation*, Oxford: Oxford University Press, 2000.

Hawkes, Nicholas, *Immigrant Children in British Schools*, London: Pall Mall Press, 1966.

Heffer, Simon, *Like the Roman: The Life of Enoch Powell*, London: Faber & Faber, 2008 [1988].

Hepple, Bob, "The European Legacy of Brown *vs* Board of Education", *University of Illinois Law Review*, vol. 3, 2006, pp. 605–24.

Herbert, Joanna, *Negotiating Boundaries in the City: Migration, Ethnicity and Gender in Britain*, Aldershot: Ashgate, 2008.

Hewitt, Roger, *White Backlash and the Politics of Multiculturalism*, Cambridge: Cambridge University Press, 2005.

Hill, Michael, and Issacharoff, Ruth, *Community Action and Race Relations: A Study of Community Relations Committees in Britain*, Oxford: Oxford University Press, 1971.

Howell, Denis, *Made in Birmingham: The Memoirs of Denis Howell*, London: Queen Anne Press, 1990.

Jackson, Carlton, *Who Will Take Our Children? The British Evacuation Programme of World War II*, Jefferson, NC: McFarland Publishing, 2008.

Jones, Catherine, *Immigration and Social Policy in Britain*, London: Tavistock, 1977.

Keith, Brian Axel, *The Nation's Tortured Body, Violence, Representation and the Formation of a "Sikh" Diaspora*, Durham, NC: Duke University Press, 2001.

Khan, Mudassir H., *Still Here, After over Fifty Wonderful Years*, Blackburn: Cremer Press, 2008.

Killian, Lewis, "School Bussing in Britain, Policies and Perceptions", *Harvard Educational Review*, vol. 49 (2), 1979, pp. 185–206.

Kirp, David, *Doing Good by Doing Little: Race and Schooling in Britain*, Berkeley and London: University of California Press, 1980.

Laguerre, Michel, *Minoritized Space: An Inquiry into the Spatial Order of Things*, Oakland: University of California Press, 1999.

Lent, Adam, *British Social Movements since 1945: Sex, Colour, Peace and Power*, London: Palgrave Macmillan, 2001.

Lenton, John, Budgen, Nicholas, and Clark, Kenneth, *Immigration, Race and Politics, a Birmingham view*, London: Bow Group pamphlets, 1966.

Levine, Josie, "Developing Pedagogies for Multilingual Classes", *English in Education*, vol. 5 (3), 1981, pp. 25–33.

Levine, Josie, "Going Back to the Mainstream", *Issues in Race and Education*, no. 39 (summer), 1983, pp. 1–3.

Lukas, J. Anthony, *Common Ground: A Turbulent Decade in the Lives of Three American Families*, New York: Vintage Books, 1985.

Mackintosh, Nicholas, *I.Q. and Human Intelligence*, Oxford: Oxford University Press, 2011 [1998].

Malchow, Howard Le Roy, *Special Relations: The Americanization of Britain?*, Stanford, CA: Stanford University Press, 2011.

Marrett, Valerie, *Immigrants Settling in the City, Ugandan Asians in Leicester*, Leicester: Leicester University Press, 1989.

Marx, Karl, *Das Kapital*, vol. 1, London: Penguin Classics:, 1990 [1867].

McAdam, Doug, *Political Process and the Development of Black Insurgency, 1930–1970*, Chicago: University of Chicago Press, 1999 [1982].

McCarthy, John D., and Zald, Mayer N., "Resource Mobilization and Social Movements: A Partial Theory", *The American Journal of Sociology*, vol. 82 (6), 1977, pp. 1212–41.

Merry, Michael, *Equality, Citizenship and Segregation: A Defence of Separation*, New York: Palgrave Macmillan, 2013.

Meyer, David S., "Protest and Political Opportunities", *Annual Review of Sociology*, vol. 30 (2004), pp. 126–32.

Miah, Shamim, *Muslims, Schooling and the Question of Self-segregation*, London: Palgrave Macmillan, 2015.

Mills, Charles Wade, *The Racial Contract*, Ithaca and London: Cornell University Press, 1997.

Mills, Charles Wright, *The Sociological Imagination*, Oxford University Press, 2000 [1959].

Milner, David, *Children and Race*, Harmondsworth: Penguin, 1975.

Moore, Barrington, *Injustice: The Social Bases of Obedience and Revolt*, New York: Random House, 1978.

Murphy, Dervla, *A Tale from Two Cities: Travels of Another Sort*, London: J. Murray, 1987.

Myers, Kevin, "Immigrants and Ethnic Minorities in the History of Education", *Paedagogica Historica*, vol. 45 (2009), pp. 801–16.

Myers, Kevin, *Struggles for a Past: Irish and Afro-Caribbean Histories in England, 1951–2000*, Manchester: Manchester University Press, 2015.

Oates, Jonathan, *History and Guide: Southall and Hanwell*, Gloucester: Tempus, 2003.

Oberschall, Anthony, *Social Conflicts and Social Movements*, London: Pearson Education Ltd, 1973.

Olson, Mancur, *The Logic of Collective Action, Public Good and the Theory of Groups*, Cambridge, MA: Harvard University Press, 1971.

Orwell, George, *The Complete Novels of George Orwell*, London: Penguin Classics, 2000.

Patterson, Sheila, *Immigration and Race Relations in Britain 1960–1967*, Oxford: Oxford University Press, 1969.

Phillips, Trevor, and Phillips, Mike, *Windrush: The Irresistible Rise of Multi-racial Britain*, London: Harper & Collins, 1998.

Polletta, Francesca, and Jasper, James M., "Collective Identity and Social Movements", *Annual Review of Sociology*, vol. 27 (2001), pp. 283–305.

Porter, Tod, *Trust in Numbers: The Pursuit of Objectivity in Science and Public Life*, Princeton: Princeton University Press, 1995.

Power, John, *Immigrants in School, A Survey of Administrative Policies*, London: Councils and Education Press, 1967.

Provenzo, Eugene F., *Du Bois on Education*, Walnut Creek, CA: Altamira Press, 2002.

Purewal, Balraj, *The Indian Workers Association (Southall): 60 Years of Struggles and Achievements (1956–2016)*, London: IWA, 2016.

Ramamurthy, Anandi, "The Politics of Britain's Asian Youth Movements", *Race & Class*, vol. 48 (2), 2006, pp. 38–60.

Ramamurthy, Anandi, *Black Star: Britain's Asian Youth Movements*, London: Pluto Press, 2013.

Rex, John, *Key Problems of Sociological Theory*, London: Routledge and Kegan Paul, 1961.

Robinson, Vaughan, "The Segregation of Asians within a British City: Theory and Practice", University of Oxford, School of Geography, Research Paper no. 22, 1979.

Robinson, Vaughan, *Transients, Settlers and Refugees, Asians in Britain*, Oxford: Oxford University Press, 1985.

Robinson, Vaughan, Andersson, Roger, and Musterd, Sako, *Spreading the Burden? A Review of Policies to Disperse Asylum-seekers and Refugees*, Bristol: Policy Press, 2003.

Rolph-Trouillot, Michel, *Silencing the Past, Power and the Production of History*, Boston, MA: Beacon Press, 1995.

Rose, E.J.B (ed.), *Colour and Citizenship, A Report on British Race Relations*, Oxford: Oxford University Press, 1969.

Rose, Sonya O., "Race, Empire, and British Wartime National Identity, 1939–1945", *Historical Research*, vol. 74 (2001), pp. 220–37.

Sandbrook, Dominic, *White Heat: A History of Britain in the Swinging Sixties*, London: Little Brown, 2006.

Sayad, Abdelmalek, *The Suffering of the Immigrant*, Cambridge: Polity Press, 2004.

Sayad, Abdelmalek, *L'Ecole et les enfants de l'immigration*, Paris: Seuil, 2014.

Schofield, Camilla, *Enoch Powell and the Making of Post-colonial Britain*, Cambridge: Cambridge University Press, 2009.

Schwarz, Bill, *Memories of Empire: The White Man's World*, Oxford: Oxford University Press, 2011.

Scott, James C., *Weapons of the Weak: Everyday Forms of Peasant Resistance*, New Haven: Yale University Press, 1985.

Scott, James C., *Domination and the Arts of Resistance: Hidden Transcripts*, New Haven: Yale University Press, 1990.

Scott, James C., *Seeing Like a State: How Certain Schemes to Improve the Human Condition Have Failed*, New Haven: Yale University Press, 1998.

Seabrook, Jeremy, *City Close-up*, Harmondsworth: Penguin, 1971.

Shukla, Sandhya, *India Abroad: Diasporic Cultures of Postwar America and England*, Princeton: Princeton University Press, 2004.

Shukra, Khalbir, *The Changing Pattern of Black Politics in Britain*, London: Pluto Press, 1998.

Simpson, Ludi and Nissa Finney, *Sleepwalking to Segregation: Challenging Myths about Race and Migration*, Bristol: The Policy Press, 2009

Singh, Gurharpal, and Tatla, Darshan Singh, *Sikhs in Britain: The Making of a Community*, London: Zed Books, 2006.

Singh, Ramindar, *The Struggle for Racial Justice: From Community Relations to Community Cohesion, The Story of Bradford 1950–2002*, Bradford: Bradford Arts, Museums and Libraries Service, 2002.

Sivanandan, Ambalaver, *Catching History on the Wing*, London: Pluto Press, 2008.

Smith, Susan J., *The Politics of "Race" and Residence*, Cambridge: Polity Press, 1989.

Spivak, Gayatri Chakravorty, "Can the Subaltern Speak?", in Cary Nelson, and
    Lawrence Grossberg (eds), *Marxism and the Interpretation of Culture*, Urbana
    and Chicago: University of Illinois Press, 1987, pp. 271–315.
Stojanović, Nenad, *Dialogue sur les quotas: penser la représentation dans une
    démocratie multiculturelle*, Paris: Presses de Sciences-Po, 2013.
Stolarski, Piotr, *Ealing in the 1960s*, Gloucester: Tignarius, 2013.
Stoler, Ann Laura, *Along the Archival Grain: Epistemic Anxieties and Colonial
    Common Sense*, Princeton: Princeton University Press, 2009.
Sugrue, Thomas J., *Sweet Land of Liberty: The Forgotten Struggle for Civil Rights
    in the North*, New York: Random House, 2010.
Talpin, Julien, *Community Organizing: de l'émeute à l'alliance des classes popu-
    laires aux Etats-Unis*, Paris: Raisons d'Agir, 2016.
Tarrow, Sydney, *Power in Movement*, Cambridge: Cambridge University Press,
    1998.
Taylor, Charles, *Multiculturalism and the Politics of Recognition*, Princeton:
    Princeton University Press, 1992.
Tomlinson, Sally, *Race and Education: Policy and Politics in Britain*, Maidenhead:
    Open University Press, 2008.
Tomlinson, Sally, *A Sociology of Special and Inclusive Education: Exploring the
    Manufacture of Inability*, London: Routledge, 2017.
Townsend, H.E.R, *Immigrant Pupils in England: The L.E.A. Response*, Slough:
    National Foundation for Educational Research, 1971.
United States Committee on the Judiciary, *Effectiveness of Mandatory Busing in
    Cleveland*, London: Forgotten Books, 2015.
Warmington, Paul, *Black British Intellectuals and Education*, London: Routledge,
    2014.
Weinberg, Mayer, *A Chance to Learn: The History of Race and Education in the
    United States*, Cambridge: Cambridge University Press, 1977.
Willis, Paul, *Learning to Labour: How Working-class Kids Get Working-class Jobs*,
    New York: Columbia University Press, 1977.
Wilson, Amrit, *Finding a Voice: Asian Women in Britain*, London: Virago, 1978.
Wray, Helena, *Regulating Marriage Migration into the U.K.: A Stranger in the
    Home*, London: Routledge, 2016.
Žižek, Slavoj, *Tarrying with the Negative: Kant, Hegel, and the Critique of Ideology*,
    Durham, NC: Duke University Press, 1993.

Index

under-achievement at school 147, 148,
    181
United States
  bussing in 2–4, 25
  desegregation in 3–4, 62, 64
  influence on British race–relations
      debates 3–4, 41–2, 97, 101, 127,
      134, 203–6
  urban ghettos in 4, 203–6
  "White Backlash" in 17, 25, 64
upward mobility 64, 98, 147, 181

Villiers High School (Southall) 184,
    188
Voluntary Liaison Committees 53, 54

Wallace, G. 25
Walsall 6, 7, 42, 82, 85, 134, 136–7
Wandsworth 102, 115, 154
Webster, E.A. 34, 185
Welfare State 6, 8, 43, 61, 88, 162
West Bromwich 2, 5, 7, 9, 42, 47, 63,
      66, 123, 127, 134, 135–6, 137,
      142

West Indian(s)
  activism 15, 109–10, 111, 112, 113,
      159, 161–2, 189
  and Britishness 62–3, 107
  bussing of 63, 112, 127, 128, 135,
      136, 137, 153
  immigrants 1, 13, 23, 43, 71, 84, 94,
      98, 101
  in ESN schools 108–9, 137, 153, 161
  stereotypes about 28, 59, 94, 96,
      111, 112, 113, 115
  under-achievement at school 91,
      95–6
"White Backlash" 13, 17, 26–7, 37, 41,
      83, 85, 86, 108, 115
"White Flight" 1, 34, 57, 60, 97
Willis, P. 148, 183
Wilson, A. 116, 179
Wilson, H. 37, 47, 61, 80, 81, 99
Wolverhampton 7, 25, 29, 43, 66, 92,
      134, 135, 136, 137–8, 142, 143,
      201

X (Little), Malcolm 118, 134

EU authorised representative for GPSR:
Easy Access System Europe, Mustamäe tee 50,
10621 Tallinn, Estonia
gpsr.requests@easproject.com

www.ingramcontent.com/pod-product-compliance
Lightning Source LLC
Chambersburg PA
CBHW052002270326
41929CB00015B/2757